RODEO STORIES III

"Hung to a Mean Bull" © Roger Langford

CHIMP ROBERTSON

NEW FORUMS PRESS INC.

Published in the United States of America
by New Forums Press, Inc.1018 S. Lewis St.
Stillwater, OK 74074
www.newforums.com

Copyright © 2017 by Chimp Robertson

Front cover Credit Dale Miller Photography, Jared Green, Cowboy.

All rights reserved. No part of this publication may be reproduced or transmitted in any form or by any means, electronic or mechanical, including photocopy, or any information storage or retrieval system, without permission in writing from the publisher.

Library of Congress Cataloging-in-Publication Data Pending

This book may be ordered in bulk quantities at discount from New Forums Press, Inc., P.O. Box 876, Stillwater, OK 74076 [Federal I.D. No. 73 1123239]. Printed in the United States of America.

ISBN 10: 1-58107-308-9
ISBN 13: 978-1-58107-308-9

Because of the dynamic nature of the Internet, any web addresses or links contained in this book may have changed since publication and may no longer be valid. The views expressed in this work are solely those of the contributors and do not necessarily reflect the views of the publisher, and the publisher hereby disclaims any responsibility for them.

CONTENTS

Dedication v
Acknowledgments vii
Prologue ix
Part I 1
Part II 39
Part III 79
Part IV 121
Part V 159
Part VI 203
Part VII 243
About the Author 283

DEDICATION

This book is dedicated to my dad, Alton Robertson,
And my brothers, Jack and Dalton Robertson

May They Rest In Peace

ACKNOWLEDGEMENTS

Many interested people helped make this book possible. First of all, I want to thank my publisher Doug Dollar of New Forums Press.

Next, I want to thank rodeo photographers Jerry Gustafson, Dudley Barker, Terri Abrahamson, Tommy Evans, Tina Williams Patrick, Tom Woods, and Dan Hubbell who were so helpful and willing to contribute their rodeo images. Many others contributed to this work as well. Their stories made this book possible and I also dedicate to them.

If we're defined by those with whom we keep company, then I'm in good shape-because my companions are rodeo cowboys and cowgirls.

CREDITS

All artwork copyrighted by the artist Roger Langford. Contact Roger at langfordart@sbcglobal.net

PROLOGUE

RODEO STORIES III. Here is a book of Rodeo Cowboys. True stories from way back in the mist of time of memories and friendships that will never grow old. The rugged color of their lives glistens for all to appreciate, like gold coins saved over the years in an old trunk.

This tribute to Rodeo Cowboys now belongs to every one who has a fondness for the days of exceptional courage, hard work, raw-boned character and bonds of friendship, told by Rodeo Cowboys themselves. They achieved distinction competing with the best in the arenas of rodeo.

This restoration of the Glory Days of the past will now never be forgotten. Every reader can appreciate the nature of Rodeo Cowboy life and the way it was lived by those whose stories are now committed to these pages. They might have been forgotten, but will now live on forever.

L. L. Waylett: Manshadow Waylett is a Salish Citizen of the Flathead Indian Nation of Montana. He is a U.S. Army veteran, and retired from IBM Corporation. As a writer his works include; A Conversation With American Indians, Shadows Talk, I Have A Feeling For This Place, and The Justice Brigade.

Rodeo Stories III

"A Classy Ride" © Roger Langford

PART 1

1. Blu Odam…I Never Heard Him Call
2. Jerry LaValley…The Fatted Calf
3. Lee Jones…I Saw A Chimpanzee
4. Mike Fletcher…Brothers of The Bull
5. Myles Culbertson…The Pick-Up Man
6. Carl Nafgzer…How It All started
7. Cory Brown…I'll Drive
8. Danny O'Haco…The Hang-Up
9. Joe Foscalina…I Will Carry the Flag
10. Larry Brady…The Rail Splitter
11. Kirk Allmon…A Long Time Ago
12. John L. Sloan…Lap And Tap
13. Lonnie Guyton…Back In The 80's
14. Doug Brown…More about The Man Who Rode Tornado
15. Red Doyal…Stolen Car
16. Redboy Schlidt…What Happened
17. Richard Flechsig…Mud and Blood
18. Abe Morris…Cheyenne Frontier Days
19. Allan Howard…Forty Below
20. Buddy Williams…Charlie Thompson Rodeos
21. Dennis Montgomery…Scottsdale, Arizona
22. Byron McNair…My Rookie Year
23. Charlie Bowden-The Hometown Cowboy
24. Rome Wager…Cheyenne-The Granddad of Rodeo
25. Ed LeTourneau…The First NFR

BLU ODAM
I NEVER HEARD HIM CALL

It was the 4th of July rodeo at Rock Springs, Texas in 1976. I was standing over my bull about to put a rope around him when Tommy Priour the stock contractor told them to open the gate and let the bull out. My friend grabbed me and pulled me back up on the back of the chute just in time.

I asked Mr. Priour why he ran my bull out from under me and he replied by pointing to the bottom of the chute and said, "Rattlesnake." I said, "I could have fallen in there and got bit." He said, "You cowboys are a dime a dozen, but that bull there is worth some big money."

A cowboy faces all kinds of danger in the arena. During the 1973 NIRA Rodeo season, I forget which rodeo, the first episode happened while Johnny Fagley was clowning. Don Graham was on a bull and Johnny slapped the bull and got him to turn back. I can't remember if Don got bucked off or not, but he was upset with Johnny and told him that if he ever needed his help, he'd call him.

Two weeks later at Killeen, Texas, Don drew Tommy Priour's bull Sleepy. During the ride Don got hung up, but finally got loose. Johnny was leaning on the chute next to the one my bull was in. Someone asked him why he wasn't in there helping get Don out of the storm and Johnny said, "Don told me that if I ever needed my help he'd call, and I never heard him call."

88 JERRY LAVALLEY
THE FATTED CALF

Sometime in the latter part of the 80's decade, I had been around and about out West on a June-July rodeo run. My old buddy Casey Backus and his wife Annette were living in Denver at the time and helped me out a bunch with some travel plans and a place to rest, when the time and situation allowed.

Just after Cheyenne Frontier Days I had a flight out of Denver, and they gave me a ride to the airport. This was before the 9/11 terrorist attack, so airport guidelines were pretty lax when compared to security standards of today. We got to the airport early, and for a little extra visiting time we parked the car and Casey and Annette walked to the gate with me.

We visited at the gate for a bit and then it was time for me to board. There was a big crowd in the boarding area and as we were saying our farewells, I told Casey that, "I owed him big time for the hospitality, and that if him and Annette came for a visit in Oklahoma that, "I would kill the fatted calf," upon their arrival.

Casey and Annette knew what I meant, but there were a couple of urban dwelling, Denver-society type ladies that overhead my farewell comment, and they both gave me the dirtiest and most evil-eye glare that I have ever seen.

One of those ladies ended up having a seating assignment next to me on the plane. When she got to her seat and saw me sitting in the seat next to hers, she quickly and urgently, asked the flight attendant to get her a seat reassignment far away from that, 'Cowboy.'

LEE JONES
I SAW A CHIMPANZEE

In 1972, we were working both the San Antonio Rodeo and the El Paso Rodeo. I was winning the All-Around saddle at El Paso, but I had to be there for them to present it to me, so we made a flying trip after the rodeo at San Antonio, back to El Paso.

I was driving and Jimmy Dix was asleep on the passenger side. Deer and all kinds of wildlife were everywhere along the road that night. And to this day, I still swear I saw a Chimpanzee by the side of the road.

I reached over and shook Jimmy and said, "Dix, wake up. You ain't going to believe this, but I just saw a Chimpanzee by the side of the road." Jimmy just shook his head and blinked his eyes then said, "Pull over. I'll take the wheel from here on out."

MIKE FLETCHER
BROTHERS OF THE BULL

In early September 1975, a bareback horse had fallen with me in Philadelphia, Mississippi, and broke my collarbone. In those days injured cowboys had first dibs at judging rodeos. About the middle of November, I got a David Morgan Rodeo in Branford Florida. I had been traveling with Jack Wiseman, and our crew varied, but Mike Waters, Gary Bruin, and I, had been with Jack all year.

This particular week Mike Duplissey, Doyle Stanford, and Shorty Wood, had caught a ride with Jack to Branford, and planned to fly somewhere the next morning. After the rodeo we all went to my room. I was judging so I had driven my truck from Louisiana, and would take Mike, Doyle, and Shorty to Tampa airport the next morning.

There were six of us in my room while 'Misty' Mike Waters was out there sleeping in Jack's camper. Jack was really tired and fell asleep fast. We were all nearly asleep when the carnival workers next door started partying real loud. I remember telling Duplissey that if they didn't quite down they were going to wake Jack up, and it would not be pretty.

The words had no sooner left my mouth when Jack hollered, "Y'all quiet down out there." Back then, Florida motel rooms had glass lattice doors so our carnival neighbors responded by kicking a hole ours. Jack was in great shape, but he was a lot bigger than the rest of us. He was sharing a bed with Gary Bruin who wore size 27 Wranglers.

That was one funny sight watching Jack trying to fit into those 27 inch waist Wranglers he'd grabbed in the dark. By the time we gathered our wits and got our pants on, it occurred to me how strange it was that even though the door was broken, nobody had to come in. We were at a great disadvantage because we were all barefooted and there was a lot of glass on the floor.

Mike Fletcher, Brothers of the Bull. [Tommy Evans photo]

When I stuck my head out the door I found out the reason no one has entered. 'Misty' Mike had heard all the commotion and crawled out of the camper with a sawed-off shotgun and wearing a Tom Mix hat. He had ordered all the carnies up against the wall and I won't say the exact words he was using.

With the situation well under control, Jack said in a very calm voice, "Okay, who kicked in the door?" Believe it or not, one of those guys was dumb enough to admit it and got a black eye for his trouble." The motel owner made the Carnage leave and we all went back to bed. Thank God, it was cool so the skeeters didn't come through the hole in the door.

The next morning I took Mike, Doyle, and Shorty to the airport in Tampa. I think they were flying to Bullhead City, Arizona. In those days, sky caps still helped you with your luggage and you can imagine we were not normal air passengers for Tampa. The sky cap was fascinated by our belt buckles and our appearance in general.

Back then, the IRA gave huge Nelson Silver buckles. Doyle had been the Bull Riding Champion the year before and he was wearing his Championship buckle. Since Doyle was a very small guy, the sky cap pointed at Doyle's buckle and said, "What's this one the champion of, riding Shetland ponies?"

We all laughed uncontrollably, especially the skycap. Doyle however, was not amused and replied, "There are ten thousand comedians out of work and this guy's telling jokes at seven o'clock in the morning." Everyone in this story is family to me. Doyle and Jack have already gone to be with Jesus.

As I think back on these crazy, but happy times, it reminds me how much we operated like the New Testament Church should. We weren't very religious back then, but we shared all things in common and took care of each other. I'm proud to say that all of my old rodeo buddies have shared their faith in Christ with me. We are brothers of the bull, and brothers in Christ, for eternity.

MYLES CULBERTSON
THE PICK-UP MAN

In the early '60s when I was in high school in Las Vegas, New Mexico we organized a rodeo club, and even had a coach. Charlie Boyles, an RCA steer wrestler who taught and coached at Robertson High and rodeo'd all the rest of the time, helped put our organization together. We paid dues, had meetings, even had jackets embroidered with "Robertson High Rodeo Club" on the back.

We were able to find a few bucking horses, mostly outlaws off of area ranches, and once in a while we acquired something to rope or a loaner herd bull to try to buck out. Anyway, we were in business and we had plenty of help from not only Mr. Boyles, but also a few local ranchers and cowboys who had gone down the road some themselves. Howard Driggers furnished horned cattle to rope and bulldog, and Dogie Jones, with all of us as slave labor, eventually even built a good arena on his place at Watrous, New Mexico.

For several months before the Watrous arena was in the works, the club used the old Rough Riders arena in Las Vegas which, because of all the history, was a kind of an awesome spot for us kids getting down in the same chutes as had some of the old rodeo legends from another era. Just about everything we had was scrounged one way or another and my classmates, Jackie Reed and Charlie Fore, had located somebody's old bareback rigging that we shared between us.

It was an old-style rigging from days long past, maybe some of Lee or Lawson Fore's old gear. The hand-hold was shallow and not rigid at all. If you stuck your hand in deep and took a palm tuck there was about a 50-50 chance of hanging up just enough to stretch your riding arm pretty good when you got off.

One Saturday afternoon we were bucking the horses out and, for a change, we had a pick-up man, sort of. Bud Linson, the foreman on a nearby ranch loaded his horse and came to town to help this little bunch of aspiring rodeo stars. There was just Bud, but if he could get the bronc to run along the fence he could get the rider off in fairly good shape. I had our community rigging on a little horse that bucked pretty dirty and could dodge out from under the rider pretty fast.

Getting down, I pushed my hand in deep and took the tuck, thinking I could ride him if I had that little advantage. The gate swung open and I had the horse conquered for about four jumps. Then he ducked hard to the right and I was bucked off. Not just bucked off, also hung up. Not just hung up, but also upside down. The horse took a couple more sideways jumps and then started running, my hand locked down by that loose handle.

From my inversed vantage point I could the Bud's horse running up behind us. What I couldn't see was Bud shaking out a loop to try to catch this runaway. I don't know that I would have, in calm reflection called roping that horse a good idea, but I do know the idea was going south fast as I felt the loop closing around my leg instead of the horse's neck. Back in those days nobody in our part of the world dallied and I guess just out of habit, Bud's rope was tied to the horn.

To complete the scene, he was riding a horse that had done a lot more roping than picking up so without needing to be pulled up, he instinctively slid to a stop. Well, that took care of the hanging up problem as my leg stretched, my hand popped out of its trap, and I thudded on the ground, wondering if I might be a couple inches taller after all this. I could feel all my fingers and toes so figured I had survived as Bud, with a sheepish look, rode up, dismounted, and helped me stand and brush the dirt off. I don't remember what he said but, looking back on it all, I'll bet it would have sounded pretty funny.

Those were great days that ended too soon as we all moved on. A few of us rodeo'd for a while after high school in college, and some of the boys, like Charlie Fore and David Craig, went down the road for a long time and made a name. But, all of us look back to the start and remember Charlie Boyles and a few other men who still had it in their blood to help share the flavor, discipline and guidance, and to open up that world to a bunch of high school kids who will not ever forget them, or that short time in their young lives.

CARL NAFZGER
HOW IT ALL STARTED

Rodeo is an exciting sport but also a dangerous sport, especially bull riding and most rodeo cowboys have the injuries to prove it. Bull riding has really become a popular spectator sport, but I'm sure most people who watch it can't understand why a cowboy would ever decide to get on the back of a 1,500 pound bucking animal that would be more than happy to run you down if he gets you off his back. When I was a kid even I thought only the idiots rode bulls.

Most of my bull riding career was in the 1960s and it seemed that during my rodeo days, the rodeo cowboys were generally guys who grew up on farms and ranches where they had experience with roping, riding, and cattle work. I grew up on a family ranch near Olton, Texas and I had plenty of exposure to cattle, including bulls. However, I never had an interest in riding them. But, when I got to high school I discovered a new interest – girls.

I didn't go see my first bull riding competition until I was sixteen. I took a girl on a date and we went to watch a guy from our class ride. I left my first bull riding competition thinking that you had to be an idiot to ride bulls. But, I did notice that girls sure seemed to like bull riders and that got me thinking that maybe riding bulls wasn't such a stupid thing after all. Years later when

I was a professional bull rider I met my wife Wanda while I was traveling the rodeo circuit.

Once I realized that bull riders were popular with the girls in high school, I got together with the guy in my class who was riding bulls and we hatched a plan. My dad had feeder bulls and we figured that we could use those for practice and get better. So, we asked my dad if we could build a bucking chute and use his bulls.

He agreed to all of this, but only if he could put me on my first bull and I agreed. Then some other classmates got interested in this bull riding plan so they joined us. We built a chute and then gathered some of my dad's bulls in a pen and started riding them. Well, I think I rode my first bull for about three jumps.

I didn't last long on that first bull, but boy it only took those few seconds on his back and I was hooked on bull riding. It was a thrill like no other. I often tell people who are trying to figure out what to do with their lives that if you think you'd love to do something, just start doing it. It's as simple as that.

That's how I got into bull riding and you just never know where your passion will take you. My passion took me all the way to the National Finals Rodeo, three years in a row from 1963 to 1965. And, it took me into the Texas Cowboy Hall of Fame and the Professional Bull Riders' Ring of Honor.

It took a few years from that first bull ride for me to make the move to Professional Rodeo Cowboy. You don't just get on bulls and go. You actually have to 'train' yourself to be good at it and I put a lot of time into training.

When I graduated from high school in 1959 I went off to college. I joined the rodeo team and every Wednesday and Sunday we'd go down to where they'd do bull try-outs. This is where they tested bulls to see how they'd do in the rodeo. We volunteered to be the test riders.

It was great experience because we'd get to ride from five to seven bulls each time. And that was important because as you ride more bulls, you develop your instinctive reactions. With each bull you ride your body trains itself to react better to the movement of the bull. So getting to test ride all those bulls helped my body develop instincts that automatically took over when I rode.

The other thing I learned was that to be a good bull rider you really had to spend time just watching bulls. So I spent a lot of time observing bulls and I learned the importance of understanding them in order to have success as a bull rider. This is actually something that I learned to apply to all aspects of my life, including when I started training racehorses.

You need to take time in your life to reflect on things and understand them. I would sit and watch bulls to see how each one moved when it bucked. Did it walk on its front feet, did the bull rear, was he flat, or did he kick while he was spinning? All of these things would influence how I set my rope when I rode a particular bull and how I would position my body and program my mind.

I do the same with horses and I think any good rider does. It's not how you ride horses or bulls. It's how you ride this horse or this bull. It's about staying in harmony and balance with the bull and you figure that out by watching that particular bull.

I wasn't in college for long before realizing that riding bulls was my passion and direction in life. Once I came to that realization, I turned professional and I just headed on down the road with a few pairs of Levi jeans to join the Professional Rodeo Circuit.

Honestly, it was a bit like running off to join the circus. And it was that kind of life – bouncing from one town to the next with a rather crazy gang of cowboys. Sometimes you had a good run at a rodeo and left town with money in your pocket. Other times, you barely had the money to get to the next rodeo. Sometimes you had no money and that's when your buddies came in handy.

To make it as a professional bull rider you really have to love the sport and the life. It's not for everyone. I laugh thinking of all the people I met who thought it was for them and discovered it wasn't. I knew a lot of young men who, like me, wanted to be a rodeo bull rider. The life of a rodeo bull rider can be great if you really want to be one, as long as you don't mind getting on the bulls and can accept the injuries and pain and the traveling.

But I knew lots of young men who wanted to be bull riders until the injuries piled up, and then they decided they didn't want to be a bull rider after all. And that's fine, because you can't figure out what you really love and want to do with your life unless you try what you think you love and see if it works for you.

Being a bull rider worked for me and while it's not a career you can have forever – it does take a toll on your body – it was a career that helped move me along to my future career as a racehorse trainer. I learned a lot from bulls and I was able to apply all that knowledge to training horses. It's much the same. You have to respect the bull and you have to respect the horse.

Carl Nafzger was a leading professional bull rider in the 1960s who earned a place in both the Professional Bull Riders' Ring of Honor and the Texas Rodeo Cowboy Hall of Fame. He went on to become a successful racehorse trainer and is a member of the National Museum of Racing and Hall of Fame.

He is also author of "Why…Discovering Your Essence is Important for a Life of Meaning" in which he shares the life lessons he learned in his careers as rodeo cowboy and racehorse trainer.

COREY BROWN
I'LL DRIVE

In 1993 my rookie year in the PRCA, Bob Logue, Lance Crump, and I, went on a run to Jackson, Mississippi and from there to Peoria, Georgia. As a rookie it was my job to drive, which I didn't mind because I could never sleep when someone else drove. That was due to a hauling partner falling asleep at the wheel while I was asleep in the back of my truck the year before, and tossing me around like a rag doll.

We left Jackson after the rodeo around 10 o'clock and I drove all night long while Bob and Lance were sleeping in the back of the van. Somewhere about halfway in the Florida panhandle, I was done. I couldn't take any more so I pulled up at a store and hollered, "Lance, Bob, someone else's turn to drive." Bob said, "I'll drive," so he went into the store to get some coffee while I crawled in the back to get horizontal.

As Bob pulled away from the store I just happened to look at my watch to see what time it was. It was about 5:30 a.m., thirty minutes or so before sun-up. Just as I fell asleep I heard Bob yell at Lance. "Lance, wake up. It's your turn to drive." I heard Lance reply, "OK". When Bob yelled, it woke me up and I looked at my watch and Bob had only been driving for about 45 minutes.

I yelled back at Bob. "Bob, you only been driving for 45 minutes." Bob, then told me to shut up and go back to sleep, laughing of course, then Lance was yelling back at Bob, "Dude, that's just wrong," then the fight was on. This went on for about 5 minutes and when I finally had enough, I said, "Screw it. I'm driving. I'm tired of hearing y'all argue."

I drove even further that time, on past the Georgia/Florida line. By this time I was spent and didn't care if we made it to the rodeo or not. I pulled over and said, "I'm done. Someone is driving the rest of the way in. I have to get some sleep." I think Lance took over at that point, and drove us on in to Peoria.

DANNY O'HACO
THE HANG-UP

Rodeo was always full of surprises and one that I recall was at the Casper, Wyoming Rodeo. I was riding my bronc when something went wrong. I was bucked off away from my hand and knew I was hung up. The horse continued to buck with me along side of him. I was trying to keep on my feet and he was kicking at me and I'm taking a beating on my right leg and ankle. This had to be the most vulnerable position I'd ever been in.

The pickup men were at a loss on how to help me get free as we go down the arena. I know I have to do something or else I'm going to get hurt real bad. The horse stopped bucking and was just running, looking for the corral while I'm dragging on the side.

He turned and heads across the arena toward the grand stands. It's a packed Saturday night and the crowd was screaming with horror. They knew that this cowboy was in a pickle. The horse was heading right toward the fence and I realize that he'd going to have to turn one way or the other.

If he turns left it would give me a second to react. My plan was to do a Pony Express mount when he stutter stepped off the fence. Luck was with me that night and in that split second when he turned left, I vaulted up on his back and pulled my hand out of the riggin' and ejected myself off the right side and landed on my feet.

The crowd went wild and were standing and clapping for my safety while I was saying a prayer that I had survived. My pants and chaps were torn to shreds and I could feel my ankle and foot starting to swell from the stomping I'd taken. I limped back to the chutes, sat down, and started reflecting how lucky I was to get out of that jam. I got my boot off before the swelling would make it impossible to remove. I slipped into my tennis shoes and figured I didn't need to see a doctor. I thought I only needed some ice.

Every cowboy that rides rough stock will face being hung up. It's not if it will happen it's when. I had a rough time after that and the next day I was at a Western Store looking for some new Wranglers when the clerk asked me if I was in the rodeo. She went on to say she had attended the rodeo last night and saw the most amazing thing happen.

She said she saw this cowboy get drug and kicked around by this horse and that he jumped back on and freed his hand and jumped off right in front of the stands. She claimed she'd never seen anything like that in her whole life. I said, "Yes, I saw that, and that guy was me." She couldn't believe I wasn't in the hospital with a cast on my leg.

I think that night was when I said to my self, "If I can do that on a bucking horse, I might have a shot at doing stunt work in Hollywood." There was definitely an overlap between the two careers.

JOE FOSCALINA
I WILL CARRY THE FLAG

In the early 1980's, at the Australian Rough Riders Association Finals during a grounds rule meeting before the first performance, the subject of the Grand Entry came up. Some of the contestants opposed the Fellowship of the Christian's Cowboy Flag.

There were strong arm threats to who-so-ever carried the flag in the Grand Entry. Graham Heffernan stood up and stated, "I will carry the flag."

In our world today, we all need to stay strong and continue to carry the flag.

LARRY BRADY
RAIL SPLITER

At Fort Leonard Wood, Missouri, on the 4th of July, 1976, the Department of Army was having a Military/Civilian rodeo, so a bunch of us decided to enter. A life-long friend of mine by the name of Buddy Young decided to go, too. He had been getting on the bucking machine I had at my house and had been doing pretty good so we said, "Buddy, you might as well enter up and go with us."

I had been to Fort Leonard Wood ten years before when Uncle Sam sent me there on a paid one-way trip to spend with him. We called in and here we go in Buddy's Dodge stretch van, seven men and three women. Bud Mayberry from Thayer, Missouri had the stock. He also put on college, and open rodeos in the Southern part of Missouri. We pulled in there on the 4th. and saw that we had drawn decent, so we were happy.

A little bit about Buddy before we get to the heart of the story that changed his life forever. Buddy worked for the Arkansas State Police as head of Governor Security for then Governor Bill Clinton. He found that he had drawn a sure enough, good, rank bull by the name of Rail Splitter. We said, "By the way you're doing on the bucking machine, you won't have any trouble with him."

That bull had a set of clown stabbers that you could almost walk through. There was no lack of encouragement from us, all the way up to the bull riding and Buddy was cocked and primed. They bucked out a couple and when it came his time, he crawled over in there with Rail Splitter and them stabbers were at least a foot above the gate.

He looked at us and said, "Son-of-a-bitch." I said, "Don't worry about them horns 'cause he can't bother you as long as you're in the middle of him." As I pulled his rope and he was getting his wrap, his left foot was doing a tap dance on the gate slat.

I said, "OK, now go get him." He nodded and the bull blew out of there for about two jumps and I mean he did turn back. He made two turns then all hell broke loose. He jerked Buddy down between them horns and when he hit the ground, the hookin' was on.

The clowns finally got Rail Splitter off of Buddy, but the bull came back and got him again. We finally got out to where Buddy was lying on his back, looking straight up and grinning. I just thought all the air was just knocked out of him so I grabbed his shoulders and drug him over and propped him up against the calf chute.

I went ahead and got on my bull and got a goose egg. When I went back, Buddy was still sitting there so we thought he was just getting' his wind back. They bucked eight or ten more bulls and some would turn buck right down the chutes where Buddy was and he just set there staring.

When I finally went over to him he said, "You drug me over here and left me and them damn bulls ran all over me and I couldn't move." We got him in the van and went to the base hospital and got him X- Rayed and they said he was more dead than alive. He had a broken collar bone, separated sternum, and four broken ribs.

He wouldn't stay in the hospital so the doctor said, "You can go, but it is against my advice." He gave Buddy a pain shot and we hit the road with him stretched out on the floor of the van. The pain shot wasn't working so he said, "Stop at a liquor store and I'll get easy."

By the time we got to Newport, Arkansas and he was sure enough easy after a fifth of Jack Daniels Old No.7. He wanted to stop and see an old friend and it was about 3:30 o'clock in the morning. We stopped at his friend's house and woke him up, but Buddy's still stretched out on the floor of the van.

The first thing his friend did was pull the door open, grab Buddy by his arm and jerk him out on the concrete driveway, not knowing he was hurt. We finally got him back to Little Rock and this time he was ready for the hospital. He had a vacation there for a week and missed a full month of work.

Buddy still went down the road with me for years and we had some of the best of times, and do still to this day. One thing for sure, the years he went with me, he never paid another entry fee. We still laugh today about Rail Splitter, and Buddy says he felt just like in the movie J. W. Coop.

KIRK ALLMON
A LONG TIME AGO

I pulled up to a rodeo in Edna, Texas, and was surprised to see the bull I had drawn was not much bigger than a roping steer. This being a PRCA Rodeo I felt the need to question my friend Roy Carter in a kidding way," so I said, "Who's the steer and does he know he's going to get spurred?"

Roy said, "Don't under estimate that little bull because he's a bucker." Never the less, I was very confidant of my prediction. Well, all I can say is, WRONG. That little bull bucked so hard the first jump out, he pulled both my groins.

The second jump, he jerked me down between them little steer horns, tearing the tendons in my riding wrist and promptly dented the arena floor with my ass going through my hat at a very high velocity.

Needless to say, old RC 1 became a very rank bull, and now you know the rest of the story. I'm not sure of the year, but it was probably around 1983 or 1984.

JOHN L. SLOAN
LAP AND TAP

I grew up bull doggin from a lap and tap start. That meant no barrier. Many small rodeos in Texas did it that way. You just had to let the steer cross a score line in front of the box.

So comes a Fall rodeo at CSU, in according to my trophy, 1969. It was in some little cracker box building so I borrowed a half-Shetland pony from Casper College rodeo coach, Dale Stiles. That little sucker could fly…for about thirty yards. That was all I needed.

We get to the rodeo and it is lap-and-tap. I don't think any of those boys ever heard of it. I'm talking some good hands like

Dave Brock, Joe Dorenkamp, and a few others. Something like 4.8 is winning it. I get Billy Reno to haze for me and comes my turn. Now up to then everybody had been sitting their horse in the back of the box like you are supposed to.

But, I ride in and put that little Shetland pony right up even with the steer's shoulder. It is about a three foot score at the most. I nod, kick and lean over and am a smooth 3.3. We are about two feet over the score line. Lots of hollerin' and such, but all 100% legal and I got the trophy to prove it.

LONNIE GUYTON
BACK IN THE 80's

Back in mid 1980, me and some friends of mine were going to Cheyenne, Wyoming, to the Frontier Days Rodeo. We had been to a few rodeos before we got there so when we got to town, which was around 1:00 o'clock that afternoon we decided to stop and have a cool beverage before we went to get a room.

As the afternoon wore on I had more beers than I planned on and eventually it turned into evening. Well, I was sitting at the bar and being the only black man in the place at the time, suddenly this beautiful black woman with long black hair and an hourglass figure walked into the bar and I thought to myself, "Wow!"

Here I was, thinking that this was kind of odd to see another black person in this town. But, I'd had a few too many so I didn't think too much about it at the time. As fate would have it, she came over and we started talking. The night wore on and we went to other places and danced and she eventually took me home with her.

As a young Cowboy in a town like Cheyenne, and having the time of your life, sometimes you do things that you wouldn't normally do and in my drunken stupor I gave her my companion pass.

Normally this would not have been a bad idea, but remember when I said earlier that she was beautiful. Well, when I woke up the next morning the woman I went home with was not the same one I was seeing now.

I tried to figure out a way to get out of there without being noticed. Her place had wooden floors so I picked up my boots and slipped out of the house. I thought I was safe and that none of my friends would ever know what I did the night before.

I made it back to Frontier Park and was behind the arena talking to one of my friends when suddenly I noticed something or someone, had gotten his attention. He turned back around said, "Lonnie, is that you?"

I said, "Is what me?"

He pointed toward a woman walking toward me and it was the same one I'd met in the bar. That long black hair I thought she had, was a wig. The hour-glass figure I thought she had, was a girdle. And, those beautiful white teeth I thought she had, were false.

I tried everything I could to get rid of her, but couldn't shake her. Finally, I ran into a crowd of people and hid under the bleachers, ending up not being able to get on my bull that day. So the moral of the story is, when it's your first time in Cheyenne, never leave your friends. From that day forward, I've never gone to Cheyenne alone.

DOUG BROWN
MORE ABOUT THE MAN WHO RODE TORNADO

In 1967 or 1968 I was riding pretty good and had made some nice rides on National Finals draws, but I wasn't winning or even placing. My traveling partners and I pulled into Burwell, Nebraska one day and it was really, really hot. All the rough stock guys were slumped on their riggin' bags behind the chutes.

Freckles Brown came bouncing in and threw his gear bag on ground and started doing pull-ups. We had met at the PI in Portland a few years earlier when he was in a full body cast from a broken neck. He asked me how I was doing and we struck up a conversation and I told him I hadn't placed for a month.

We were joking around and I asked him if it would be alright to tell everybody he was my Uncle. He laughed and said, "Sure Doug, if you think it would help you out." I swear, if I didn't start winning right away. I won some All-Arounds, and placed at some major rodeos.

Later that Fall I ran into Freckles again at Pendleton. He said, "Doug, come here I want to talk to you. Look," he added. "I haven't placed for three weeks. Would it be alright if I told everybody you were my nephew?" We had a great laugh and I said, "Sure."

It was the apex of my rodeo career. He smiled and said, "See you at the Cow Palace," and winked. I thanked him and we both had a successful Fall run.

RED DOYAL
STOLEN CAR

One year during the winter rodeo a group of us entered Tucson, and a rodeo in California, because we were not up at the big rodeo until the next week. It was me, T.J. Walters, and a couple other young guys.

When we got stranded in Tucson with no ride to California, I ran into an old friend George Eads from close to El Paso. I borrowed his car and took him to the airport to fly home. I went back and picked up the others and we headed for the California Rodeo.

We never talked about the car, but later the story got around that I had stolen some guy's car and took it to California. When asked about it, I would just say he got it back, and never told anyone I had known George from college rodeos.

Last summer, my son was judging a rodeo with T.J. and T.J. told him about me stealing a car in Tucson to go to a rodeo. We took the car back to the Texas Rodeo and later, I got it back to George. I guess the other guys still think I stole it. A lot of them rodeo tales are like that.

REDBOY SCHILDT
WHAT HAPPENED

Back a few years ago I was asked to help out with a Nevada High School Rodeo Team since they had no one to assist with the bareback riding event. Most kids were turned onto bulls due to all the fame of the PBR. Well, being a bareback rider and having volunteered my soul to rough stock events, I dove right in.

I was standing behind the chutes at a practice session and this kid walks up and asks if I'd help him. I said, "Sure." I looked at his gear and when I noticed he was trying to ride a right handed rigging, left handed, that kind of got my attention. I tried to explain, but he wouldn't listen. It was a soft rag handhold anyway. He needed everything from a hatpin to a spur rowel.

He was the toughest kid I ever saw. He'd get up at 5am to feed his mother's Shetlands, ride his bike a mile or two to school, try to make rodeo practice after school, then work as a part time dishwasher at a truck stop at night. At one practice they let him get on a saddle bronc and I got there just in time to see the wreck. He'd gotten on with his boots tied on and bucked off over the front left shoulder.

Packed both stirrups and was hanging upside down asking now what do I do? As luck would have it the young horse just stood there. About scared that colt to death he was riding. It took a few guys a while to get him untangled. Finally, I decided I better have a talk with this guy before he got himself killed. I took him under my wing and eventually got him some gear, but he refused to give up that old soft handhold, probably for the better.

The kids snickered as kids do, but I could see change coming in his riding. At a high school rodeo in Lovelock, Nevada, he drew a pretty fresh, snuffy horse about 1100 lbs. When he nodded, that horse blew up and jumped about high as the chute gate, kicking over his head. About the third jump, Joe came loose and peaked at about 10 or 11 feet in the air.

He did one flip and hit square on his back when he met the ground. The air was cold that spring and the ground was hard as a tabletop and that fall would have killed the average man. You could hear that horse bellerin' and kickin' and when the dust cleared I could just barely see Joe.

I was wondering if his vertebrae were all in place, but before I could ask, he jumps up on the chute gate and screams in my face, "Well…what happened?" I had gone over the basics with this kid for two or three months, but trying to keep a straight face was really hard that day.

The best I could come up with was, "You nodded." I backed away and went for some coffee. You know, we went through some pretty tough tests that spring, but Joe came through at the Silver State Finals and placed in the rodeo. Joseph came through from not knowing a shadow from a hurricane in the riggin' event in just a few months, and he did OK.

Joe didn't come from money and not having any, he graduated that year and enlisted in the US Navy. His plan was to get through the Service and save money so he could rodeo. Last I heard he was talkin' about rodeoin' down in Texas and qualifying for the National Finals in Vegas.

Time went on and we all scattered doing our life things. I saw him a few years later in a Nevada Wal-Mart Store with a full shopping cart. It was a nice surprise to run into Joe. He introduced me to his pregnant wife and one small kid. I wanted to ask him,

"What happened," but I figured he already knew. I guess Joe decided to retire and tell Wild West Tales. God bless him.

RICHARD FLECHSIG
MUD AND BLOOD

In about 1997, I judged a rodeo for Kenneth Auger in Eldorado, Arkansas. The rodeo was on a parking lot covered with about fourteen inches of dirt. The Friday night performance was canceled as a tornado had been sighted in the area. It rained cats and dogs so we had slack next morning. The rain couldn't drain out and the arena was a sloppy mess.

We only had calf roping slack and I was flagging the roping, but before we started one of the ropers asked me if they had to wear cowboy hats and I said, "Yes. Slack is like the rodeo." They roped, and to their credit did a heck of a job taking two or three places. Also to their credit, they all wore one hat and about ruined it so they all kicked in to get the owner a new one.

That afternoon we were going to have an afternoon performance because of the rained out one on Friday night, but not many hands showed up. I was flagging the dogging and one of the horses was a little skittish because it was real windy. There was a canvas tape that the trick riders used that was hanging on the fence flapping in the wind and he didn't like it.

On the last run of the dogging, that horse spooked and threw his head up. I was pulled forward and his head hit my face. I rode back to chute and the other judge said, "Damn, Dick, your nose is bleeding," and indeed it was, as it was broken.

Fortunately, everyone else in the other events except the bull riders had turned out so all we had left was the bull riding. My wife was with me so she had the EMS guys get some gauze and wet it with saline solution and pack my nose.

I got my judges book and we started riding bulls. I'm dripping blood on the judge's sheet, plus mud spatters. Donnie Gay was announcing and half way through the event, I told them to hold up for a minute so I could get my nose repacked.

When they rode the last four or five bulls I went into the office and gave Mildred Farris my judges sheets. I told her be sure to tell the head office that this was a wild rodeo and if they didn't believe it, to take a look at the mud and the blood on the judges sheets. Donnie was sitting there and asked me how old I was. When I said, "Sixty-two," he started laughing and said, "Well, you're a tough old sumbitch."

ABE MORRIS
CHEYENNE FRONTIER DAYS

I have a fond memory of Doug Vold that happened at the Cheyenne Frontier Days Rodeo in July 1983. Rodeo fans that are familiar with the layout of that rodeo are constantly entertained because of the arena, as well as the race track events, that are held during the performance. Many of these are simultaneously held and the astute fans need to pay attention and constantly be on their toes.

Doug had successfully ridden his bronc that had bucked straight across the huge arena at Cheyenne. Right before his horse got to the other side, a bunch of race horses blazed by on the track right in front of the grand stands. Not wanting to be left out of the big race, his bucking horse leaped over the small rail fence with Doug still aboard and immediately gave chase.

Doug being the character that he is started to ham it up, wildly whipping his bronc rein in an over and under fashion in order to urge his trusty steed to run even faster. His spontaneous antics were very crowd-pleasing and the rodeo fans ate it up. A rodeo committee man had to open a gate to allow a couple of pick up men to join in the great race. It was pretty funny.

People that are familiar with Cheyenne know that the race track encompasses the entire rodeo arena, one infield grand stand

and all of the livestock holdings pens. During the wild horse race, the riders disappear from view for about a minute or so before reappearing towards the end of the race.

Well, the rodeo action continued and all of a sudden for no apparent reason, there was a huge roar from the crowd. At first, many of us cowboys didn't realize what was going on. Then a few seconds later, we all figured out that a pick up man had finally caught up to Doug and rescued him. He was being escorted back to the main arena and received a standing ovation.

ALLAN HOWARD
FORTY BELOW

Several years ago in late December I was wintering my cows about 3 miles north of where my buildings are located. I decided to bring them home to treat them for worms and lice. I also wanted to sort off some older cows and take them back to the winter pasture the next day, so I called my brother Norman and my cousin Duane to help me.

It was fairly cold and we had some snow on the ground, and if there was anything Duane hated it was a northwest wind in the winter time as it is always cold and coming straight out of Canada. Saturday was a good day. It was cold, but we were driving the cows south with the wind to our backs so it wasn't all that bad. We got the cows home and got them treated and sorted the way I wanted to, but since it took a while to get that done, I fed them hay and decided we would head them back to the winter pasture the next morning.

Sunday morning after we caught the horses and saddled up to drive the cows back north to the winter pasture, I asked Duane if he had enough clothes on because that wind was going to be tough. He said he did, so we took off and got the cows moving north. It wasn't too bad until we got about half way there. When we got out of the hills and gullies and into the open it had to be 35 to 45 below with the wind chill.

My brother and I were dressed pretty good for the occasion, but Duane wasn't ready for that good old northwest wind. We rode a ways and I looked back at Duane and his nose was white as could be. I stopped and said, "Duane your nose is white. It's freezing on you." I don't think he even realized it. So I took off my scarf and wrapped it around his face. It's funny because all you could see were his eyes looking at you. Those cows walked in single file thru the snow right into that wind just like they were going to water in the summer time, and it would have been quite the picture.

When we got the cows to the pasture, my wife Lisa met us with the stock trailer and we loaded the horses and headed for home. After we got home and unsaddled the horses I told Duane to come in the house to warm up and have some whiskey to get his blood flowing again. I told Duane if someone had punched him in the nose when it was all white like that, it would have shattered.

He laughed and said that was the coldest ride he had been on for a while. I saw Duane a couple of weeks later and his nose was peeling and was all red. We laughed about it and figured that the next time we would wait for warmer weather. Duane was around 70 years old when this happened. You just had to like the guy. RIP my friend.

BUDDY WILLIAMS
CHARLIE THOMPSON RODEO

In the summer of 1982 I was living in Lubbock, Texas with my two room mates, Karl Hanlon and Bret Carter. We were headed to one of Charlie Thompson's rodeos in Amarillo on Sunday afternoon. I think it was the 4th of July run and we had already been to a couple other rodeos that weekend.

We were running a little late of course, so we were flying along in Bret's Chevy Blazer. We were right outside of Plainview when we heard a loud pop. We had a blowout so we pulled over to the side of the road and Bret just sat there for a few minutes. Karl looked at him and said, "You don't have a spare tire do you?" Bret quickly responds with a, no.

Now, we're in the middle of nowhere and you can see for miles and there is nothing in sight. We are a little mad at Bret because we were already running late and now we may not make it at all. As Karl and I were sitting in the Blazer while it is up on the jack and the radio blasting a Bob Seger tune, we watched Bret disappear over the horizon rolling the flat tire towards civilization.

As we sat there listing to Bob, an old cowboy pulling a 32 ft. stock trailer pulls up behind us gets out and asked if we were ok. We tell him our dilemma to which he quickly replies, "We need to get you boys going so you can make that rodeo." He tells us that he is sure the spare tire on his cattle trailer would fit the Blazer and sure enough, it did.

We thanked him, got his phone number and told him we'd return the tire after we got another one. We sit there for a minute and Karl and I make decide to head on to Amarillo, thinking that we will see Bret on the way.

Well, we make it a long way without seeing Bret and I have to admit we were really trying harder to make it to the rodeo than we were looking for him. I was driving pretty fast, trying to make it in time for the rodeo and Karl looked at me and said, "Hey, there's an old car behind us and someone is hanging out the window waving his arms trying to get us to pull over."

We slowed down, thinking there is something wrong with the car. We get pulled over and looked back to see an old Mexican man in a 1952 Chevy that was so full of junk that Bret was having to sit in the front seat with the tire in his lap, waving his arms to get us to stop.

We told Bret that we were driving fast to try and find him and I don't think he believed us, but that's our story and we are sticking to it. I think Bret and his new friend had been chasing us for awhile and Bret was not too happy with us. We were a little late getting to the rodeo, but Charlie let us ride anyway. I did get my bull rode and ended up one hole out of the money, but still left there with a great memory.

DENNIS MONTGOMERY
SCOTTSDALE, ARIZONA 1987

At the first open of the World Bull Riding held in Scottsdale, Arizona in 1987 the prize money was $10,000.00. I was just twenty years old and although I wasn't entered, I had gotten on a turnout the night before.

Cody Custer said, "Hey, Dennis. Do you want to get on some more turnouts today?" I said, "Absolutely," and headed for my truck to get my gear bag. On the way back I realized I'd forgotten something in my truck, so I put my gear bag on a table by the barn.

When I came back Lane Frost was sitting on the table, leaning back on my gear bag talking to Cody Custer. I just walked up and stood there silently while they talked. Lane said, "Is this your gear bag?" I said, "Yeah," and he said, "Cody, I'd better get off his bag before that big sum bitch whips my ass."

We laughed and introduced ourselves, shook hands, and I went on about my business. He always remembered me every time we saw each other after that, until we lost him in 1989 at Cheyenne.

Let me add something here. In the past three months we have also lost some other greats in rodeo, Richard Tavenner, Hadley Barrett, and Harry Vold. Thanks for wanting to hear my story, and God Bless America.

BRYON MCNAIR
MY ROOKIE YEAR

In 1977 I was at a rodeo talking to Donnie Gay and he asked if I was interested in getting my card. Of course I said yes, so he told me to meet him at the Cow Palace in San Francisco in October. He said he would introduce me to the man who owned the rodeo stock called RSC. His name was Bob Cook.

I met Donnie in October at the Cow Palace at a big party they called the Hookers Ball. Of course, I wasn't dressed in rodeo attire; I had on my bell bottoms, platform shoes, a shirt and jacket my mom had made for me, and as always, hair down to the middle of my back.

When I saw Donnie he was talking to Bob Cook. He called me over to introduce me and Mr. Cook couldn't believe what he saw. He said, "Is this some kind of a joke?" By the looks of him, he probably don't even know what a rodeo is." He just kept cussing Donnie and sayin', "There ain't no freakin' way."

Donnie finally talked him into at least trying me so the next year, 1978, the first rodeo was in Clements, California. I had met Rob Smets the year before and he wanted me to teach him how to fight bulls. I ran into him the next night at the Cow Palace. They had cowboy boxing. Smets said, "You teach me how to fight bulls and you can be my boxing coach." I said, "Boxing coach?" He said, "Yeah, I'll show you."

Rob walked over to this great big guy and said, "I'm sorry," and knocked him out. I said, "Well, if it's that easy, I guess so." The next year Rob and I worked the Clements Rodeo together. I worked rodeos by myself 80% of my career, but Rob and I worked a couple together then he went on to become the five-time World Champion. But for what it's worth, I didn't teach him how to jump bulls without the barrel.

Anyway, Mr. Cook liked the way I fought bulls and let me work his rodeos and I got to see Alan Jordan ride Oscar. That was an amazing bull, not very big in size, but had a heart much bigger than most other bulls. When it came time for Salinas California, Mr. Cook didn't have the rodeo. But, because it was one of the biggest shows they did ask him to bring some stock out there.

I wasn't working it; Jerry Mariluge, Wilbur Plaugher, and another bullfighter who worked the first day, but couldn't work the last three performances, had it. They asked me if I wanted to work in his place and like a kid in a candy store I went crazy.

First bull out I heard the announcer say, "I don't know who this long-haired kid is, but I think he's having a good time." I didn't mean to, but I think I kinda hogged the next three days.

Then we went to Red Bluff and it was probably two feet deep in mud. My feet kept getting stuck so I took my shoes off and worked it barefooted. I saw Don Gish a few years later and he said, "I tell rodeo stories every day and you're always either the first or the last story. I don't know how you fought bulls in the mud barefooted the way you did."

At the last rodeo I worked for Bob Cook I broke my ankle. He told me I was fired when the rodeo was over, so I taped up and worked three performances with a broken ankle. At Fort Worth the next year I saw Wacy Cathey. He told me the Top 15 bull riders had voted me to work the Finals the year before, until they found out I had broken my ankle.

I had no idea, and if I'd have known I would have taped up and worked the NFR my rookie year, which to my knowledge has never been done. I'm pretty sure it would have been a career changer. It was still an honor to know that the Top 15 cowboys had voted me to work the Finals, with me havin' hair down to the middle of my back, the first year I had my card.

I kept my card, but I went back to Montana and worked for Dale Small for three more years. If a bullfighter got hurt I'd go work the Pro show, but I was happy just fighting bulls and the younger guys were the ones that needed the most help.

A man interviewed me once and asked if I regretted not working the Finals my Rookie year and I told him that I work the Finals every year. I treated kids and upcoming bull riders the same way I would have treated the Top 15 at the NFR. I loved what I did and was very lucky to be able to do what I loved.

CHARLIE BOWDEN
THE HOMETOWN COWBOY

Those of us who were around rodeos back when, have seen 'em. The hometown cowboys who had possibly never even been on a bronc or bull before, and looked very out of place at the arena. But, since the rodeo came to their town, these gunsels always entered the pitchin'. Heck, some of us may have even started out in rodeo the very same way because we all had to start somewhere.

It was a local 4th of July rodeo sanctioned by the State Association in 1990. I had never seen this young man at a rodeo before and I had been going to them for a long time. If he had any experience it had been somewhere that I hadn't been.

Not a bad looking youngster, I judged him to be early 20's and he seemed quiet and timid. He wore somewhat shabby jeans and a simple pale colored Western shirt. I'm sure his beat up straw hat was a Resistol, but it wasn't shaped like that of a rodeo cowboy. He definitely looked like a farm boy.

Then, there was the gear. His bull rope was the kind of flimsy grass rope you would find at a hardware store. He wore rough-out shotgun chaps and the spurs on his cheap cowboy boots were the basic spurs you would buy down at the feed store. I do not think he even had the rowels locked.

Now, all that would seem laughable if it weren't for the fact that this young man had drawn the worst bull in the pen. This bull was really tough. I only recall seeing him ridden twice over the years. There was no tellin' what he would do, which way he would turn back, or if he would be doing back flips. He had no set pattern, and on top of that he would hook you.

I had never drawn him and was grateful that I hadn't. I cringed at the thought of a beginner on this bull. I struggled with the thought of trying to talk him out of getting on that mean booger, or at least do what I could to help him, but in the end I did neither. I didn't watch this guy in the chute so I don't know if he knew what he was doing or not, but he apparently got his rope pulled and nodded his head in a timely manner.

I almost couldn't watch. That ol' bull blew out just a little past the end of the gate and commenced to spin and this guy was weathering the storm. I can't say it was pretty, but this new comer was putting it on the bad bull and had him ridden, until his rope broke at about the 6 second mark.

I never got the guy's name and as far as I know I never encountered him at another rodeo. But, for six seconds he made a whale of a bull ride. It is cliché' to say, but you certainly can't judge a book by its cover.

ROME WAGER
CHEYENNE, THE GRANDDAD OF RODEO

In 1973, I was 18 and entered at Cheyenne, Wyoming, at the Granddad of Rodeo in the last event called, "The Amateur Bronc Riding," before it became the, "The Rookie Bronc Riding." I was up the 1st performance as I remember it and at the time, I was driving an old 6 cylinder Ford that at 600 miles, not 620 miles, I had to pull over in the ditch and clean the spark plugs or it would hardly drive.

Later, I got 2 sets of plugs so I could run 1200 miles without cleaning them. I'd hit the ditch and yank one set out and slap in the other set less than 18 minutes. I could have worked in an Indy Pit crew if they'd been runnin' 6 cylinder Fords.

I was green as could be. Fresh off the Reservation, I was so painfully shy I almost couldn't ask for help. I drew a horse called C36 El Capitan. Someone had stolen my chaps two weeks before and the guy I'd been borrowing from needed them back, so I was asking to borrow chaps from everyone.

I'm at the biggest rodeo I'd ever seen and only one guy would let me use his chaps stood 6'4" and weighed about 200 pounds. He had legs bigger around then me. I stood 5'2" and weighed 119 lbs with a 26.5 waist. I could borrow his chaps, but onlyafter he rode. When my bronc came in, I went to the flank man and asked if I could wait on this big fellow on the other side so I could use his chaps.

You have to understand, in the RCA at Cheyenne they had not yet determined if the amateur bronc riders were part of the human race, but he mumbled something so I pulled my horse and ran to get the chaps I was borrowing. The big guy had bucked off right in front of the chutes which helped in swapping the chaps except it was about a foot of mud where he hit. I'm running around tying to clean the mud off and put rosin on that mud, but I don't know why.

Back then, hardly anyone pulled their latigos from both sides. I pulled mine from the gate side and asked the flank man to pull the latigo under the saddle. Before I got the guy's chaps I pulled my back cinch and measured my rein and by now they are speaking harsh words toward me because I was using time and oxygen that I wasn't yet qualified to have possession of.

I climbed on and nodded my head and mark the horse out. I held my mark out for 3 jumps the way John Mcbeth had taught me to, if I wanted a score at an RCA show. I spurred him alright for 2 or 3 jumps then my saddle goes to jumping up and down in the front and trying to move side to side.

I went to doing what was called back then, bicycling the horse with my spurring motion, meaning spurring forward with one foot and simultaneously spurring back with the opposite foot to get control of my saddle for a jump or two, then back with the regular spurring motion, which after a jump or two had to be repeated all the way across the arena till the whistle blew.

When I got off on the pickup man my saddle slipped way back and was flanking the horse so the pick up man undid my back cinch the saddle just fell in the mud. I hadn't checked ck my front latigo.

The flank man hadn't pulled it tight all the way under my saddle and it had totally come unraveled in the eight seconds. So, I'm carrying my old Hamley that still had a saddle horn on it back across the arena, trying to run, but had to stop as they bucked two more horses while I was crossing the arena.

As I get closer to the chutes I saw Mr. Harry Knight who was at that time honored as one of the greatest men in the history of rodeo. He had a big comfortable chair up above the chutes where this eighty plus year old monarch sat and watched his rodeo operate.

But, he had walked down a flight of stairs to the arena floor and was walking in that terrible mud toward me. I thought, "Oh, no. What did I do?" You have to remember I'm this little kid off the Reservation and I'm thinking I'm in big trouble. As I get to this man who had been a saddle bronc rider in the early 30's and had produced some of the greatest rodeos that had ever been in the history of rodeo, He extends his hand and shakes my mine.

He said, "Young man. In all my years in rodeo, I've never seen anyone spur and ride a bronc with nothing but a back cinch. You, my friend, are a bronc rider. Did you get a reride?" I said, "I don't know, Sir. I don't think so." He said, "Let me talk to the judges." I didn't get a reride because the horse bucked, and I didn't deserve a reride, but I still ended up one point out of the short go for the, "Amateur Bronc Ridng."

But, for that great old gentleman to come down that long flight of stairs and walk through all that mud to shake a little Indian kid's hand that just wanted to ride at Cheyenne, the Granddad of Rodeo…in the next 32 years that I rode broncs, without a doubt, this was the greatest compliments I ever received.

ED LeTOURNEAU
THE FIRST NFR

I joined the RCA in 1957, using my college card because I could join and not have to pay the initiation fee. I joined in September when school started, having had a fairly successful year in the amateurs. You could work RCA Rodeos on your college card, but not amateurs. The next year I paid my RCA dues and never went amateur again.

At the Cow Palace the guys were talking about a new concept where the top fifteen cowboys at the end of the year would compete at a National Finals rodeo against top bucking stock in the world.

Wow, that sounded like a great idea, but I knew I wouldn't be able to compete in that because I was planning on going to Vet school and it wouldn't allow me to go to enough rodeo to make the top fifteen. The first year of Vet school was six days a week so I could hardly make any rodeos.

But, when school ws out in June I went to as many rodeos as I could get to until school started up again. I flew to a lot of rodeos with Jim Madland in a Cessna 140, the same plane that Larry Mahan learned to fly in, and also the same one I turned upside down on a landing at Grants, New Mexico.

By the time school started in September I was in the top twenty, pushing close to qualifying for the first NFR. So I traveled back and forth to the Pacific International Rodeo in Portland, taking class mates with me to study on the way and won it, then placed deep at the Cow Palace and made the top fifteen, in thirteenth place.

So, here we were in Dallas, Texas at the first NFR in 1959. The first go-round had the top fifteen riders against the top fifteen bulls. There had only been seven qualified rides on those bulls all year long. Some had never been ridden, and some only once. Everyone was saying, "Pity the bull riders," but eleven of 'em got rode that night.

Then they were saying, "Must be the sand in the arena, or they weren't used to bucking in a building." But we said, "It must be the bull riders." I rode eight of ten bulls, won two go-rounds, placed in some others, and was the reserve NFR Champion. It wasn't a lot of money to win compared to today's payouts, but it went a long way to help pay my college expenses. One of the best times of my life.

"Crankin' It Up" © Roger Langford

PART 2

1. Pistol Pete Hawkins...I Made The NFR In A U-Haul Truck, Pullin' A Cadillac
2. Steve Scott...Ellie Lewis Scared Me To Death
3. Tom Ray...Sarge Was His Name
4. Robert Driggers...Drinkin' With Your Friends
5. Ned Londo...We Cleared The Fence
6. Lee Jones...Rat Shot
7. Melvin Smiley Sierra...Round Two At Cheyenne
8. Neal Heaslet...The Flyin' L Rodeo
9. Randy Magers...Belle Fourche Re-Ride
10. Rhett Hardcastle...Butler's #314
11. Rod Sinclair...The Calgary Stampede
12. Shari Korff-My Companion Is Watching
13. Mark Sanchez...Cosmic Cowboy
14. Jay Foscalina...Ground Rules Meeting
15. Kevin Busche...The Drunk Tank
16. Richard Flechsig...We Were Just Kids
17. Abe Morris...Downtown Denver
18. Allan Howard...My Cousin, Duane
19. Bryan McNair...My First Real Break As A Bull Fighter
20. Buddy Williams...Water Skiing In A Cotton Field
21. Don Mellgrean...Characters You Meet Along The Way
22. Charlie Cook...Travelin' Partners
23. Joe Lifto...IRA Board Meeting
24. John L. Sloan...Have To Tie A Stick In His Mouth
25. Ed LeTourneau...The Bull Rope Pad

PISTOL PETE HAWKINS
I MADE MY FIRST NFR IN A U-HAUL, PULLIN' A LINCOLN

The 4th of July, 1996, I was 20 years old with the dream of making the NFR. At the time, I was maybe in the top 30 in the World Standings. I went to Pecos, Texas, but did no good. I went to Belton, Texas, but still no good. The only rodeos I had left were Springdale Arkansas, St Paul, and Molalla, Oregon.

I didn't have the money to get to Oregon, so Springdale was my last chance to win anything over the 4th. I left Weatherford in a Lincoln Town Car that I was trying out and possibly purchasing from a family friend for $1000 bucks. I had $200 cash to my name, my dad's gas credit card, and a cheerleader that wanted to go to a rodeo. I'll call her Pom Pom.

We were late for the rodeo, but made it just in time to hear them playing the National Anthem while we were waiting in the line to get into rodeo. I bailed out of the old Lincoln and gave Pom Pom my Companion Pass and told her to park in Contestant Parking, then go find a seat and I would find her after I rode. (Mind you, this is her first ever rodeo).

I took off running toward the arena and made it just in time to put my riggin' on. I ended up winning first place and a $5,300 payday, the biggest check I ever won riding bareback horses at the time. After I got my check I asked Pom Pom if she had ever been to Oregon, and she said, "No." I said, "Me neither, but we're fixin' too."

"We left right away and got on the road because I was up at St. Paul the next night. It was an all night drive and we barely made it again. As luck would have it, we gained two hours because of the time change or we wouldn't have made it. I scored 84 and won 2nd place and made another $6,200. My new, biggest check ever, for riding bareback horses.

We left soon after I rode to make it to Molalla, just fifteen minutes down the road where I placed and won another $1000. So now, me and Pom Pom are on the west coast and I have no cash left, dads credit card is getting close to max, but I do have close to $13,000 in checks!

We get the old Lincoln headed south to take Pom Pom home from her vacation. I'm up at Santa Fe, New Mexico, and Casper, and Sheridan, Wyoming, the next weekend. We get to Twin Falls Idaho and the transmission goes out in my test car I'm thinking about buying. We limped into town going about 5 mph. We get a room and I take the car to the Ford dealership.

The guys said $5000 for a new transmission, and it will be done in maybe a week or two. Hell, that isn't going to work so I called the family friends that still owned the car that I was trying out, and told them what had happened. They said to get the car back to them and they would make it right. Only thing is, they had no idea I was in Idaho, and was in a long way away.

I tried to rent a car or truck, but was too young at the time. We stayed the night and the next day I was walking back from the dealership when I saw this huge U-Haul truck with a car trailer/hauler hooked up behind it, for rent. I ask the man how old I had to be to rent it and he said, "Twenty," so I said, I'll take it. I filled out the paper work and drove the U-Haul back to the dealership, loaded the Lincoln onto the trailer and went to the room to get Pom Pom.

We headed out the next day, but I realized there is no way we can make it back to drop her off and me get back to my first horse at Santa Fe. So, I figured we would just go on to Santa Fe, and drop her off and take care of the car and U-Haul when I got down in Texas. At Santa Fe, I scored 86 and ended up winning the 1st round.

I can still remember calling my dad and saying, "I have my car on a trailer and I'm pulling it with a U-Haul truck and I'm winning a check everywhere I go."

After a moment of silence my dad starts laughing and says, "Don't come home. Keep entering. We'll worry about the car and the U-Haul later. Just keep entering." So, me and Pom Pom and the U-Haul and trailer head north to Casper, and Sheridan, Wyoming.

I placed at Sheridan and then we came back for my 2nd horse at Santa Fe, still driving the U-Haul. By this time word had got around about this young kid moving up in the World Standings traveling with a cheerleader and driving a U-Haul. I ended up winning Santa Fe as well, and over that two week span I won somewhere around $14,000.00 in 14-15 days. I was now in the Top 15 in the world and never looked back.

The best part of the story is after I dropped off Pom Pom and headed to the U-Haul drop off place in Weatherford Texas, when I checked in the guy behind the desk said, "Did you come from Twin Falls Idaho?" I said, "Yes Sir. I came from Twin Falls." Well the person who filled out the paper work in Twin Falls must have made a mistake. You couldn't have driven all these miles in 8 days!"

I smiled, paid my bill with no extra mileage, drove the old Lincoln 5 mph back home, and she stayed there until I sold it for scrap a year later. When I think of the first year I made the National Finals, or hell, even my whole career, I can't help but think about those 2 weeks and how I made the NFR rodeoing in a U-Haul truck, pulling a trailer with an old Lincoln on it. Needless to say, my bareback riding career lasted longer than Pom Pom and the Lincoln both.

STEVE SCOTT
ELLIE LEWIS SCARED ME TO DEATH

I was working with Ellie Lewis hauling rodeo stock into Salinas for RSC Inc. We got to the arena and dropped off our load and were headed back to Clements, California, to pick up another load. It was about lunch time so Ellie stopped at a Mexican eating joint as we were headed east toward Los Banos.

We parked the rig on the side of the road and went in to have some lunch. When we finished eating, we were just sitting there sipping our tea and shooting the bull. Ellie said, "You about ready to roll?" I said, "Yeah, but let me go to the bathroom, first."

While I was gone, Ellie decided to play a trick on me. He stepped up to the cash register and paid us out, then told the lady that when he ran by her, for her to yell out, "Hey, hold on there." Then he hurried back and sat down.

I came out of the bathroom and just as I started to sit down Ellie jumped up and hollered, "Run," real loud. I said, "Do what?" and as he ran by me he said, "I said, run." I said, "Holy crap," and lit out right behind him. The waitress played it up real good and reached out and tried to grab me by the arm as I flew past and hollered, "Hey, hold on there, buddy." It scared the fire out of me.

Ellie rode saddle broncs, and was the World Champion back in the fifties. This was the seventies and he was so crippled up and bow-legged he could hardly run. He was going as fast as he could, but he was more or less just hobbling along like a crab. I sailed past him and jumped in the truck, flipped off the air, and got her in gear before he got there. When he got up on the running board I was already moving.

He hollered, "Well hell, let me get in the damn truck." When I pulled back up on the highway and looked over at him, he was looking in the side mirror, looking back at the restaurant. We went a ways and when he looked over at me I said, "Why in the hell are we skipping out on a ticket for? I had enough money." He didn't say anything, just kept chewing on the toothpick in his mouth and looking back and forth between the road ahead of us and the mirror, back and forth.

I kept thinking the law was going to overtake us and shoot us through the window or something. After a while I looked over at him and said, "Why did we run out of there? We could have paid out easy enough." Ellie looked at me, still chewing on that toothpick and said, "I don't know why you were running. I paid up out while you were in the crapper." He started laughing and it took a while to sink in, then I started laughing, too. We laughed all the way back to the ranch.

I was looking at Bill Putnam's web site called, "The Bull Pen," one day and saw a picture of Ellie smiling, and that's when I found out that he had passed away. It was quite a shock because I sure did like him. He was a heck of a bronc rider, a heck of a hand, and a heck of a nice guy. He would give you anything he had if you needed it. Ellie was the only guy that Bob Cook trusted to flank his great bull, Oscar.

TOM RAY
SARGE, WAS HIS NAME

This a story that honors the great animals that to most spectators go completely unnoticed. They're never introduced, but without them there would be no rodeo. In 1972 or 1973, at the Amboy, Illinois Pro Rodeo, Bob Barnes was putting on the show. At a lot his rodeos the arena and pens were portable. This was the last performance. It was a sellout, and the stands were full with standing room only. The arena was just outside of the town and it was time for bull riding.

Here, I'll introduce the hero of the story. Sarge, was his name. He was a bay pickup horse that probably weighted about 1300 lbs and stood about 16 hands. He could do it all and do it well, but he had to be used sparingly do to being tender footed.

Bob Barnes sent just few regular horses so, Sarge picked up the barebacks and the saddle broncs. Bob used one of the other horses to clear the bulls out of the arena. As I said, everything outside the arena was packed with fans and the arena fence was only about 4 feet from the first row of bleachers.

Bob had a bull numbered 55, and he had a habit of jumping out after being bucked. I rode my bull before 55 was to go and was standing in the corner where they had tied Sarge, talking to David Shadock and Bobby Kurten.

When 55 bucked, he bucked to the middle of pen. The secret to getting him out of the arena was ride to him and keep the pressure on him. The pickup man missed his chance and 55 ran toward the bucking chutes then made a sharp right turn.

He headed down the arena fence 'till he had enough speed then his 1700 lbs. cleared the fence with room to spare. He landed right in isle between the fence and the first row of seats and never missed a step. Coming toward him was a lady pushing a little child in a wheel chair.

With my chaps and bull spurs on, I untied Sarge and climbed on. I headed toward the other end of the arena where the roping chutes were, and all the time formulating my plan and keeping my eyes on 55.

People are scrambling up into stands and the only thing that was blocking 55 was the lady and the little kid in the wheel chair. At the last possible moment and without missing a beat, 55 jumped right over the woman and the kid in the wheel chair.

I can only imagine that everyone was amazed as I was. I got to the far end of the arena about the same time 55 did, so he made a left into the parking lot. Ducking between the cars and trucks, my skills with a rope left much to be desired and there was not much chance of getting a second loop.

The gravel parking was hurting Sarge's feet and I could almost feel his pain with each stride he took. It was impossible to follow 55 behind between the cars so I tracked him parallel, hoping for some kind of shot. He zigged in and out between the cars while I stayed along the edge awaiting for a chance to rope him.

Through the rows of cars and out into the open space approximately 25 yards or so, then we would be in the street. Sarge is hurting and sweating, but still going and I had thoughts of giving up to spare him the pain. I figured as poor as I rope, this probably be over pretty soon.

I got as close as I could, wanting to catch him as deep as possible. I took the shot and it landed as if I did it everyday. I dallied off and tried to keep the rope as tight as I could to try and cut his wind.

Sarge was soaking wet and he groaned with each step. I thought, "Will he quit and fall? Should I un-dally and just let 55 go?" Finally, Old 55 stopped, and with his head down, nostrils flaring, he searched for air, but Sarge gave him no slack.

Some of rodeo committee guys were now at scene so I asked one guys what we were going to do. He was the guy who drove tractor around in the arena to keep it level, so I told him to go get it. When he returned with the tractor I had Sarge pull 55 up close and un-dallied my rope and handed the guy. He tied it on the drawbar hitch and started back toward the arena. By the time he got there old 55 would damn near lead.

I rode back to the arena, stepped off of Sarge, and loosened the cinch. His head was down and he was panting hard. One of Barnes' men said, "I'll take him," but I said, "No. I got it."

I took him out back and unsaddled and rinsed him off. I sprayed water on his feet, put him in an empty pen and gave him a big scoop of feed and a block of alfalfa hay, and in a little bit he laid down to rest.

I've ridden lots of good horses, but, Sarge was hero. I took my spurs and chaps off and caught a ride back to Texas. The last I heard was that Sarge was just fine and was back doing his job.

ROBERT DRIGGERS
DRINKIN' WITH YOUR FRIENDS

I'm not much of a story teller, but as I remember it, a bunch of us would enter Eddie Puckett in the steer wrestling at some of the college rodeos just to watch him get down and get drug all over the arena.

Also, one year at Sul Ross, and I'm not sure but I think it was Red Doyle who talked me into entering the bareback riding. To the astonishment of everyone, including me, I was winning it after the first performance. I was only out of the money by one spot when it was over.

I hadn't been on a bucking horse in a long time and my bucking horse career was over. A person usually learns something from everything that happens and learned you shouldn't make life threatening decisions when drinking with your friends.

NED LONDO
WE CLEARED THE FENCE

In 1966, Bill Smith, Chuck Swanson, and I, were working the rodeo in Billings, Montana, and also the Home on the Range for Boys Bronc Riding Match in Sentinell Butte, North Dakota. We hired Bill Greenough and his small plane to fly us to Sentinell and back to Billings. We were riding at the match during the day, and riding at the rodeo in Billings that night. Bill was from Red Lodge, Montana.

When we left that morning it was cool and the flight was smooth. There wasn't an airstrip so we landed in a hay field. When we left to go back to Billings it was quite a bit warmer, almost hot, and with the weight of our saddles and gear, plus the four of us, the plane had trouble taking off.

Bill took a run at it and we were nearing the end of the hay field and coming up to a fence, so he got it to hopping and we cleared the fence and finally got airborne. I looked back and Chuck was white and his fingers were embedded in the seat. We were all shaken, but Chuck was the worst. I don't think he ever flew in a small plane again, but we did make it back to Billings.

LEE JONES
RAT SHOT

Back in the early 1970's, two bareback riders, Charlie Burns and Johnny Trout were living with me. Charlie wanted to learn to bulldog so I was teaching him. We had this old horse that did not want to go by the steer very fast. So, I told Charlie I would go get some rat shot and put in my 22 rifle and about the time he started down on the steer, I would shoot the old horse with rat shot.

Well, I went to the hardware store and they didn't have any rat shot, but the man told me that bird shot would work just as good. It was twice as big and had little bb's in it.

Charlie gets out a little late on the steer and runs him to the far end of the arena. I take my shot and by then, Charlie was way down the arena so the pattern was very big.

Charlie got 16 little bb's from the middle of his back all the way down to the calves of his legs and he was one mad cowboy. He came back to the chutes and said, "I'm going to whip your ass!"

I said, "No, you're not," and I jacked another shell into the chamber of the 22 and said, "No, or I'll shoot you again." I really had to keep my eyes on him for about a week, afraid he was going to retaliate. It wasn't a pretty sight having to pick those little bb's out of Charlie's back.

MELVIN SMILEY SIERRA
ROUND TWO AT CHEYENNE

As most everyone knows, at Cheyenne the Daddy of 'em all, there are many performances and many sections that a cowboy can be in. In round two at the 1992 Cheyenne Rodeo, it just so happened that I was in the section of bulls that I was a little bit familiar with. I had drawn a bull that had bucked me off once before.

Melvin Smiley Seirra, Cheyenne, 1992. [Dan Hubbell photo]

I'd drawn him at the Garden City, Kansas PRCA Rodeo, just a month before in the rain and mud and that night he had my number. It seems Cody Lambert had either won the rodeo on this bull or he had bucked him off the night before, I don't recall.

The bull had a kind of rolling move right out the gate as most bucking brindles do. A couple of friends of mine, Troy Hipsag and Dan, helped me down on him and he bucked out two jumps then turned back around to that right. He rolled me into my hand right away, but I crawled back into the middle of him with a strong left arm and a good spur hold with my right heel.

I was only 78 points, but I tell you it seemed like 95 points to me, and I thought I should have won first place. I heard the buzzer sound for the completed eight seconds and just as I started to get off, the bull switched gears. He went from being a righty bucking dude to now a lefty, spinning really flat and fast.

He jerked me down on his head and threw me about fifteen feet in the air, bent my belt buckle and gave the crowd a good show. As I twisted in the air like a catty bull rider usually does at that altitude, not so surprisingly I landed on my feet about the same distance behind him.

As I walked back to the chute, which was only a few feet away, Tuff Hedeman said, "Hell'uva ride, Smiley." Now, I don't know if it was because of the a great ride, or the acrobatics it took to get off safely with a ten-point landing, but I like to think it was because of the ride.

NEAL HEASLET
THE FLYIN' L RODEO

In 1987, me, Junior Goss, Darrell Kirby, and the late Kenny Cook and Bubba Lee, had laid out partying and was up all night after the rodeo. Somehow or another the following Sunday morning, we all wound up out at the flyin' L Rodeo arena in Mount Vernon, Arkansas. The Flyin' L Rodeo was Arkansas' oldest hometown rodeo to date and is still in operation.

Bubba Lee was the son of the late, great Roy Lee, who owned the arena. He was a fine man and was also preacher at his church. Well, we decided to run some bulls up and buck 'em while Preacher Roy Lee was preaching. Me and Darrell Kirby got on and Darrell messed his hand up, and I went down in the well.

When I freed my hand from the rope, the bull kicked me in the face and broke my jaw. And, if that wasn't bad enough he also stomped me in the same place he'd kicked me, therefore shattering my jaw thirteen places

I guess that was God's way of letting us know there were better places we could have been on a Sunday morning. I miss those days, and all the people I've run across that have come and gone through the years.

RANDY MAGERS
BELLE FOURCHE RE-RIDE

When I was rodeoing with Jerome Robinson and Gene Bightol, we went to Belle Fourche, and I drew a bad bull and was awarded a re-ride. I had some time so I went on to Livingston. After the rodeo I caught a ride and made it back to Belle Fourche, about 7:30 o'clock Sunday morning.

The motels were full so Gene was asleep in the car with both doors wide open and his legs sticking out. I grabbed him by one leg and gave him a jerk. When he sat up, I asked him what re-ride bull I had. He told me that my re-ride bull had gotten crippled and that my other re-ride was a Hereford bull that had bucked off Ronnie Rossen.

I went over to the pens to try and get a look at my bull and was walking down the alley way when I saw Jerome Robinson up on the catwalk above the pens. I asked him where my re-ride bull was and he pointed that way. When I walked around the corner, the Hereford bull was lying in a pen close to the fence.

I asked Jerome, "Does he buck?" and he said, "I think so." I reached through the fence panels and touched the bull on the head and he shook his head, snorted, and blew snot all over me.

After the rodeo started and it was my time to get on, he was the smallest bull I'd ever been on. But, hey, if this sonofagun could buck off Ronnie Rossen, I'd better be ready. I got on and nodded for the gate and the damn bull walked out of the chute and just ambled all the way to the catch pen. I had to stay on the full eight seconds or I wouldn't be given a re-ride.

So I stayed on him until he got to the end of the arena then bailed off and ran for the fence. When I got back to the chutes everyone was having a laughing fit. I soon discovered it was all a prank, and that the bull was Wiley McCrey's little clown bull.

Sonny Linger said it was the funniest thing he'd ever seen, me trying so hard to ride that walking bull, and after that, he always kept a picture of it on his wall. My wife always said I was gullible and I guess she was right, but I got another re-ride bull and this time, I won first place.

RHETT HARDCASTLE
BUTLER'S # 314

When I was fifteen years old, I entered the Odessa Sand Hills Rodeo and got on Butler's #14 in the slack. He jumped out and made two rounds right in the gate and jerked me down and hooked me in the chest, then stopped.

I spurred him in the neck and made a few more rounds and he threw me off right at the buzzer. My dad said, "Son, you're damn tough, but you'd better stay that way if you want to be a professional bull rider.

ROD SINCLAIR
THE CALGARY STAMPEDE

This is about the second time I drew Calgary Stampede's Bucking Horse #231 Moon Rocket. He was one of their best at one time, and was selected to go to the Canadian Finals Rodeo nine times and the National Finals Rodeo eight times.

In 1976, Moon Rocket was named the best bareback horse at Calgary, the top bareback horse in Canada, and also the World Champion bareback horse. He was also named the best bareback horse at Calgary Stampede again in 1981.

The first time I drew him was at Calgary Stampede's Rodeo Royal in the spring of 1980. I was 81 points and won the round. The second time was at the 1980 Calgary Stampede, later that summer. He wasn't a real big gelding, but he was still pretty strong. He really got in the air, kicked really high and hard, and had a lot of drop, trying to pull you down over his head. You didn't dare stub your toe on him or he would make you pay.

This particular time I had him at the Stampede, he was having a bit of a mad on. When I started to set my riggin' on him, he started leanin' back against the buckin' chute. I managed to get him pulled, but couldn't get but one foot down because he was leaning so hard against the back of the chute.

Winston Bruce rode up and said, "Let a couple go in front and we'll roll him. But, you'll have to hurry or he'll do it again." Well, we got him rolled and he decided to stand up just long enough for me to set my hand in the riggin' and start to slide up on my hand hold.

Then it happened. Just as I was about to nod, I lifted on my hand hold and it hit me right in the middle of my chest. Turns out when he was leaning he strained so hard that it broke my cinch at the D ring and there were only a few strands holding it when we rolled him. Had it held for just a second or two more he would have made that first jump and I would have been out the back door with my riggin' in my hand and dirt in my mouth.

Jack Duce ran and got the cinch off his bronc saddle and we re-pulled him. It all worked out because I was 79 points and won the round. The next day Bob Schall said, "I heard you won the round yesterday." I said, "Yep." He said, "I heard the good Lord had both hands on your ass too." Well, he was right because sometimes the good Lord is in your corner for sure.

SHARI KORFF
MY COMPANION IS WATCHING

I've always been amused by the animal rights people. The thing they really don't understand is the reason we do what we do is because we love being with these animals. Rodeo is a chance to make a living at something you love with an animal you love.

I definitely did not do it for the money. Barrel Racers feel that way probably more than any other event and are not shy about that fact. Here is a good example (no names are given to protect the innocent)

I was traveling with another barrel racer and it was several hours after the performance at Ellensburg, Washington. We were getting ready to go have dinner. As we were leaving for dinner, my companion notice a calf horse still saddled and tied up to the fence. We knew the horse belonged to one of, if not the top, cowboy in the world at that time. We had seen him earlier and he was not happy about how the horse had preformed.

Well, my companion decided the horse had been disciplined enough so she went over and unsaddled the horse and we went to dinner. When we returned from dinner the horse was saddled again. My companion went over took the saddle off and put the saddle back on. The next morning the thing everyone was talking about was the horse belonging to this top notch cowboy.

Everyone who saw the cowboy was laughing and giving him a hard time. You see, when she put the saddle back on the horse, she put the saddle on backwards. I know he was not happy with all the attention and I never saw that horse tied late at night to the fence again.

I tell you now, cowboys and cowgirls fully realize and appreciate that for any animal to compete at it best it must be given the best care possible. The biggest enemy is the miles we have to travel. No one is going to do anything to keep an animal from performing at its absolute best. If they do, my companion will be watching.

MARK SANCHEZ
COSMIC COWBOY

1975, several of us entered at the Texas State Fair in Dallas, and also entered a Matt Dryden Rodeo in Florida. We left in

Nicky Wheeler's pickup which had a camper on it. Of course as was sometimes the case, we had to stop by the Cosmic Cowboy in Huntsville Texas. We were there for quite a while that night, then all six or seven of us loaded up in the pickup and headed to Florida.

Outside of Liberty, Texas we were running at top speed to get to Florida because we'd stopped for too long at the Cosmic Cowboy. It was very foggy and suddenly the three-lane highway narrowed down to a two-lane. We left the road at a high rate of speed and wrapped Nicky's pickup around a tree.

As everyone was scrambling out, we started counting people and Roy Carter was missing. We heard Roy, and he was still in the camper and couldn't get out. He'd been sleeping on the floor of the camper when we hit the tree and all the riggin' bags and clothes bags had buried him under the bed against the cab of the pickup.

Everyone was in good health by a miracle except Roy, who had a few broken ribs. It was pitch black, foggy, and about three o'clock in the morning and as we watched the truck steam, we were wondering, "What now?"

We heard a clunking sound, sort of chugging sound, and suddenly up pulled a guy in an old station wagon. He asked what was wrong then he saw the wreck. We told him we were headed to Florida to a rodeo and he said, "I'll take you to Florida." And, here it begins.

Nicky stayed with the truck while several of us jumped in the old station wagon and off to Florida we go. Well, with small talk and naps, on through the rest of the night we go. About mid-morning that next day we realized the station wagon was only running 50 to 55 miles an hour. At that point, I think it was Bo Ashorn, asked the driver, "Is this as fast as this piece of shit will run?" and the reply was, "Yes."

So, alternative plans began brewing and with no rental car places around and the nearest airport a few hours away, we headed for the airport. I think it was Atlanta. Anyway, I was up in the next performance, as was Bo, and I'm not sure, maybe Travis Hudson or Mark Smith. So, Roy and someone else got on the plane and the rest of us that couldn't make it in time in the old station wagon, headed back to Texas.

Bo said to the driver, "We aren't riding in this piece of shit all the way back to Texas," and the driver said, "You guys are getting me back to Texas." He reached under the seat pulled out a pistol and said, "Yes, you will."

Well, a few hours later we stopped for gas and when the driver went in the station, Bo looked at us and said, "I'm going to get his bullets," and he did. Then, if you know Bo, he immediately began telling the driver, "We're getting out and getting a rental somewhere," and the driver pulled his pistol and reminded us that we were getting him back to Texas."

Bo grinned and said, "That don't mean anything. I have your bullets." The driver checked, then reached under the seat and pulled out another gun. But, Bo never let up and ribbed on the guy continually. About day two and a half, we are back in Louisiana in the middle of nowhere and at a gas station straight our of a movie.

Only one light in the parking lot and June bugs and every other kind of bugs were flying around the light as we pull up to the pump. It was late at night and the wheel falls off the car, right in the driveway. We put the spare on, got gas, and proceeded off at 50 to 55 miles per hour and Bo never weakens.

Anyway, we are finally back in Liberty, Texas and the driver, at about three o'clock in the morning said, "My dad owns this building." He walked around it and comes back to the car, but doesn't say much. We disperse somewhere around north of Houston,

While lying in a motel the next morning, the local morning news said that our driver, who was an escaped convict, had been arrested. That is a three-day experience that I will never forget.

JAY FOSCALINA
GROUND RULES MEETING

At our NHSRA rodeo district meeting, a motion was put before the members to change the colors of our team vest from red to black. The vote was real close so it was decided that the voting be postponed and should take place at the next rodeo when all the members were present.

Before the next rodeo began, we had our typical grounds rule meeting which was held in the arena in front of the bucking chutes while the elected officials were up in the announcers stand. With about 100 contestants, some on horseback, the vote on the changing of the team vest colors was brought before the body.

The announcer said, "All those in favor of changing the color of the team vest to black, raise your hand." About half the contestants raised their hand. Those in the announcers stand made a feeble effort to count the hands after which he said, "All those who want to keep the red vest the way they are, raise your hand."

Again, the other half raised their hands. It was hard for them to count because the contestants kept moving around and the vote was real close. So the announcer comes up with the idea to help with the counting and said, "All those who want black, stand on my right side and all those who want red, stand off to my left, so we can accurately count."

The contestants split up into two groups with about twenty feet of space between them. By this time they were all getting bored of the whole process. All it took for the ensuing chaos to start was for some fool to pick up a dirt clod and chuck it across at the other group. All of a sudden dirt clods were flying everywhere, people were scattering, horses running amuck, and it was anarchy in the arena. After it all settled down, the red vest won and it remains red to this day.

KEVIN BUSCHE
THE DRUNK TANK

In late April of 1978, my buddy and I had entered two indoor spring rodeos in Fox Creek and High Prairie Alberta. Fox Creek is about 150 miles northwest of Edmonton and High Prairie is another 120 miles or so northwest of there. Daryl and I were up in the Saturday Night performance at Fox Creek, and Block Brothers Rodeo Company had the stock.

I'd never been to one of their rodeos before and didn't know the stock, so I asked the bullfighter Rusty McLean about my bull. I had known Rusty for several years as he worked a lot of rodeos for Ted Vayro of Grass Lands Rodeo Company. Rusty said, "Oh, he's just a big high-loper. I'll meet you at the far end of the arena."

Well, when they loaded the bulls he was right about one thing, he was big. He was the biggest bull I had ever seen to that very day, more like an ox. His back was level with the top rail on the chute gate and he filled it up full width. You couldn't get your feet down alongside him. I let the knot in my bull rope out as small as it could go and when I pulled it, the tassel on the end of the tail was just barely sticking out past my palm.

I figured a bull that big couldn't be very fast, and seeing as I couldn't get my feet down in the chute, that I would just jam them down when he was turned out. There weren't any other options, so I nodded. Man, he blew outta there and turned back so hard and fast while trying to kick the lights out that I don't even think I made it halfway through that first round.

He fired me over the back side of the still open gate and I landed on top of my head with my feet straight up in the air. When I regained my senses, I looked at Rusty and he was laughing. He said, "I've never seen him do that before." I still don't know if he was pulling my leg or if that monster was just feeling his oats that day.

When the rodeo was over, we decided to head to High Prairie and see if we could make the dance. We drove as hard and fast as my Cutlass Supreme with a 455 could go, and pulled into High Prairie at around 11:00 o'clock that night.

We pulled into the first gas station we saw and went in to buy dance tickets. The clerk told us the dance had been cancelled by the RCMP, as the local natives were restless and the RCMP was afraid of a clash between them and the cowboys. So, we cruised around town until we recognized a couple of vehicles outside one of the bars belonging to some cowboys from home.

We went inside only to find out we had missed last call and the bartender wouldn't serve us. There were about six or eight cowboys at one table and the rest of the patrons were all local natives. They were playing pool and eyeing us up and you could feel the nervous tension in there big time.

One of the cowboys we sat with was Wayne Eithier. He was about 5'7" and maybe weighed 140 lbs. He rode bulls and was a bullfighter. In spite of his size, he was a scrapper and had super fast hands and feet. Wayne had bought a couple of cases of off sale beer before we arrived at the bar and when the bartender wouldn't serve us, Wayne opened the case, popped the tops off of two beers and handed them to us.

We each had a drink and the bartender came flying out from behind the bar, grabbed them and the two cases of beer and threw them behind the bar, then instructed us to leave. Everybody was caught off guard so Wayne asked what the problem was.

The bartender said, "You opened off sale beer in here and that's against the rules. So, get out." Wayne apologized and told him he didn't know that and if he would just give us the two cases of beer back we would leave peacefully. They exchanged a few more words, but the bartender was in a foul mood, plus the fact that he was a big dude.

Wayne was sitting on the table top with his feet on a chair and the rest of us were sitting in the chairs when all of a sudden the bartender jumped at Wayne. What happened next was a blur because the next thing I knew, Wayne had launched him self up onto the table and kicked that bartender right under the chin. He went down like a fat kid on a see saw.

That was it. The natives swarmed us and we were outnumbered at least 5 to 1 so we all bolted for the doors. There was the front entrance that we had come in from the street, and a side door that went into the parking lot. We scattered outside. Now, everybody in that group of cowboys, myself excluded, were a tough bunch of guys and had been in our fair share of scraps. But, this was shaping up like the little big horn so we retreated hard and fast.

I had parked down the street nearly a block away and Daryl and I made it to my car unscathed. The other guy's vehicles were right across the street from the bar and too close to the mob that followed us out, so they had scattered in several small groups. As all this was happening there were several RCMP cars cruising by, but they made no effort to help and just kept on going.

We drove around and found three of our buddies several blocks away. The others had also outran the mob and waited for things to settle down and went back for their vehicles later. The three I picked up were Rocky Moore, Alan Hunt, and Todd Jones, who was my regular traveling partner, and a cousin to four-time Canadian Bareback Champion Jim Dunn.

We eventually drove them back to Alan's pickup, but he was nearly out of gas and the three of them were all up in the slack at Fox Creek at 8:00 o'clock Sunday Morning. In those days, the gas stations in the small towns were all closed by 10:00 or 11:00 o'clock at night so they were in a jam.

There were a couple of bulldoggers that worked for a rock bit company and they were allowed to take their company trucks to the rodeos. Because they were always traveling to remote drilling rigs, they had 100 gallon tidy tanks on the box, so we drove around until we found the motel they were parked at.

When we got out of our vehicles Rocky said, "Buschey, you got any beer?" Well it just so happened I had a cooler of beer in the trunk so I opened it and handed everyone a beer. I don't think we had taken more than two sips when out of nowhere three cop cars came screaming into the parking lot in a four wheel skid. They all jumped out with Billy clubs and seemed very anxious to whack somebody with them.

As they came tearing into the parking lot everyone started ditching their beer cans. I set mine in the trunk and closed the lid and everybody else tossed theirs under the vehicles. It was raining out and we were all wearing slickers and had just been having a beer and deciding who would go and wake up the motel desk clerk.

We needed to see if we could find out what rooms the bull-doggers were in to get some gas for Alan's truck when the po-po arrived, and you would have thought we had just robbed a bank. There were two of 'em in each car, so six altogether, and the one who seemed to be the boss was a big dude. Not fat either, just a big tough looking guy and he was waving that Billy club around a lot.

He wanted to know what we were up to and Alan was trying to explain to him why we were there. He didn't seem too interested in actually hearing the truth and told Alan to shut up. Then he looked at me and said, "Whose car is this? Do you have any alcohol?" Of course, I denied it and he knelt down and started pulling half full beer cans out from under it. Each time he would say, "Is this your beer?" and each time I would say, "No, that one's not mine."

The slicker I was wearing was one of the yellow long riders and he kept calling me yeller! "Hey yeller, is this your beer?" Well my old buddy Todd was nearly peeing his pants laughing at me, fibbing to the cop when the cop turns to him and says, "You think this is funny?"

Todd straightens up and now looking a little nervous says, "No. I don't think it's funny." The cop says, "Which one of these beers is yours?" Todd perks up and says, "None of 'em. I don't drink!" The cop says, "Why don't you drink?" Well' ol' Todd, he's pretty fast on the draw and looking real proud now says, "I'm religious."

The cop says, "What religion are you?" Todd says, "Well I'm a Christian." and he's got a big smirk on his face like he's won when the cop lifts his Billy club up over Todd's head and hollers, "Oh yeah, well Christians drink. So get in the damn car." Well, he nearly sprained his ankle he spun around so fast ran and piled into the backseat of that cop car and pulled the door shut. Then it was me who was trying not to laugh out loud.

The cop turns his attention back to me and says, "Open the trunk!" I fumbled around and pretended I couldn't find the keys and he says, "You open it or we'll pry it open!" Well, that's was all it took. I pulled out the keys and unlocked the trunk. He picked up the open beer I had set in there and says very calmly and sternly, "Is this your beer?" I said, "Yes sir, that one's mine."

Now he's smiling and says, "I knew you had one here somewhere." So he made me take the cooler out of the trunk and take it to his car where he had me open all the rest of the beers and pour them on the ground. Then he put all the empty cans into the cooler and put my cooler in his trunk. He confiscated my beer cooler, too.

Then he asked for my driver's license and that's when he discovered I was only 17 years old, the legal drinking age in Alberta was, and still is eighteen so he wrote me a thirty-five dollar ticket for minor in possession. I had quit school a year before and worked on the drilling rigs. Funny, that at that age the government thinks you're old enough to work with the men, but not old enough to drink with them.

After he wrote out the ticket he says, "What do you think I should do with your smart ass buddy?" I said, "Well, I dunno. What were you gonna do with him?" He says, "Well, I should put him in the drunk tank for the night to teach him a lesson, but if you think you can keep him out of trouble I'll let him go".

I thought about it for a minute, pondering that if the tables were turned and it was me in the back seat of that cop car, he'd let me go to jail? Hmmmm. I looked over at him in the car and he looked like a lost pup in the back of a dog catcher's van with his nose pressed against the window. He didn't look nearly as humorous as he thought he was ten minutes before, so I told the cop I would make sure he was good, and he let him go. They got in their cars and left.

Alan woke up the motel clerk and she phoned the bulldoggers' room and they came out and fueled his pickup up with gas. They headed out to Fox Creek at about 2:00 AM. One year later to the day we are back at the High Prairie Rodeo, but this time they didn't cancel the dance. For a small town there was a lot of good looking girls and one of them picked up my buddy, Todd.

Seeing as they had both been drinking, they were walking back to her place. He had a belly full and they had taken a shortcut through somebody's back yard. In the backyard was a garden so he was staggering around in the garden, trying to help himself to some carrots or whatever. It just so happened that the lady who lived there was awake and using the bathroom and heard the commotion in the back yard as the girl was trying to coax him out of the garden.

Well, as luck would have it, her husband was an RCMP officer on night shift. She called him and a couple of minutes later the police cruiser pulled up. Her husband got out, handcuffed my buddy and he got to spend the night in the High Prairie drunk tank after all. That was nearly 40 years ago, and every now and then we still laugh about it.

RICHARD FLECHSIG
WE WERE JUST KIDS

When I was seventeen me and two buddies went to look at a horse that was for sale. I had really just started riding bulls. When we arrived at the farm we noticed a good sized bull in a pen by the barn. My buddy Joe Courtney, a bulldogger, said, "There's a nice bull Richard. Ask the man if you can ride him." The man showing us the horse laughed and said, "Sure, but I don't know how you'd get on him."

We were just kids and would figure out a way. I had my riggin' bag in the car so I got my bull rope and put my spurs on. We had a lariat so we roped him and tied him off to a gate post and tried everything we knew, but no way were we going to get a rope on him.

Joe spied an old, and I mean really old, wooden shotgun chute by some old working pens so got the bull into the pens and then into the shotgun chute. The gate hinges were barely hanging, but our other buddy Jack Beaver said he could hold it closed. Nice try Jack.

By now, this once easy to handle bull had about enough and was losing his temper. I hurried and got my rope on him and using a jury-rigged chute hook made of baling wire, I get on him and Joe pulled my rope. Now friends, here is where you need to stop and say, "What the heck are you thinking?"

I figured if I did get out on him he was going to really put a hurt on my knees coming out of a shotgun chute. This bull has had it by now and is big time mad and is leaving with or without me.

When he put his head down and lurched forward I let go of the rope, the smartest thing I had done all day and he hit the gate with his head and about fourteen hundred pounds of weight. Sadly, Jack's 160 pounds were no match for holding this big fellow.

The hinges came off and he came out over the gate and Jack. Have you ever seen a cartoon where the guy gets run over and the door is laying on him and all you see are arms and legs? That was Jack.

Joe and I are dying laughing as we help Jack stand up, and except for a few scrapes and a bruise or two, he would live. Fortunately, we had taken the lariat rope off the bull while he was in the chute.

When I stop now and look back at that day it was marked for a wreck. Had the gate held and the bull cooperated I would have probably busted at least one kneecap and possibly two. However, Jack saved the day and I rode home unscathed.

ABE MORRIS
DOWNTOWN DENVER

Years ago I worked in the phone center for a Fortune 100 Financial Services Corporation in downtown Denver, Colorado. My shift didn't end until 9:00 pm. Getting back and forth to work was pretty easy. I drove to a nearby Park n Ride in Northglenn, Colorado and rode the RTD transit bus. After work we would either walk or ride, depending on the weather to the free bus shuttle at the 16th Street Mall, then back to the RTD bus station.

In January of 2002 I got off work as usual and a female coworker and I walked to the curb to wait for the next shuttle bus. It happened to be during Denver's PRCA National Western Stock Show and Rodeo. There was also a gigantic Western Marketing Show that took place during the same time.

The weather was cold, and as I boarded the bus I noticed a couple of rodeo cowboys who were in town for the Stock Show and Rodeo. I was in professional office attire because jeans weren't allowed, and was wearing a ski hat. Immediately, I recognized the 1998 All-Around World Champion Dave Appleton.

I hadn't seen Dave for about 12 years and I knew he wouldn't recognize me dressed in casual business attire and all bundled up for winter, as well. Right away, I started harassing him and asking him if he was a real cowboy or was he was just wearing a cowboy hat because he wanted to look like one.

My co-worker kept staring at me in amazement, just knowing that sooner or later these cowboys were going to get fed up with my taunting and beat me up. No matter what response I received from Dave I kept saying, "Yeah sure. That's what they all say." The punch line, so I didn't get punched out was I finally said, "Dave, the next thing you're going to tell me is that you were born in Australia and they also call you the Lone Roo."

You should have seen the look on his face because he knew there was something else behind this chance encounter. I finally asked him if he had ever heard of a black bull rider by the name of Abe Morris? Right away, he knew who I was and gave me a big bear hug and we both got a kick out of that little escapade.

A few nights later I saw Bob Logue at the annual Wrangler Party in downtown Denver. He said Dave had already told him about seeing me a few nights before on the shuttle bus. I didn't see Dave Appleton again until his PRCA Hall of Fame induction ceremony and then again at Harry Vold's Memorial service in Colorado Springs, a few weeks ago. We still get a good laugh about meeting each other on that shuttle bus in downtown Denver.

ALLAN HOWARD
MY COUSIN DUANE HOWARD

This story is dedicated to my late cousin Duane Howard, but it strays away from the rodeo arena a bit. Late in the fall I was doing some work for a fellow south of where I live. He had a 3 year old stud that was barely halter broke that needed castrating. The guy was feeding him oats twice a day and all he did was chase him in and out of the barn.

I told the guy that his horse was kind of good built and good looking. That's all it took for him to insist I buy the horse from him. I told him that I didn't need another horse, but he kept on and the price got lower and lower so I ended up buying him.

I got him home a few days later and was going to start some ground work on him, and boy was he snorty and was acting like a bronc. There was about 8 inches of snow on the ground at this time and I didn't want to get bucked off on the frozen ground and get hurt, so I quit him for a few days.

I was telling Duane about this horse that I had bought and how snorty and full of oats he was. I told him I didn't want to get into a wreck and get hurt for I was the only one here to feed and take care of 250 cows.

Duane said, "Do you still have the lease on that 400 acres two miles south of here?" I said, "Yes, I do. That's where the rest of my geldings are, out there roughing it to get something to eat."

Duane said, "I tell you what you do. Take that horse down to that pasture and turn him loose with the rest of the geldings. Just leave him for a month or so and when you go back to get him he'll treat you right."

So in about 5 weeks I went back down to the pasture to get the horse, which I had to walk about a half mile to get there because the snow was much deeper now. When I got there, the first horse that wanted to get caught was this one. I told Duane I could not believe it for he wasn't the easiest horse to catch in the first place since the guy chased him in and out of the barn all the time.

I got the horse home and after a few days started messing with him again and he was one of the easiest horses to break, and I ended up riding him the rest of the winter in the snow and cold.

Thanks to Duane for his advice and wisdom. I can remember Duane calling and asking how that horse was doing, and if that little 5 week vacation to that pasture had taken the oats out him. I'd always laugh and tell him what nice horse that was.

One day a guy drove in the yard looking for a young horse that was already started with no buck in him, because he could finish him the rest of the way. I showed him this horse and let him ride him. I told him the story that the horse had never bucked, but that when I first got him he was pretty snorty.

The guy ask me what I wanted for him and I figured, being I started him that my time was worth something so I doubled the amount I paid for him and the guy got out his check book and bought him on the spot.

Duane and I talked and laughed about that horse deal often and he told me not to forget about that trick when you get a horse full of oats. Duane was my friend and my hero, and a go-to person for advice. I'm glad I got to spend time with him. He was quite a guy, to say least. Rest in Peace, Duane.

BRYON McNAIR
MY FIRST REAL BREAK AS A BULLFIGHTER

I used to go to a buck out in Boyd, Texas on Thursdays and Sundays to help put on flanks, get horse flanks out of the arena, and just whatever needed to be done. One day while I was putting on bull flanks some dumb-ass hung up on a bull they called Snake. It happened right in front of me so like a dumb-ass I jumped in and got him off. It was a 'high' I can't explain.

I still haven't found that kind of high, even to the last bull I ever worked. So I figured that was my purpose in life-to, fight bulls. At age 15, still going to Boyd and fighting bulls, Curtis Nail and I started working all the high school rodeos. We averaged 500 bulls a weekend at $35.00 a performance which wasn't much money, but some kept saying it was good experience.

Then I started working for Bernice Johnson at Northside Coliseum. With hair down to about the middle of my back he wasn't real fond of my hair, but he liked the way I fought bulls. He would buy three truck loads of swamp bulls that had never seen a man before, and they had quite a different attitude than most bulls.

Those swamp bulls taught me a lot about fighting bulls. Actually, they taught me everything about fighting bulls. One day a kid showed up wanting to learn to fight bulls. It didn't take him long to catch on and I asked him if he was superstitious about the color yellow. Most cowboys don't like yellow, but he became the "Bumblebee."

Bernice called me one night and said a man he used to rodeo with had a rodeo company in Montana so he told him he would send me up there if he wanted a bullfighter. His name was Dale Small from Pompey's Pillar, Montana. Bernice failed to mention to Dale anything about my long hair and I thought it was a for-sure deal, so I quit school the next day and had my mom drop me off at the highway to hitch hike to Montana.

When I got to Kansas a State Trooper pulled over and told me it was illegal to hitch hike on the Interstate. He asked me where I was going and what I planned to do and I told him I was headed to Montana to fight bulls. He just laughed and said I looked like an overgrown Charles Manson.

He looked at my pictures for about an hour and said. "Well, it's a $1,000 fine, 10 days in jail, or I can take you to a U.S. Highway where hitch hiking is legal." Of course, I said OK and the highway he took me to was barely wide enough for two cars and it dropped off on both sides of the road.

After seven hours of sitting there, two older women and their three grandchildren stopped and asked how long I'd been there and if I needed a ride. I told them I'd been there for seven hours and about the State Trooper. She said, "Well, you look like an overgrown Charles Manson, but you look like an honest one. I bet that State Trooper didn't tell you about the three State Prisons right down the road." So, they got me out of Kansas and into Colorado.

When I got to Montana I found out where Mr. Small lived, out in the middle of nowhere. It was Mothers Day and there was not a soul around. I sat there on my riggin' bag until nearly dark and finally a car came up the driveway. I got some of the strangest looks I've ever seen on the faces of these people.

I went to the door and knocked and Mrs. Small answered the door. In Montana, they greet you either with open arms or a shotgun. About that time Mr. Small came around the corner with a double barrel and asked me who in the hell I was, and what in the hell was I doing on his property.

I told him that Bernice Johnson had called him and told him I was coming up there to fight bulls for him. He said, "Bernice wouldn't send no **##** hippy up here." I said, "Bernice don't like my hair either, but he likes the way I fight bulls so he lets it go."

I finally talked him into letting me stay and he put me in an 8 ft. by 8 ft. horse shoeing shack across the pasture. The first rodeo was to be in Hardin, Montana, but it was two weeks away. Thanks to the rest of the Smalls, they provided me with food and drink while I stayed in the horse shoeing shack.

In a couple of days they started working calves and steers getting them ready. A steer got loose and I was able to grab him and dog him while Dale's son Guy, grabbed his tail. Dale grabbed the steer's horns and told me to get up and I said, "I can't, you're on my hair." Dale told Guy to get this son-of-a-bitch off my land and he meant it.

So, Guy took me to Billings, Montana and introduced me to the man who ran the Yellowstone Exhibition Coliseum. I explained what happened and the man was kind enough to let me stay in a real nice bathroom and shovel shit until the first rodeo at Hardin.

Finally Hardin came and every time Dale saw me he just shook his head and looked down. I didn't get ready until right before the bull riding and I was getting some pretty weird looks from everybody. Finally, the announcer said it was bull riding time. I asked Mr. Small what to do on the first bull. It was a 1,700 pound Charolais named Charley.

He said, "You can stand in front of him and wave your arms up and down and holler Charley." So when the chute opened I did just as he said, never budged, and when Charley ran right smack over me I was still on the ground waving my arms, hollering Charley.

I worked that bull for five years and I could stand over by the fence and holler, "Charley," and he'd turn back every time, never went straight. Mr. Small rode up to me, slapping his knee and laughing. He asked me why I didn't get out of the way and I told him the guy I work for said he would turn back. I think Charley heard him and wanted to help me out.

Mr. Small said, "Hell, if you're going to be that dedicated you can work all the rodeos I have." A couple of bulls later he told me I really had to dive on this one's head to get him to turn back, so I did. And when I knocked the bull rider off he said, "Okay, I get your point."

So, we got through that rodeo and everything was pretty good. By the second rodeo he was asking me what we should do to the bulls to turn them back. But, if it wasn't for old Charley, I don't think we would ever have made it. I worked with the man for five years and we became like family.

BUDDY WILLIAMS
WATER SKIING IN A COTTON FIELD

In the spring of 1982 I was living in Lubbock, Texas and we were headed to one of Charlie Thompson's rodeos in O'Donnell. We had been getting a hard rain for a good week and all of the streets in Lubbock were flooded. Karl Hanlon, Phillip McCarty and I headed out for the rodeo in Karl's truck which has no back glass.

He'd had a camper on his truck with a boot between the camper and the cab, but had sold the camper and I think that's when the glass had been broken out. We were a little south of Lubbock when we saw flashing lights ahead. A Highway Patrol Officer flagged us over and told us the highway was flooded, but since we were in a truck he would let us go through.

I think we are some where between Tahoka and O'Donnell and the water on the road was getting pretty deep, so Phillip crawled through the back window that had no glass and grabbed a shovel and started paddling.

Well, now we look like a canoe going through the water. After a good laugh, he got back in the cab as we headed on down the road. We all knew that that area of Texas was pretty flat, but we came to a big low spot out in the cotton field and we saw a ski boat riding through the cotton field.

Not only do we see a ski boat going through the cotton field, but it was also pulling a skier. I guess the guys in the boat thought it would be funny to buzz by us and spray us with water and thank goodness, none of the water came through the back window so we remained dry. I have to say it is quite a sight to see a ski boat pulling a skier through a cotton field in west Texas.

If my memory serves me right the rodeo arena is on Highway 87 in O'Donnell. As we pulled up we are running a little late as always, so Karl thought he'd save time by cutting across the median between the Highway and the arena.

Well, after all that rain his truck made it about half way before sinking all the way up to the axels. We grabbed our riggin' bags and ran on over to get on our bulls. I ended up winning third, Karl lost his rope because of the mud, and I don't remember how Phillip did.

After the rodeo it took two dually trucks and about forty-five minutes to get Karl's truck out of the mud, but what a great memory and one I'll never forget. I have not seen Phillip since I left Lubbock, but Karl and I stay in touch. We have a great laugh every time we talk about that trip.

DON MELLGREN
CHARACTERS YOU MEET ALONG THE WAY

In the early 1970s I had two good young horses and I saddled them both up to go work them in the hills. I rode one and led the other one to my back pasture gate. Just as I opened it up a guy rides up the poorest horse I had ever seen.

I knew of him from town, and his reputation wasn't all that good. He had a cheap black saddle with taps, spurs made out of tin, a two-dollar black hat, and a black shirt with white fringe.

He said, real load, "Hi, Don. Been doin' any bullin' lately?" I had no idea how he knew my name or even that I used to ride bulls, so I really had to fight to not laugh. I thought I'd have a little fun and said, "No, not for several years. How about you?"

He said, "No, not for several months." I knew I had him, so I said, "Do you like to ride with your toes in or toes out?" He said, "I like to ride with my toes straight." I said, "Do you use those spurs?" He said, "Oh, yes. And they're good for bucking broncos, too."

I don't remember the rest of the conversation, but he talked real loud. I didn't ask him to ride with me and he didn't ask to join me, so I just rode off. I didn't think his horse could have made it up the big hill I had to go up, anyway.

I bet every one of you has run into very loud phony's in your travels. A few years later, someone murdered the guy. I was sorry to hear it, but it seems like some people work real hard to be made fun of.

CHARLIE COOK
TRAVELIN' PARTNERS

Joe Campos and I have been good friends for 25 years and it would have never happened had it not been for rodeo. We had both been competing at the Edinburg, Texas Rodeo in early January of 1992 and I had won second place. After the rodeo Joe approached me and said that he had just gotten his PRCA permit and asked if he could travel with me. I said, "Sure. The next PRCA Rodeo I'm planning on entering is Lafayette, Louisiana if you want to go." He said, "Yeah, I definitely want to go."

Two weeks later I left McAllen early that morning and picked Joe up in Kingsville, and off we headed for Lafayette. By the time we got to Refugio we hit a driving, coastal rainstorm that stayed with us the next 400 miles. Because of the heavy rain we were running late and when we arrived at the rodeo coliseum, there was no nearby parking.

We finally found a grass lot with some trucks and decided to park there. My truck sunk as soon as I pulled on to the lot, but I told Joe we would worry about it later as every truck parked there was going to be stuck. As it was still pouring rain we made a mad dash for the coliseum, and got soaked along the way.

When we arrived inside the lights were down for the National Anthem and we couldn't see much of anything. Once the lights came back on we made our way behind the bucking chutes. Once there, I asked Troy Kibodeaux what he could tell me about my bull, Harper and Morgan's #45 Gunsmoke. He told me that he was a really good one with lots of action and spun to the right.

Troy was certainly right about #45. He blew out of the chute and every round he made was probably three feet off the ground. I started spurring him pretty early and was in such rhythm that I spurred him with both feet the last three rounds. I ended up winning third place and after driving 400 miles in a blinding rain, I was glad to pick up a good check.

When we left the coliseum, everyone parked in the grass lot pitched in and helped one another get their vehicles unstuck. Troy had invited us to a country bar so we joined him and his Louisiana buddies for a good time. It was quite funny when Joe and I arrived at the bar. They let two girls about 16 years old walk straight in, but checked our both our ID's before letting us in and I was 32 years old. I told Joe, "Welcome to Louisiana."

Joe and I continued to travel together until I called it quits on my 37th birthday in 1996. We continue to be close friends and hunt together on a regular basis. Rodeo introduced me to many friends that I probably would have never had, and for that I am thankful.

JOE LIFTO
IRA BOARD MEETING

Ronnie Martin and I had to fly back to Paul's Valley to make an IRA board meeting, so we left Johnny Roberts to drive my orange and white VW "hippy van" with California plates on north, by himself.

Being as this was during the easy rider days, somewhere in Mississippi he finally had to put his long hair up under his hat. He might be able to give you the story over the phone if you want to hear it. He has never forgiven us for it.

JOHN L. SLOAN
HAVE TO TIE A STICK IN HIS MOUTH

So here it is, maybe 1969. I'm sitting behind the chutes in Ft. Collins, Colorado. A little, skinny guy named Joe Alexander sits down and starts messing with his rag of a riggin.' He always was bad to be rubbin' stuff on the handhold.

So, me being a friendly kind of guy and knowing Joe pretty well, I says, "Draw good, Joe?" You know, you say that kind of thing even when you don't care and I didn't, 'cause I had already drawn the best of 'em as we use to say.

Well Joe, he takes a minute, the way those guys from that side of the mountain do then says, "John, he is so dang rank they have tie a stick in his mouth before they can run him in the chute." Then, he commences to rubbin' on his riggin'. That was a new one on me so I thought a minute and says, "Joe, why they do that?"

Now back then, Joe would take a chew of Red Man and that's what he did. He worked it good then spit and says, "They do that to keep him from jumpin' plumb through his ass when they crack the gate."

I never forgot that, but I did win the go. We split the average, but he won the flip for the buckle. I figured he'd give to me, but as usual I was wrong.

ED LeTOURNEAU
THE BULL ROPE PAD

I went to a rodeo in the LA area back in the early 1960's and drew Andy Juareguis' bull #81 Andy's Pet, a NFR Bull that had recovered from an illness, but was still quite thin and his back bone was still pretty prominent.

When the bull rope was pulled tight Andy's Pet would buck good at firs,t then slow down and stop. I went over to some ropers and asked if they had an old saddle blanket I could have a piece of.

So, I got one and made a pad to put under my rope and over the bull's back bone. Andy was on his horse and saw the pad under my rope and said, "Look, you guys. He wasn't to win the bull riding."

Sure enough, Andy's Pet bucked real good, and I won first place. That was the beginning of the pad under the bull rope. No one had ever used one before that I had ever seen.

"Big Rear Out" © Roger Langford

PART 3

1. Joe Foscalina…Jeff Jones
2. Joe Bob Nunez…Cowboy In A Toolbox
3. Darryl Davis…Out Of My Slump
4. Casey McGlaun…Mike Cervi's #A-14
5. Beau Mayo…Where's Me Bec
6. Steve Scott…Rooty Toot Toot, Open The Chute
7. Chuck Sasser…The Cowboy And The Trick Rider
8. David Brown…The Notorious Bull Cocaine
9. Corey Brown…Screw You, Bob
10. Chimp Robertson…You Wanna Eat
11. Joe Lifto…The Golden Rodeo Trail
12. Mark Dennis…The IRA World Championship Buckle
13. Johnny Garza…Double Dink
14. Jim Liles…A Bronc Rider's Dance
15. Johnny Rivera…The Bull Rider
16. Mark Simmons…IRCA Finals Trick Pulled on Doyle Wooke
17. Joe Foscalina…Definition Of A Hero
18. Dwayne Jett…What Dreams May Come
19. Dennis Merrell-Miserable As Hell
20. Jesse CR Hall…Eastern Love For The West
21. Don Mellgren…Panquich, Utah
22. Richard Flechsig…The Judge's Test
23. Rob Hendrickson…Ballet Dreams
24. Steve Scott. The First RCA Rodeo I Ever Clowned
25. Clint Ford…The Mayor's Party

JOE FOSCALINA
JEFF JONES

The year was 1981, and we had just joined the Australian Rough Rider's Association. Jeff Jones and I were entered in the bull riding at the Springsure Rodeo. This is where they stopped the show during the saddle bronc ridding and everyone left the arena. Off in the distance you could hear drums beating as the crowd moved towards the steady beat, which was located next to a big circus-like tent.

As I was watching I couldn't help but wonder what was going on. The announcer, judges, and even the stock contractor were also heading in that general direction. I was a little confused. The rodeo wasn't over yet and everyone was leaving. Jeff had just got back and noticed my befuddled look. He then told me to relax because it's just a short break and that we should go watch.

So Jeff and I walked to the tent. When everyone was there the drums stopped beating and prize fighters came and stood on platforms. A producer came out and stood next to the first boxer. He than announced the weight by saying, "This boxer weighs 14 stone and who wants to go 3 rounds with him?" Someone out of the crowd hollered. "I'll fight him, mate".

This went on until they were matched up. All the boxers and challengers then went around to the back of the tent to get ready for the big event that was just about to take place. The producer told us if we pay one dollar we could enter the tent and watch the boxing matches.

This was all new to me. I had never been to a rodeo where they did anything like this before. I was excited and quickly paid my dollar. In fact, everyone paid to satisfy their curiosity. Once inside, the producer instructed the crowd to form a human boxing ring. So, to my amazement a bunch of sweaty, smelly rodeo cowboys huddled together to form a crude ring.

While we were waiting for the fighters to get ready they had two young blokes put on a little pre-show boxing match. After they finished their bout the producer put a blanket down in the ring and said, "These little guys put on this pre-show for free and if you want to show your appreciation, you can throw something out on the blanket."

So, we threw money and the little fighters grabbed the blanket and took off smiling and giggling with their loot. Then, the main event started. With fist flying, a fighter would fall into the human ring we created and we would just push them back into the center for another go at his opponent.

When the matches were over, everyone went back to the rodeo with big grins on their faces and back to wild rodeo riding we all went. I will never forget this memory with a fantastic rodeo friend, Jeff Jones. May you rest in peace brother... You will never be forgotten.

JOE BOB NUNEZ
COWBOY IN A TOOL BOX

One year in the early eighties, me, Guy Murphy, Ramie Harper, and Buck Harris, (RIP) went to the Strong City, Kansas Rodeo. We had to borrow a truck from Bucky's brother L.P. Harris to get there. It was a little crowded in the truck so we cleaned out the tool box in the back and one of us would ride back there.

It's a pretty good drive from Gallup, New Mexico to Strong City, Kansas and we were running late. Guy was first up in the bareback riding event so we put him in the back so he could get taped up. We photo finished it to the rodeo just as the bareback horses were being loaded.

Bucky pulled right up to the arena gate and Murphy jumped out just as his name was being announced. Needless to say, the crowd was quite surprised to see the next cowboy jump out of a tool box in the back of a truck and run into the arena ready to ride.

They'd held the rodeo up so he could ride. I guess Harry figured he'd give him a chance and I'm pretty sure Guy spurred one, as he was one of the most under-rated three-event cowboys to rodeo.

I believe it was 1996 that Robert Etbauer asked me to give him a ride from Window Rock, New Mexico to the Gallup airport. I said I would and asked him if he'd like to stop by my parent's house to get something to eat and he said he would.

My mom had some great red Chile with beans and tortillas made, and she was famous for her cooking. I can remember sweat pouring off of Robert as he enjoyed his meal. Thinking it might be a little too hot for him I offered him a paper towel and more Chile, and he gladly accepted both.

DARRYL DAVIS
OUT OF MY SLUMP

Back in the late 70's and through the early 80's I traveled to rodeos with a lot of people. There were about eight of us who were pretty tight with each other. We might not be in the same vehicle, but we ended up at the same rodeos. Between us, we had all the rough stock events covered.

I was on a dry spell and was trying to figure out what I was doing wrong while all my buddies who rode bulls were weighing in on what I needed to do. I was getting real serious trying to concentrate in the chute on every ride. I'd call for the gate and hit the ground before the buzzer. Things were not going my way.

We were at a show close to home one time and met a bareback rider named Darrell Larson. He had a Cajun type accent and I think he was from Louisiana. We helped him on his horse and he rode pretty well. While we were waiting for the bull riding, Darrell and I talked about my dry spell and he asked me what I was doing before I called for the gate.

I explained about being wound up like a nine-day clock every time I called for the gate. He said, "Try something different. Don't get serious. Just have fun. That's how you probably got into bull riding in the first place so just go back in time to your younger days."

I thought about it, but thought it best to continue what I was doing. As my bull was coming down the alley I started getting my serious game face on. I put my rope on a high-horn bull and started walking back and forth behind the chutes talking to myself while my buddies were talking to me with encouraging words.

The chute boss yelled, "Let's go, here," and pointed at my bull. I climbed over in the chute and slid down on the beast while Ronny Ashley pulled my rope. The announcer was saying a lot of kind words about me as I burned my rope, took a wrap, and right before I called for the gate Darrell Larson looks thru the chute bars and with that Cajun voice of his, said, "Hey, Hey, Hey, I wish my name was Darryl."

The chute boss, the flank man, the gate men, my buddies, and me, all busted out laughing. Not that he was Darrell and talking to a Darryl, it was just that Cajun accent. I got my composer back and called for the gate and won the bull riding…I was out of my slump.

Darrell Larson traveled with us from that day on. He made it a ritual to always say those same words before I called for the gate. "Hey, Hey, Hey, I wish my name was Darryl." It helped a lot and I started having fun again. Darrell lives up in Anderson now and we talk every now and then. He always answers the phone when he sees my number with, "Hey, Hey, Hey, I wish my name was Darryl."

CASEY MCGLUAN
MIKE CERVI'S BULL, A-14

The year was 1984 and the city of Las Vegas, Nevada was 'romancing' the PRCA to move the National Finals Rodeo to Vegas. In order to show the PRCA that they meant business the city added a record purse to the regular season. The Elks Helldorado Day's Rodeo in turn, received a record number of entries, especially in the bull riding. I was living and rodeoing with Jay Cochrane at the time.

Unarguably, the best bull to draw was going to be Mike Cervi's bull #A-14, Sunni's Velvet, named after Cervi Rodeo Company's secretary Sunni Deb Backstrom. A-14 was a small bull by that day's Standards and was mostly of Hereford decent, with very little Brahma in him.

A little side story that I always found interesting was that A-14 was sired by the great bucking bull of the year #44 General Issamo of the Beutler Brothers and Cervi string. The Story goes that PRCA stock contractor Howard Harris from New York State leased General Issamo from Cervi and turned him out with some cross-bred cows on an island off shore of the State of New York. They had to be barged over to the island and A-14 was a product of this 'pasture arrangement'.

The day before the stock draw I told Jay that I would draw A-14. He jokingly stated that it wasn't possible because he was going to draw him. That night I wrote A-14 on a sheet of paper and put it under my pillow, as this had worked a couple of times in the past.

Jay was the one that called PROCOM the next day to get the draw for Vegas. I had been in town running errands to get ready for a week long rodeo run and when I came back home Jay blurted out, "You've got A-4." I figured he was joking and had to call for myself. Sure enough, I had drawn the rankest bull at what was to be the richest PRCA Rodeo to date.

What turned out to be the longest week of my life finally ended when we landed on the airstrip in Las Vegas. I had only watched A-14 buck two or three times, but had never seen him ridden, or even heard of him being ridden. When I got to the rodeo office the first thing Sunni Deb said to me was, "Well, you've drawn my bull."

I had ridden him a hundred times in my mind and figured all I had to do was go through the motions. I didn't want to appear too cocky so I replied with, "Yes, ma'am. I can ride him." The next couple of hours seemed to move like molasses. I kept going back to the pen where they had him isolated by himself, and starring at him.

He was known for a bad attitude, was bad to hook, and bad in the chute. I'd seen him flip over in the chute earlier in the year with Lane Frost at Omaha, Nebraska and had heard of him rearing up and flipping over on a couple others. Each time I went back to look at him he hadn't moved an inch. He just stood in the corner of the pen and starred back.

When the time finally came and they ran the bulls in the chutes, I got my rope on him and waited….and waited. Finally, when it was time to crawl down on him, I tippy-toed around as to not make him rear up or flip. He stood like a statue as I slid up and nodded. He turned back to the left right in the gate and was pretty bucky, with lots of drop and kick, while he was spinning.

Like on all rank bulls, things were happening fast and I never felt like I had him tapped, nor did it ever feel like I was bucked off. About the six-second mark he reversed the spin and went to the right. I made the adjustment and was damn glad to hear the buzzer.

This was only the second performance with several performances yet to go, but everybody knew I had won the rodeo. That night I hit the blackjack tables and won three hundred and sixty dollars. The next day I doubled for Steve Ford in a made for TV movie called 'The Cowboy and the Ballerina' with co-star Lee Majors, and was paid another three hundred dollars.

When it was all said and done, with day money, bonus's, and first place prize money, I left Vegas with over ten thousand dollars. That held the record for the most prize money at a regular season, one-head PRCA Rodeo for thirteen years. A-14 went on to win the Bucking Bull of the NFR, bucking off Don Gay and Randy Queen.

BEAU MAYO
WHERE'S ME BEC

Me and Denny Mclanahan traveled together for several years. In about 1999, Australian bareback rider Darren Clarke asked to join us. Clarkie was a great bareback rider and was very entertaining. He had a thick accent and had many funny sayings. He had a girlfriend back in Australia named Rebecca and was always taking about her. He called her, "Me Bec."

Well, she decided to fly over to visit Clarkie and go to some rodeos with us. Bec was about nineteen years old, very attractive, and she wore short shorts and a tank top most of the time, and she was a head turner. It was July when she flew over, the busy time of the year, and we were entered up and had a rodeo about every day.

Denny had a white Dodge van with a bed built in the back. We would take turns driving and me and Denny would usually visit with each other while they slept in the back. One night at around two o'clock in the morning Denny was driving and I was in the passenger seat.

We were on the Interstate between Salt Lake City and Cheyenne in a very desolate area. Clarkie pops his head up and says, "Where's me Bec?" I looked back and didn't see her anywhere. We pulled over and looked everywhere. No Bec!

Oh, no! Apparently she had gotten out of the van to go to the restroom when we stopped at a rest stop about 100 miles back.

No one had seen her get out and Clarkie was in a panic, Denny was furious, and I was laughing my tail off. This was before anyone had cell phones. Bec was in her shorty shorts and tank top, no shoes, no money, wallet, purse, or cell phone, at a rest stop in the middle of nowhere, and in a foreign country that she had been in for only about three days.

We had to try and remember where we had pulled over and go find her. Well, you don't just turn around out there and exits are few and far between. I think we drove another 20 miles before we came to an exit to turn back to the east and head back to the rest stop. When we pulled back into the rest area about two hours later, there was Bec.

She was alright, but was crying and very scared. She had befriended a trucker who was willing to give her a lift if we didn't come back for her. She was real glad to see us and hopped back in the van real fast. She stayed in the U.S. and rode with us for the next couple weeks, but she never got out of that van again without telling everyone where she was.

STEVE SCOTT
ROOTY TOOT TOOT OPEN THE CHUTE

I was working for RSC Inc. at San Jose Firefighters Rodeo, fighting bulls with Jerry Mariluch, when a bull rider got hung up on RSC's bull Typhoon. He was a big brindle with a sizable rack of horns and he would camp out on you if he could. Somewhere in the melee I got knocked down and got under the dog pile and the bull stepped on my right leg and broke the small bone in the bottom of my leg.

I knew it was broke because it hurt so bad. I didn't think it was the big bone so I figured I could make it. I could jump and hobble on it, so Mariluch told me to take it easy and he'd take care of the rest of the bulls. This was the first performance of five performances so I had four more to go and Bob Cook was paying a hundred a perf. I needed the money because my wife was pregnant.

I didn't have any insurance and I had to have eight hundred bucks to give to the hospital before the start of the third term of her pregnancy. Anyway, I needed to work those other four performances. Mariluch told me that he'd do the bull fighting and I could just kind of stay up by the chutes.

I hopped and skipped and stumbled my way through the whole five performances and along the way, I ate every pain pill that I could bum from anybody who had something. If it was for pain I ate it. Hell, I would have eaten a birth control pill if I thought it would help.

I'd hobble around and help Mariluch with the acts and Bob Tallman would make jokes on the microphone asking me if I had got my trailer hitch broke. I could hardly sleep and by the last performance I was a mental and physical wreck, but I made it to that last performance.

I don't know how it is in the PRCA now, but in those days it was the RCA and they would let the locals enter up with the idea that their wife, kids, mom, dad, cousins, and buddies would all buy a ticket to cheer on their bull riding hero. So this local cowboy had drawn Bob Cook's good bull Tuffy. He always went two jumps and then went to the left.

He was a pretty good bucker and he would go out of his way to hook you if he got the chance. He was real quick too. Well, this guy got on and somebody pulled his rope and all of a sudden, he just screams out real loud, "Rooty Toot Toot, open the chute!" He screamed so loud and so all of a sudden that it scared me. I thought he'd got a leg tore off in the chute or something. I remember thinking, I'll bet he practiced that in the mirror for a week.

It was left hand delivery and the bull was going to his left so I was on the end where I'd be behind the gate when they opened it.

They opened the chute gate and this guy lost his nerve and peeled off on the gate, hanging by both hands on the top bar of the gate.

Tuffy felt him come off on that side and came back to his right instead of his left, looking for this guy, but he came around the end of the chute gate. I'm jumping on one leg, looking like I'd been shot trying to go up the next chute gate when Tuffy caught up with me. He stuck a horn in my ribs about the same time somebody stepped on the top of my head which seriously impeded my escape. I think it was the gate man.

Tuffy slammed me into the chute gate which was still open. I remember that idiot staring wild eyed at me and Tuffy through the top of the chute gate. The bull got on me hooked me for a while down the next two chute gates where Mariluch was finally able to get him off of me right in front of the announcer's stand. Bob Tallman was busy explaining to the folks in the grandstand how they should hide their kid's eyes for a while.

So, now I have a broke rib and broke leg. I grabbed the bottom bar on that portable panel and drug myself through that fence and just laid there under the announcer's stand. Tallman was telling the crowd how I had saved this guy's life and I was just trying to make sure that I wasn't dead.

They took me to the emergency room and my wife showed up with fifty bucks that Bob Cook sent up there with her. They were checking for internal injuries and told me that they were worried that maybe that rib had tore something else up. I told them that they ought to check that broke leg. They x-rayed it and the bone was already growing back together, but it was lapped over and not end to end so they had to re-break it and re-set it. That was another whole rodeo right there.

While I was recuperating I ended up driving a truck and hauling stock for Bob Cook. It was hard to drive with a cast on my leg where I couldn't bend my ankle. It was about two weeks later and I was driving with Ellie Lewis, going to another rodeo. We stopped at the Ryder Truck place in Fresno to get something fixed. While we were waiting, I got an old hacksaw blade out of a garbage barrel and cut that cast off my leg so I could drive.

Another week and I was back fighting bulls, kind of hopping and hobbling, but I did it. Bob Cook paid me to finish out that rodeo even though I wasn't much good. He also paid me to drive and haul stock and do what I could do 'till I got back to where I could fight bulls.

I always appreciated the fact that he helped me keep my head above water when he didn't have to. Our baby was a boy and we named him Jason Paul Scott. He's 43 now and lives in Boise, Idaho with his wife and three kids. He made a good man and I'm proud of him.

CHUCK SASSER
THE COWBOY AND THE TRICK RIDER

It was September and nearing the end of the rodeo year in Washington, Idaho and Oregon. As a bareback rider I had been following the Christensen Brothers stock for one very good reason. The weather was chill and spitting rain in Moro, Oregon a little town out in the Blue Hills, as I eased down into the bucking chute.

Barebacks are generally the first event of a rodeo and I was the first rider out in the first event. The announcer went into his spiel from above the chutes—"Our first rider is an Oklahoma cowboy Chuck Sasser, riding a rough one call The Mop. . ." I pounded my gloved hand into the bareback riggin' handle and winked at the reason I was following the Christensen's.

Linda was watching from the shelter of the announcer's stand. She flashed me the sweetest, most promising smile. A little contract-act trick rider with roan-colored hair and riding a chocolate-colored horse. She had caught my eye—and, incidentally, the eye of every other young cowboy on the circuit.

Each show, there she was in her short red skirt putting that horse through his paces.

Chuck Sasser, The Cowboy and the Trick Rider.

She was a cowboy's main attraction. I was one smitten rodeo hand. Dashing, too, I thought, with my bright red, rough-out leather chaps and wide hat with the peacock feather in it. But dashing or not, it seemed like every time she walked near and flashed that smile I immediately lost all dash and went tongue-tied with a deer-in-the-headlights look.

Finally, at a show I girded up my nerves and sauntered up to her, gallantly sweeping off my Stetson so the feather fluttered like it was still strutting for its former owner.

"Say, girl," I mumbled. "I bet we could sure show 'em something at the rodeo dance tonight." It wasn't like I was suave and sophisticated. I was nothing but a country boy from Oklahoma.

"You ain't showed 'em much riding barebacks," she said, as she turned in her little red skirt and walked off.

I was nothing if not persistent. Other cowboys said the girl liked my style, but her protective papa thought I was just another rodeo bum going nowhere. But, at last I won Pop over. Now her smile from above the chute assured me of a first date at the street dance tonight after the show.

With my grin on Linda and my mind not on business, I eased down on The Mop's back and settled in with my spurs at his shoulders for the 'mark out.' I nodded my head and Mop's eyes walled back at the feather.

The chute gate swung wide—and for a few seconds there, I thought I was riding a cougar instead of a horse. The Mop mopped up the arena with me. He tossed me so high I almost got a nose bleed before I hit the ground.

And when I did hit, my face digging a trench in the wet plowed ground and my cowardly hat turning peacock and flapping off, ol' Mop was waiting for me. He tattooed me with all four hooves from my spurs all the way to my ridin' glove.

He moved on, kicking and bawling in triumph and passing explosions of wind every time his front feet struck the earth. I lay where I lay, in the mud, unable to get up. The beast had stomped both arms and both legs and I was paralyzed. I thought I was some messed up. I couldn't move anything except my head.

As they will, cowboys ran out and hoisted me up to carry me off to a waiting ambulance. One cowboy had one of my lets and another cowboy had the other one. That was when I became aware to my chagrin that my jeans were split open all the way, exposing me to the grandstands—and to my trick rider.

Linda had climbed up on the fence gate as the cowboys carried me through—and that look, all wide blue eyes and red skirt. I was totally humiliated and ended up in The Dalles Hospital with bad bruises, but no serious permanent injuries.

And Linda? I think she went to the street dance with a calf roper.

DAVID BROWN
THE NOTORIOUS BULL COCAINE

As Saturday night came around at The Round-Up in Simonton, Texas they had an event called 'Hard Money.' It consisted of wrapping a nylon string around a bull's neck and turning him out into the arena where people paid a fee and signed a waiver to try and get the string off the bull's neck.

College guys and wannabe cowboys tried their luck. I had bucked off my bull and needed money to get to the next show so I tried my luck at getting the string off the bull's neck and that was a really big mistake.

The bull Cocaine was a good bucking bull, but he was also a head hunter. I helped out and fought bulls from time to time, but this bull had radar and could take you down quick. They let Cocaine out into the arena and right away he hooked a couple of guys.

Bullfighter Don Zachary had his hands full saving those wannabe cowboys and college boys left and right. When I noticed that Cocaine tired out a little bit, I made my move for the string.

I reached over his head between his horns and got a good grip and tried to pull the string off, but he unleashed on me. He lunged at me, slammed into the left side of my rib cage and broke three ribs and sent me flying. I know I could have cleared a pick-up truck from front to back.

I hit the ground on my feet and at a full run, with Cocaine almost in my back pocket. Luckily, Gary Edge another great bull fighter happened to be out there and he stepped in and saved my hide. I learned my lesson the hard way.

As I said, Cocaine was a head hunter, but these college boys were trying to impress their girl friends. The hard money event was nasty at times. When they let Cocaine out of the chute, instantly like a domino effect, three guys were standing behind each other and Cocaine freight trained 'em all. I won't go into details, but they were hauled off to the hospital. One guy wound up with a broken back, the second guy lost an eye, and the third guy was busted up real bad. It didn't pay to mess with Cocaine.

COREY BROWN
SCREW YOU, BOB

Bob Logue, Brian Evens, and a friend of mine, Heath Cook, and I, were at two rodeos down in Florida. I believe it was Bonifay and Kissimmee. Bob had nicknamed Brian 'Spike Muffin' which of course Brian hated. That being said and since he hated it so much, it stuck, of course.

The rodeo in Bonifay, heck it may have been Tampa as it was a long time ago, so I'm not real sure, anyway it was an indoor arena in a metal building and the bleachers were about half full. Bob, Brian, and I, get on our horses. None of us had good horses, but Brian's was worse so he got a re-ride.

That year 1993, Bob was the bareback director and of course, being Bob, and being in the game as long as he had, he knew everyone and I'm not kidding, everyone. So, he had a little chat with the announcers before Brian's re-ride.

They ran Brian's re-ride horse in before the bull riding started and Bob, Heath, and I pulled his riggin' for him. Just as Brian is starting to slide and ride, the announcer says, "Here's the re-ride from the bareback riding. From Greely, Colorado, SPIKE MUFFIN."

Brian heard this as just as the horse bolted out of the chute, and yelled, "SCRRRRRRRREW YOUUUUUUUUUUUUUU BOOOOOOOOOOOOOOOB, as loud as he could. It echoed all through that metal building, and of course everyone in the arena heard it. Bob, Heath, and I, almost fell off the bucking chutes we were laughing so hard.

CHIMP ROBERTSON
YOU WANNA EAT

I was workin' for a Seismograph outfit in the Oklahoma panhandle and usually got off on weekends to rodeo. My travelin' buddies were down in Texas somewhere so I decided to make a show out in New Mexico.

Three local guys asked if they could ride with me. I said OK, but I'd have to leave when it was over to get back in time for work. That was fine as long as they didn't have to drive. We loaded up Saturday morning and just as I pulled out on the highway one of 'em said, "You wanna eat?"

I'd never traveled with any of them before so all three of 'em leaned back and went to sleep. I knew I'd have to drive hard and fast to make it in time so I kicked it up to ninety and never let off except to go through a small town. I ran low on gas and pulled into a convenience store and just as I got back on the road, the guy in the back hollered, "Uou wanna ?"

The bareback ridin' had already started by the time I slid to a stop behind the chutes. I jumped out and grabbed my riggin' bag and ran in the arena just as they called my name. I yelled out that I was there, so they bucked another horse while I put on my chaps and spurs and got my riggin' on my bronc.

I rode about six seconds before my hand popped out of the old limber, leather hand hold. I hadn't had time to wrap tape on it and just couldn't hold on long enough and went out the back door and almost got kicked in the face. It was hot and windy and I couldn't even see the chutes because of the dust the bronc and the pickup men were making.

All three of my passengers bucked off of their horses, so we sat on the ground inside the fence and watched the rest of the rodeo. When the bull riding started I climbed up on the chute and dropped my rope down the side of the bull, but my passengers were still sittin' on the ground by the fence.

The chute boss reached under and hooked my rope, but I had to pull it myself. I made the whistle and jumped off, picked up my rope, and walked over to the fence and sat down. All three of my passengers bucked off their bulls and when the first go-round was over, the rodeo committee shut the rodeo down for a Bar-B-Que and a whole slew of matched horse races. It was well after dark before it started up again.

With over forty bareback riders and eighty some bull riders, by the time the rodeo was over it was two o'clock in the morning. We grabbed our gear bags and ran for the car. Just as I spun out in the dirt behind the chutes the guy in the back said, "You wanna eat?"

I didn't answer because I knew I'd have to drive as fast goin' back as I did comin' over. I kicked it up to ninety and tore off into the dark. The crew I worked with pulled out right at seven o'clock each morning, and I knew I'd be lucky to make back in time.

My passengers were asleep so I drove hard without slowing down. I pulled into a gas station in Boise City, Oklahoma about five-thirty and slid to a stop. I jumped out and topped off the tank, ran in and paid, got back in and peeled out, and just as I got back on the road the guy in the back leaned up and said, "You wanna ?"

I didn't say anything, so he sulled up and went back to sleep. I was drowsy and really fightin' it so I rolled down the window, turned up the radio, and was singing at the top of my voice just to keep from falling asleep at the wheel.

After a while it seemed like I was drivin' between two rows of tall, white grain elevators and that they were right up against highway, so I slowed down and eased off the road. I didn't even turn off the lights or the engine, just leaned my head down on the steering wheel and konked out.

It felt like I'd only been there about a minute when someone tapped on the side of the door. I opened my eyes and it was the biggest State Trooper I ever saw. I explained the situation so he said, "Alright, but turn off the key and stay here. Don't drive sleepy." He got in his patrol car and turned around and took off. As soon as his tail lights were out of sight I peeled out and the guy in the back woke up and said, "You wanna eat?"

It was right at seven o'clock when I roared into the motel parking lot. The crew had already warmed up their trucks and was ready to leave. I bailed out and hurried to my room, grabbed my hard hat, and ran back out the door. The foreman drove the front truck and I always rode with him so when he saw me slide to a stop in front of my room, he waited.

As I ran by the car my passengers were still asleep so I just kept on goin' and climbed up in the truck with the foreman. He knew I'd been off to a rodeo somewhere so when we stopped at the only red light in that small town, he nodded toward an old Café and said, "You wanna eat?"

JOE LIFTO
THE GOLDEN RODEO TRAIL

We were our way south to start David Morgan's Florida circuit, Doyle Stanford, Jackie Maroney, Shorty Woods, and I, and we had a four day layover so we stopped at a beautiful ranch in Northwest Florida that was owned by a stock contractor. When we arrived at about 1 o'clock in the morning, Doyle noticed a horse saddled and tied to a post. When we checked it out, we saw he had dug a hole almost up to his knees.

They put us up in a big house and fed us while we were there. When they asked if any of us broke colts, Doyle and I readily volunteered to help with two of their horses. The next morning Doyle had an un-broke three year old and I took the horse that was still tied to the fence.

Doyle got his bronc lined right out, but mine was a different story. I eased up on him and when I hit the seat on that slick stock saddle, all hell broke loose. I grabbed the horn and it was all I could do to stay centered. He had thrown me off twice, but I luckily landed back in the saddle.

As time went on he was not weakening and a matter of fact, he was getting worse. After a while I was running out of air and was about to bail off when he finally gave up so I ran that SOB around for an hour. The owner was peeking around the barn so I knew we were being tested a little. Doyle and I rode those two horses every day that we were there and although we went round and round every time, it was nothing like the first time. Doyle figured they had set us up with the best one in their bucking string. If that was the case I hope I took some of the buck out of him. That horse was one of the toughest broncs I had ever ridden in all the twenty years on the Golden Rodeo Trail.

MARK DENNIS
THE IRA WORLD CHAMPIONSHIP BUCKLE

In 1971, with myself driving, packed four other cowboys into the car I had at the time and headed for the Anadarko, Oklahoma, Little Britches Rodeo, a three-day event. My oldest friend Otis, and I, had grown up trading cowboy hats and such all the time, just for the day, usually.

The second day at the rodeo, Otis started hanging out with this Oklahoma roper and they'd traded buckles for the day. The trouble was, Otis's buckle was a World Championship Buckle, one of many that an Oklahoma Cowboy had won in the IRA. He had gotten the buckle from his sister, who knew the Champ well, from back in her barrel racing days in the IRA.

After the final day of the rodeo we waited for several hours at the fair grounds by the only other thing there, the trader's horse trailer. Everyone had left, contractors, everybody, but the trader never did come back. We never forgot about losing that IRA World Championship Buckle.

JOHNNY GARZA
DOUBLE DINK

I began riding bulls right before entering high school in South Texas. The year was 1975. There were three pens that I mostly rode at before later traveling around, that offered practice bulls, jackpots, event type bull ridings, and full rodeos. These three arenas were Bandy's, Vic's, and Kicker's Korner.

The owners and hands of these arenas were and still are some of the best people you could ever know. Around 1975, or so, me and my buddies were on our way to Bandy's arena to get on some practice bulls. We and others all knew the bulls, so if a new one got added to the herd, it was obvious.

When we got to the arena we noticed a new bull back in the holding pens. The riders were asking plenty about him, but no one really knew anything about him. To me, this bull looked familiar. A few other guys also said that the bull looked just like a bull they had seen before.

Finally, the riders had put an identity to this secret mystery bull. They claimed that this bull was Sunshine from the movie, Junior Bonner. In the 1972 movie, starring Steve McQueen, Sunshine was the rankest and meanest bull going at the time, according to the movie's story line.

The Bandy's were not saying much on this bull, they just wanted someone to put a rope on him. Well, weeks and months went by, but no one wanted to try him. Even in jackpots this bull got turned out. Eventually, the Bandy's sold this marked bull to the owners of Kicker's Korner arena.

Oddly, the same thing was happening at that arena, too. Riders did not want this Sunshine bull. One Sunday afternoon, not too long after the arrival of Sunshine to Kicker's Korner arena, a cowboy stepped up and put his rope on him. As the cowboy was settling in on Sunshine, everything became quite. The bull was difficult in the chute just as he had been in the movie. Everyone wanted to see this bull buck.

Finally, when the cowboy nodded for the gate the bull came out of there running like he was the last chicken on earth and Col. Sanders was after him. For all this time folks had believed this bull was the rank Sunshine from the Junior Bonner movie.

The bull could have made a good race horse if you could call it that. Trip after trip he ran like he was trying to break the record for the fifty yard dash, and probably did up to a point. The bull's name was changed on the spot, from Sunshine to Double Dink.

JIM LILES
A BRONC RIDER'S DANCE

This ain't no Texas two-step and it ain't for city cats
This dance requires some grit and growl and a feather in your hat
You ease down in that bucking chute, first one pedal then the next
Screw yourself down in that Hamley, lift on the rein and nod your head
Your feet are locked up in the neck when she leaps into the sky
You duck the bar across the top, it's like this bronc can fly
That first jump it's a big one as she drops off to the left
When she hits the ground with a terrible bound, I thought she broke my neck
I'm not settled in that kack just yet I'm just a shade behind
Spur high in the neck and drive em' back, that speed I'm sure to find
Circle right and jump and kick, I'll beat her to the ground
Jump for jump, neck to cantle, a dancer I have found
A high leap up into the air as our dance comes to an end
We turn away with a grin and a wink I think I've found a friend
We will dance again I'm sure, at a place on down the road

Where we'll all tell our rodeo tales at the Pearly Gates of Gold

RIGGINS'-N-RHYMES: Every cowboy or cowgirl that ever went down the rodeo road has a different way of remembering those times. Not long after developing the Crash Pad and getting it on the market, I started to reflect on rodeo life. Not through a book, but through my cowboy poetry. Some of the poems are about my own rodeo experiences and all are meant to be a true reflection of rodeo cowboys.

The "Riggins'-n-Rhymes" exhibit is a unique exhibit of over fifty bareback riggins' from the 1900's to the riggins' used by cowboys going down the road today. In addition, there are vintage rough stock spurs made by Bobby Blackwood, Kelly, and many others.

We also expanded the exhibit to include vintage rodeo equipment from the bull riding and saddle bronc riding events, and photos and articles about the history of bareback riding round out the display. It is the only exhibit of its kind in the world and is displayed in a private museum in congress, Arizona.

It is our wish to share this exhibit with the public with showings at major events like the WNFR and the Cowboy Hall of Fame. The uniqueness of this exhibit and the items in it, make it extremely attractive to the cowboys of the past, as well as the present and also to the general public, as they can no9w see up close exactly what the cowboys used both today, and 115 years ago.

Our exhibit is named "Riggins'-n-Rhymes because I'm also a cowboy poet with a book published titles" The Cowboy Way," which has many great poems about rodeo life. When showing the exhibit, a little cowboy poetry fits right in. An educated audience is what we as producers and participants need to promote our sport. Long Live Rodeo.

JOHNNIE RIVERA
THE BULL RIDER

One time we had a bull rider show up at our house, telling us his car had broken down in Arkadelphia. He said he'd left it in a parking lot because the lights would kill the battery and it wouldn't start. My room mate told him it was probably just the alternator and it wouldn't cost more than a hundred bucks to fix it.

We offered to go with him and help him fix it, but he wouldn't do it. He told us that if we wanted it we could have it. My room mate said that he would go get it and fix it and sell it. Then, he asked the bull rider how much he was going to want for it? Needless to say, we dragged him with us, to repair his car.

MARK SIMMONS
IRCA FINALS TRICK PULLED ON DOYLE WOOKE

The Snowbird Rodeo Company had a paint horse that they always used in the bareback riding. I drew that horse several times and you could always win the bareback riding on him. Usually, he was the very last horse to go out and after the ride one of the pickup men would rope him, step off of his pickup horse, throw his saddle on the paint bareback horse and ride him to pick up saddle broncs.

As long as you didn't touch him with your spurs, he was pretty handy. One year at the Marshalltown State Finals, Doyle Wooke from the Grand River Rodeo Company, (R.I.P. my friend), needed a horse for the Grand Entry so they pulled the paint horse out of the bucking string.

I was carrying the Grand River Flag and was riding beside Doyle. As we rode into the arena I touched my spur against the paint and he started bucking. Doyle rode him for about three seconds before he got dumped. He remembered it for a very long time, and we sure had a lot of laughs about it.

At the Eddyville, Iowa Rodeo, Doyle showed me how to pull my riggin' down on a horse named Polka Dot. He was one of the most famous horses in the Midwest, and I drew him seventeen times that year. When Wendell got done pullin' my riggin' I could lift it off Polka Dots back, about five inches.

Two men had to hold the horse so I could put my hand in and I thought he was goin' to kill me in the chute. I called for the gate and got him rode. If you look at my Face Book page, you'll see a polka dotted lookin' bareback horse that Joe Simmons offered Doyle thirty-five thousand dollars for, but Doyle turned it down.

JOE FOSCALINA
DEFINITION OF A HERO

I've told this story many times and some of you have probably already heard it. I think it was in the early 1990s at a California bull riding. My friend Jay Cheatwood just got off his bull and was still standing in the arena holding his bull rope when they opened the chute gate and the next bull came out.

The unknown rider was thrown to the ground and knocked unconscious. The bull fighter had distracted the bull only for a brief moment and the bull was coming back at the cowboy. Jay dropped his rope and sacrificed his body to cover the cowboy without a second thought.

When I think about what he did, I am very proud of him. When I relive that day in my mind and wonder what I would have done, I pray I would have done the same thing. Jay Cheatwood you are the definition of hero, and I am truly honored to call you friend.

DWAYNE JETT
WHAT DREAMS MAY COME

Every now and then, a movie comes along that moves me like 'Ghost,' 'Field of Dreams,' and this one, 'What Dreams May Come.' All three of them deal with the death of a loved one and what may occur afterwards. I would like to think that their authors or whoever came up with them has a great insight into the afterlife and that they're right.

I hope that when we die, wherever it is we end up, that we might be able to help protect and perhaps guide our loved ones on their journey. Not to control what they do, but to help them make their journey complete and fulfilling. Or that we may fulfill our own dreams or see ourselves as we would like to be.

So for me, the one thing that I would hope to finish would be a successful rodeo career. To have done what I chose to do, ride bulls, and be a Champion. To have been able to provide for my family, and not to have seen the hard times that we all shared. And to walk with legends of rodeo and to maybe be one of them.

Who knows, maybe the things I went through were a lesson to someone, somewhere, or will be when it's over. I have known what it feels like to be a Champion Bull Rider. Having won Mesquite twice, maybe that was all I was to accomplish as far as my riding was concerned. Maybe that was my fifteen minutes of fame. If that's the case, then I'm satisfied with it.

Now, what I'm trying to do is create a place where others who want to learn to ride bulls might come and begin their journey. Maybe I can show and tell them what I did and how to avoid some of the things I did. Also to provide a living for my family so they can see their dreams come true. To make it easier for them to do the things they choose to do, whether they carry on what I start or have someone else run things.

But no matter what, I hope after we die we are able to be around or be in touch with our loved ones in some way. Sometimes, I know that those who have gone before me are still around. I can feel them. When mama sent me Papaw's pocket watch, and it slipped out of the eyeglass case she'd sent it in and fell into my hand, I felt Papaw's hand holding it. When I touch my father's branding iron, I feel his hand.

Dwayne Jett, What Dreams May Come.

Although my mom has now passed on, I know when something moves me or touches my heart it's her love I feel in my heart.

The love she had shown me all my life will never end. Maybe that's why I hope the hereafter is somewhat like these movies, so we'll never be apart.

So, if only in memory we touch our loved ones, I believe we truly do come back and play a part in others lives because of what I feel in my heart. For my family, friends, and those I have met on my journey, I will tell you where you'll find me.

You'll find me in your children when they pout and when they do things that they shouldn't.
You'll find me when you drive down the road and see a bull that you know I could have ridden.
You'll find me on the radio in a country song.
You'll find me when you pass an arena in any town
You'll find me when you hear a cowbell, or a buzzer go off.
You'll find me in a beat up old pickup truck.
You'll find me in Texas, and you'll find me in the mountains of Colorado.
You'll find me when you hear of someone who's sober.
You'll find me in a drunk somewhere that needs help.
You'll find me when the sky is clear and the stars so bright you can almost touch them.
You'll find me when you stand up for what you believe, no matter what anyone says.
You'll find me when you struggle or when you're down to your last dime.
You'll find me when you lose everything and have to start over.
You'll find me in the eyes of your children, your husband, your father, your brother, your sister and mother.
You'll find me when you gather together as a family, because you know I believed in family.

To all of you who have been a part of my journey and me a part of yours, you'll find me in your heart when you try and succeed, or when you try and fail. When the world is on your shoulders, know that I am there with you. Reach down and pull your boots on and walk on. You'll never fail as long as you dig down in your heart to your soul and find the answers you're seeking.

My life has been full of twists and turns, peaks and valleys, but you always stood by me, believed in me, and helped me be the person that I am. These three movies will always bring me to you. You'll feel my love for you when you watch them. So dare to dream, because who knows 'What Dreams May Come.'

DENNIS MERRILL
MISERABLE AS HELL

I was at the Louisville, Kentucky Rodeo sitting behind the chutes watching my bull fighting partner Steve Williams trying to put on his makeup, with a major hangover. His hands were shaking and besides that, he stuttered real bad.

We were sitting there shooting the breeze when a nice young family stopped by to watch Steve as he held his mirror in one hand and his grease paint in the other. With rapt attention a young boy about five years old watched Steve intently while the parents looked on.

Steve's clown face had the corners of his mouth painted downward. The young boy noticed that it resembled a frown so he spoke up and said, "Hi, Mr. Clown. Why are you so sad?" Steve replied, " Uh, uh, uh, 'cause I'm miserable as hel,l kid. Leave me alone." I felt like hiding as the parents grabbed the boy by the hand and left. That was probably those folks' last rodeo.

JESSE CR Hall
EASTERN LOVE FOR THE WEST

I started rodeoing in 1963, at amateur rodeos through out the east coast. After several years I finally got my PRCA permit and filled my card in two years in bareback and steer wrestling. In 1968, I broke three vertebras in my neck and was laid up for two years.

I started back by going to Larry Mahan's Rodeo School s, one at Tommy Steiner's ranch in Austin, Texas, and two at Neal Gay's place in Mesquite, Texas. During the 1972 season I was on the road mostly in the bareback event, making Louisville, Kentucky, Chicago, El Paso, Odessa, Denver, the Cow Palace, and a few more. Mahan endorsed my riding as, "Keep coming. You're knocking on the door."

In 1973, I was entered at Fort Worth in the bareback riding, but had to turn out because I broke the wrist on my riding hand at a jackpot in Dewey, Oklahoma. Opportunity lost. I came home and met Marie in the Bronx and decided to stay home and start a career in the retail supermarket business, eventually working my way up to store manager.

Marie and I got married and bought a trailer for our first investment in a home. When our first son was born we named him Alexander, after Joe Alexander, the World Champion Bareback Rider from Corey, Wyoming.

Throughout my career I've had a torn cartilage, dislocated shoulder, broken ribs, broken nose, broken foot, broken neck, and fractured eye socket.

In 1978, an APRA Rodeo came to the town where I lived in Lakewood, New Jersey. The rodeo ran every week-end throughout the summer at the Red Pony Academy. APRA sanctioned other rodeos through the northeast, south, west and eastern states.

I joined the Association and started competing whenever I could get away from my job. I was in the lead in the bareback and steer wrestling, but broke my foot and had to sit out the remaining two months of the season, but still ended up in second place.

I healed up for the 1979 season and had a solid year, winning the bareback event and second in the steer wrestling. In 1980, I won the All-Around and Bareback Championship. I decided to step back from actually competing and get into the business end of rodeo, not only because I was thirty-eight years old, but also because I had finally reached the goal I had set out to do. It was time.

Tom Harvey was elected President of the APRA and I was elected Vice-President, serving two terms. I also started producing PRCA and APRA Rodeos throughout the east, under Hall and Sons Championship Rodeo Inc. 1991 was the end of my rodeo company, and also the end of me chasing buckles.

I believe the only critical obstacles in my rodeo career that stopped me were the injuries. My play ground was the Howard Harris Cowtown Rodeo. That prepared me for the success I had everywhere I went.

My full name is Jesse CR Hall. CR stands for Charlie Reno which I started out using on my permit, then later I used C.R. Hall. I was introduced to rodeo by cowboys who were already rodeoing. My family became the most important thing in my life, and that's where I want to be.

DON MELLGREN
PANQUICH, UTAH

In 1962 Pat Russell and I got to Panquich, Utah about a week before the rodeo. We needed entry fee money so we found some work with a rancher named Jim Peterson. He rodeoed in the 40s and 50s and was a really good cowboy. He and his wife were very nice to us, and boy could she cook.

One of the things he had us do was to go out to a corral in a great big pasture where he had a big old wild cow that lost had her calf. We were to milk her out once a day. The first day we went out and looked things over, and decided to rope her and snub her to a post.

We decided that Pat would mug her and I would milk her out. One thing I remember about driving out there that day in Pat's Ford Ranchero was that I spotted a big Jack rabbit about 6 feet away in some grass. Pat stopped the car and handed me his 45 pistol that he kept under his seat.

I'd never shot any thing that big before, but I cocked it, took careful aim, and KABOOM. It hurt my wrist, my ears rung for two days, and I missed, and the rabbit ran off. There was an old barn at the corral and it had a real old saddle hanging in it. We got the great idea that since we were cowboys we'd put that old saddle on the cow and ride her.

We got her milked out and now it was time. Pat mugged her and I was going to saddle her. I gently raised the saddle up touched her back with it and she let out the loudest beller I'd ever heard and jumped so high that saddle flew about 25 feet in the air.

It was like time stood still as I watched that saddle go up and come down. I looked at Pat and he still had her mugged, but his hat was all sideways and his eyes were quite big. I started laughing and Pat started laughing and I'm sure we were quite the sight.

Yes, we changed our mind about riding the cow, but at least we both placed at the rodeo. I was only out there that one time, but Pat went back the next year and became great friends with Jim. He went back for many years and helped Jim with his ranch and his cows. Boy, those are some great memories.

RICHARD FLECHSIG
THE JUDGE'S TEST

On time I worked a rodeo in Belleville, Illinois, with Quail Dobbs and Jack Lynn for Bob Barnes. Jack had a car act, as many did back then, and he had trouble keeping it running. He worked on that thing all day and Bob was right there making sure it would run. Those that worked a Barnes rodeo knew Bob called everyone Charlie, and it was, "Is that thing going to run tonight, Charlie?"

Quail and I were talking one night before the performance and I said, "If I ever look like I wanted to have a car act to kick me square in the rear." Quail said, "Yeah, I feel the same way."

However, a few years later, Quail bought a car act from Jerry Olson's dad and that old car took Quail to Cheyenne, and on to the Pro Rodeo Hall Of Fame.

In 1985 or so, I was asked by Bill Crowder to serve as Judging Commissioner for a new rodeo association in the Southeast called the American Cowboy Association and I said I would. The ACA held rodeos in the Southeast and put on a really good rodeo. I was also judging PRCA rodeos at the time, but in all honesty the ACA Rodeos paid better.

I wrote a judges test to use at judging clinics that I would hold around the Southeast to guys that wanted to judge ACA rodeos. The test was long, but covered every event well.

After a while I noticed I wasn't getting as many PRCA rodeos as I had been, so I called Jack Hannum, the PRCA Judging Commissioner and asked why?

Jack said, "Well Dick, you need to decide which side of the bread you want your butter on." The PRCA follows a right to work law, but this was a veiled threat if I had ever heard one. So, I decided to quit as ACA Judging Commissioner and did so, and Joe Haydock took over as the new Commissioner.

I wanted to keep judging ACA rodeos on weekends when I didn't have a PRCA rodeo, so I bought a card. Joe put out an article in the ACA news letter that anyone wanting to judge ACA rodeos had to take the judges test. I called Joe and said, "Do I have to take the test, too," and he said, "Yes, everyone."

He was giving a seminar in Decatur, Alabama, one Saturday morning and I was judging a PRCA Rodeo in Lauderdale, Mississippi about two hours away, so I got up at 6:00 am drove the two hours to Decatur.

We watched some film then Joe passed out the test, the one I had written. It took me about fifteen minutes to complete it, but most guys were still on the first page when I handed Joe my paper. When I went back and to get my things to leave, one of the guys asked how I finished it so quick. I just smiled and said, "I wrote the damn thing."

ROB HENDRICKSON
BALLET DREAMS

Having the wind knocked out of you, sucks. And that can happen, and does happen if you don't prepare properly. Gripped hand violently jerked from your rigging, swells stolen from your clenched knees, your thick leather riding glove ripped away from your bull rope's rippled edge.

Gravity and opposing weight separates you and the twisting animal, the horse's hunching, solid spring legs, diving yet again, into the sky. The bull spins and turns in acrobatic arches away; hopefully away. And you, tossed into the air like discarded laundry. A silk scarf floating up, the hard packed earth collides with your skin. The soft layers of vessels retreat. The solid hinges of your rib bones act as the battering ram against the lungs and the blow forces every single ounce of air... out.

You gasp. The lung sacks fill with air, but you can't push it out. Vocal cords rasp and squeal. Having the wind knocked out of you, sucks. In order to avoid this airless calamity one must prepare. Follow the rituals you were taught by your mentor who was taught by his mentor, older rodeo hands that you admire. Not too old because too old and you consider many of their rituals and their techniques to be outdated. Gray and faded like the pictures of rodeo arenas of long gone.

Yet, you take it all in. Learned all the rituals, test the techniques, new and old. No wind will be kicked out of your lungs without a fight. One such method has stood the test of time. You hold a dirty sack in your left hand and squeeze a pinch of the golden nuggets between your thumb and forefinger. You gently place the rosin in the crack where a thick leather glove meets the rope.

You drag the two slowly together, feeling the crackle of the rosin pebbles breaking into dust. It makes a thin line down the plaited, stained surface. Sliding your hand faster, the dust begins to liquefy and grab, and the friction brings heat. The heat morphs rosin from a solid, ochre colored gemstone into sticky glue. This is the effect you desire. This is what keeps your hand in your rope, locks your palm to the rigging, and your knees to the bronc saddle swells. Thus, rosin protects your lungs from being raped by the arena floor.

Your father gifted you his leftover rosin. When he closed up his rigging bag for the last time, it was pulled and tossed to you like a sack of gold. The use of rosin to keep things tight and in place goes back as far as anyone could tell.

Your father's father showed him how to apply the stuff and rub it sticky. His father's father showed him. And if you go back far enough, so your grandpa says, in the past was a cavemen that dug rosin up out of the ground, slapped it on the back of old T-Rex and gave that God-like beast a good shankin'.

But you're not thinking of Grandpas or dinosaurs. You toss the sack to the ground and watch it belch snowy sparkles into the air. You're thinking of baseball players and gymnasts, ballet dancers and orchestras. Rosin is a common denominator between you and them, their world and yours.

The pitcher fumbles a rosin-filled sock as he eyes a catcher's intricate signals. In a leather glove tucked behind his back he secretly turns a baseball, matching his grip with the signals. Fans lean anxiously over ketchup-stained chairs. The anticipation palpable for this is the last throw of the last game. The rosin holds a sliver of skin to the ball's thread as the pitcher rares back and rockets it home.

The gymnast torques shoulders and arms are covered white with rosin and talc mixture. Muscles bounce as his head and feet change places. Arching high above the floor he crisply grabs the rings and is held fast. Rosin squeaks. His dismount is emphasized with a slap of powdered hands, making a glorious cloud.

The Ballet dancer skips feather light across a New York stage. Rosin holds the feet and allows her muscles to become movement. Her movement becomes a story. The story is hundreds of years old and has been retold by lithe dancers over generations. Hers is a retelling now. But, she speaks like no one has seen. People have come from around the globe to see her spin, pirouette, and prance, to tell the story in her own way.

The violinist pulls a bow that not for rosin would be silent; sad. Rosin creates a bond between the metal strings and filaments of the bow. The filaments, ironically, are made of horse hair. The vibration expands, dives deep into the bowels of the violin and turns wood into sound. The violinist turns the sound into music. Sophisticated people gather to hear the music. If not for the rosin the fancy dressed crowds would be disappointed, the music halls silent. The violinist's dreams are sprinkled with the sounds of cheering crowds and smells of rosin.

And there you are, standing close to a dusty, hot, arena at the bottom of a ravine. The arena is old, weathered. You are young, ambitious. There will be no stadiums filled with cheering crowds for you. Not yet. Your bareback riggin', bronc saddle, and bull rope surround you with powdered white with rosin, ready and waiting. The practice horses load. Hooves and steel muscle pound out a thundering beat that jump starts your heart.

You pick up your riggin', riding glove, and of course the sock filled with powdered rosin. You turn toward the excited brute. Daydreams of Ballet dancers and violinists fade from you. You smile and walk toward your own destiny.

STEVE SCOTT
THE FIRST RCA RODEO I EVER CLOWNED

I was entered in the bull riding at Lake Isabella, California, on a military ID. I'd been clowning Indian Rodeos and Military Rodeos for Cotton Rosser and Bob Cook. I'd met them at Camp Pendleton at the All-Service Military Rodeo where I was clowning and fighting bulls. I was still in the Marine Corps and was trying to get my RCA contest/contract card so I could both, ride in and clown, RCA Rodeos.

Back then, I had to have letters from two RCA bull riders and three RCA clowns in order to apply for my RCA card. I had a letter from Wilbur Plaugher, Jerry Mariluch, and Chimp Taylor, but I still needed letters from two bull riders. The problem was, I hadn't clowned any RCA rodeos so no card holding bull riders had ever seen me fight bulls.

Cotton Rosser's chute boss came up to me and said that their bull fighter was hurt and that they needed a bull fighter to work with Wilbur. He asked if I had my bull fighting stuff and I told him I did. He said if he could get permission from the RCA, would I fight bulls there at Lake Isabella.

You talk about being stoked. This was gonna be my first RCA rodeo as far as clowning was concerned. So the chute boss called the RCA and they agreed, under the circumstances, that it would be fine. It was really the only thing they could do right then.

Everything went fine because I had worked with Wilbur at Military Rodeos before, so we knew each other pretty well. I rode my bull in the slack, but didn't score much, but I was really stoked about fighting bulls.

Larry Mahan had drawn a black, motley-faced bull with one horn that belonged to Cotton that was named Captain Hook. He was a mean one and had hurt Wick Peth not long before that.

He came out and turned back to the right and ended up right by the fence.

When the buzzer sounded, Larry bailed off and landed on his feet right up against the fence. The old bull stopped and went back to his left to catch Larry who was trying to get up on the fence. I got between them and the bull hit me pretty good, but I stayed with him and took him on around with me. Larry got away clean, and all was well.

As I was walking back to the chutes, Larry caught up with me and shook my hand and told me I did a good job and that he appreciated it. I told him thanks and that I appreciated him saying so. Larry said, "If you ever need anything, just let me know."

I said, "Well, there's one thing I do need if you don't mind, and that is a letter of recommendation so I can apply for my contest/contract card." He said, "See me behind the chutes after the bull riding." I did, and he wrote me a letter with his card number. I couldn't have gotten any higher if I'd been on an airplane. My Marine buddies couldn't believe I'd gotten a letter of recommendation from Larry Mahan.

Larry, as most of you know was, always and still is, a great guy. Not just a great hand, but a great guy. He sure didn't have to take up any of his time to help someone like me, but he did and he was glad to do it. I can't thank him enough, to this day.

CLINT FORD
THE MAYOR'S PARTY

With all the head injuries and hangovers through the years, some stories and occasions just can't be forgotten and this is one of them. One weekday in the Spring of 1994, while I was living in Grandbury, Texas, I stopped by my folk's place to use their phone to call into some rodeos, Billy Bob's being one of them.

While I was getting entered in the weekend bull riding, Bo Jamason told me they were putting together a little show for the

Mayor of fort Worth, Kay Granger. She was welcoming a large group of young Asian college girls here on a transfer program. He said they needed some bull riders for a little jackpot of $500.00 winner-take-all, and I couldn't say no.

When I got there I saw some of the regular faces, Dean Wilson, Kent Cox, and of course, Sandy Kirby, and a tough little dude named George that hung out with Dean and Sandy a lot. I can't remember his last name, but this cat would get on Godzilla. This was the perfect opportunity for Sandy to try out some young bulls since we weren't paying entry fees.

I drew a read bull that apparently never been in a bucking chute and he sure as hell didn't like it. Sandy didn't like you being slow or stupid when you were in the bucking chute, even on a young gull…get in and get out. So, I hustled up the best I could with the bull laying down and banging around.

Just as I was about to call for him he lunged to the front of the chute and stood straight up and turned around like a big-ass ballerina. My feet were still in the slats of the chute and I barely got my hand out of the rope when he lunged forward. I was trying my best to get the hell out of there before he came down on top of me.

I was moon walking on those slats while guys tried to help me, but he came down right as I hit the back of the chute. I was lucky because just his front hooves scraped my chest pretty good and ripped open my shirt. But, I got out of there with my shirt torn to hell, bleeding a little, and my bull is now standing backward in the chute.

Sandy said, "Well, I guess you want to turn him out, huh?"

I said, "Hell no. Spin that sumbitch around."

Sandy told me that's all he needed to hear and kept saying something about being tough like old timers. He was plumb fired up.

Just a young nobody and Sandy Kirby, says you're tough. Why, that makes you think you're a real bad ass. Anyway, I finally got on him and he was a miserable piece of junk, but I got him rode. Kent Cox won it on a good little spinner and he deserved it.

Back in the dressing room packin' up our gear, me and George are talking about all the pretty girls up there in the crowd when Bo Jameson walks in and says the mayor is having a party in the VIP Room and wanted to personally thank all the cowboys for putting on such a good show.

I didn't want to meet the mayor in a ripped up shirt, but I didn't bring my clothes bag, so off we went. When we jerked those big ol' double doors open we couldn't believe it. A room full of pretty girls with cameras started taking our pictures and asking for our autographs, and we took full advantage of the opportunity.

Hell, the only person to ever ask me for my autograph was a cop when he pulled me over. Then out of nowhere, the mayor herself comes in to take a picture with us and she even bought us a beer. She has my vote to this day.

Me and Kent Cox and a few others were headed to the parking lot after the party, but when I got to my car I realized I'd locked my damn keys inside. Kent assured me it was no big deal because he knew a trick. All he needed was the plates off the car to use like a Slim Jim.

While he worked his magic I stepped behind a horse trailer to get rid of a beer and while walking back towards my car, I saw a cop car creeping in our direction. I flagged 'em down and told 'em some crazy SOB was tryin' to break into my car. They got out and started toward Kent with flashlights and guns drawn and that feller could sure run. I was about to wet myself I was laughing so hard.

I had to chase the cops who were chasing Kent to tell them I was just kidding, but the police didn't seem to have the same sense of humor as we did. I just wanted to add this part since I couldn't attend Kent's funeral. He was a good cowboy, with a great attitude, always helpful, always fun.

Chimp Robertson

"Belly of the Beast" © Roger Langford

PART 4

1. Jesse Christensen…Bull Riders On Sunset Strip
2. Frank DuBois…Roping With Cary Culbertson
3. Barney Brehmer…He Did Drive A Lot
4. Abe Morris…The Fort Worth Rodeo
5. Barry Gullo…The Finest Travelin' Partner
6. Mike Stone…Speeding Tickets
7. Ned Londo…436 Miles to Kalispell
8. Red Doyle…Adventures With Charlie Thompson
9. Sean Baker…Sounds
10. Robert Driggers…Jack Ruttle
11. Talonna Rossen McNab…Memories Of My Dad
12. Wes Ward…The Wrong Ferry
13. Ty Rinaldo…John Shey, My Rodeo Buddy
14. Redboy Schlidt…Surprise
15. John Sloan…Truck Fishing
16. Randy Magers…Indianapolis
17. Rhonda Foscalina…My First Bull Ride
18. Mike Jones…The Flyin U Horses
19. Scott Fletcher…Ridin' Broncs in the Dark
20. Joe Foscalina…How Four Cowboys Became Friends
21. Richard Murray…Stupid Is, As Stupid Does
22. Rick McCumber…Rode And Songwriting
23. R.J. Preston…The Arena Pass
24. Mike Duplissey…Those Wild Days
25. Ed LeTourneau…Bull Ridin' Bull Fighter

JESSE CHRISTENSEN
BULL RIDERS ON SUNSET STRIP

In 2000 I was on my rookie card. I'd been staying the winter in Wickenburg, Arizona with my cousin Brett Tatum. We'd been working and rodeoing a bit out of there. Since I was in the California Circuit, and nothing was going on for Brett in the Turquoise Circuit, we decided come April we'd head out to Northern California and stay at my dads for a bit, and hit all the Spring rodeos.

Early April came and we headed out. Brett had recently acquired the use of a brand new Capri camper from his sponsor, with his and their names on it. On the way out, we entered two Professional Rodeos in Burbank and Camp Pendleton, California.

Brett rode bulls and I rode bareback horses so we had to be strategic when entering. I also 'buddied' that weekend with a couple of friends of mine and fellow bareback riders from Oregon, Jimmy Mclean and Lee Lantz.

Brett was up at Burbank on Friday night and we were all up at Camp Pendleton on Saturday afternoon. On Sunday, all of us bareback riders were up at Burbank for the last performance there. Upon arrival at Burbank Friday night we met up with another bull rider (I can't remember his name) from Colorado, who jumped in with us. After the performance Saturday at Camp Pendleton and a short stop at the beach in Oceanside, we headed back to the rodeo grounds at Burbank.

After sitting around for a while and being bored, we decided to go for a drive and check out Hollywood. Brett's truck with the new Capri camper offered the most room so all five of us piled in and headed over the hill to Tinsel Town. It was dark by then and nearing 9:00 o'clock.

We had no idea where to go or which street to take, so we exited on the one that sounded most familiar....Sunset Strip. Not knowing what to expect, it wasn't long before we were in bumper to bumper traffic with BMWs, Lexus', Mercedes Benz's, and many other name brand luxury cars.

With all the traffic and the many people in long lines on the side walks, it didn't take us long to realize we were right in the middle of the Club District and boy, did we stick out like a sore thumb. So there we were five twenty-one year old cowboys 'hanging' out the windows of this Crew Cab Ford Truck with a camper that said, "Professional Bull Rider Brett Tatum rodeos with Frontier Trophy Buckles," on both sides.

People were cheering and yelling at us, "Woo Hoo. Bull Riders." We were all eyes. I think we went into two different Clubs that night. Parking that truck in that town was a task in, and of, itself. We were not dressed up fancy or anything and several people came up to us and said that we could get into any Club just because of how we were dressed. It was an interesting night, to say the least.

The last place we went into had a bucking machine and of all people, Brian Hawk, former NFR bareback rider was in there. He was also up at Burbank on Sunday. Well, like I said, there's no real significance to this story other than just the funny visual of five young rodeo cowboys in a big truck and camper, stuck in traffic on Sunset Strip, during the busiest night of the week in Hollywood.

FRANK DuBOIS
ROPING WITH CARY CULBERTSON

Frank Dubois served as the New Mexico Secretary of Agriculture from 1988 until 2003. DuBois is a former Legislative Assistant to a U.S. Senator, a Deputy Assistant to the Secretary of the Department of Interior, and is the founder of the DuBois Rodeo Scholarship at New Mexico State University.

The picture above was posted in Cary Culbertson's Facebook page. It was taken in 1973; right after his horse had bucked him off face first into a cactus. His brother, Myles, said that he was thrown off over the horses head, and the pony was really hard to bridle after that. Cary's Dad said that landing on his head was a good thing because he did not sprain his ankles that way.

Cary Culbertson

The picture got me to thinking about the one time Cary and I roped together. You know how certain memories are permanently implanted in your brain and you can call them up at any time, and how some events, although they happened in a rapid fashion, appeared at the time to happen in slow motion and thus your memory is in slow-mo too? Well both of these apply to this one run with Culbertson. Call it cowboy instant replay.

Cary had a 5 year old buckskin gelding he called Cody. He said he had done some pasture roping on the horse and would like to see how he would react in an arena. So we met at Skip Pritchard's arena in Las Cruces, New Mexico, where I was a member of the Riff Raff Roping Club.

Here is how this particular run is replayed in my mind's eye, always in slow motion. I back my horse into the headers box; Cary positions his on the heeler's side. I call for the steer. My horse blows out of the box and runs to my favorite hole.

I throw. The honda knot hits just below the left horn, my curl comes around just right and I jerk my slack. I got my dally and was shaping the steer as I went left. And then I saw a Zippo cigarette lighter falling from the sky. I remember thinking to myself, "Is that a lighter falling from the sky?"

It was followed by a pack of cigarettes which was immediately followed by Cary, head side down and heading for the dirt. The next thing I know the buckskin bucks into the rope between me and the steer, so I quickly let go of the dally to keep the wreck from getting any worse.

Now folks, I wish I could tell you just where the buckskin started bucking, how hard he bucked or just how high he sent Culbertson, but I can't. All I saw was the lighter, cigarettes, and the upside down Culbertson.

This happened over twenty five years ago and I don't remember if this was our first run or the last. No, all I remember is the Zippo lighter… the cigarettes…and Culbertson heading head first for tierra firma, and that he still had his hat on as he whisked past my line of sight.

BARNEY BREHMER
HE DID DRIVE A LOT

We were on the road from Red Deer, Alberta, Brian Claypool, Witch Holman, and me. We were in Brian's pickup that had a topper on it with two gas tanks of fuel down the sides. Witch was in the back in a mummy sleeping bag. He was a heavy smoker, but there was no smoking in this situation.

We were speeding through the canyons and curves and it woke him up from his nap. He was scared, but he couldn't smoke because of all the gas. And yeah, he was beating on the windows and cussing and yelling. We acted as though we didn't notice him, and just kept gassing it.

When we finally pulled over in Idaho, he was one hot, mad, bronc rider when we let him out. After he got out and lit a cigarette we got a cussing like we'd never had before. We all remained friends, but we could never get Witch to ride in the back again… but he did drive a lot.

ABE MORRIS
FORT WORTH RODEO

Paul Gallegos and I were both living in Colorado, and had traveled to Fort Worth, Texas to the rodeo in late January, 1989. Paul had drawn and ridden well enough to qualify for the short go-round in the bull riding. The tradition at Fort Worth was that they took a group photo of the all of individual event winners right before the bull riding event.

Because the bull riding winner hadn't been decided yet, the current average leader stood in to represent the bull riders. The group photo was taken in front of the bucking chutes by rodeo photographers and media representatives and by that time, the bulls for the short go round had already been loaded.

I was standing up on the bucking chute gate helping Paul get ready, and had my back to the arena. Neal Gay was the rodeo producer and Don Gay was the chute boss. I was surprised when Don Gay came up to me and tugged on my jeans and said, "Abe, come with me. I need you for minute." He escorted me over to the group photo and I had no idea what was going on.

He said, "I need you to stand in for Sylvester. We can't find him and the show must go on. Just don't say anything and they'll never know the difference." NFR qualifier Sylvester Mayfield from New Mexico had won the tie-down calf roping event and was late for the group photo. Apparently, he was still out in the parking lot, tending to his horse.

So, I pretended to be Sylvester Mayfield and shook hands and was congratulated by several members of the media for such a sterling performance in the tie down calf roping event. If anyone were to go back in the archives of the photos of the winners of the Fort Worth Rodeo in January 1989 they'll be surprised to see Abe Morris, even though the caption says Sylvester Mayfield.

BARRY GULLO
THE FINEST TRAVELING PARTNER

Gene Lyda had left the RCA and joined the TRA so we teamed up and traveled the TRA trail in 1974. One evening when we were talking he said, "You know, there's a pretty good bull riding coming to Kerrville and I was thinking that with all that added money, we should go." Well, we got entered up and went to a few other shows during the next few weeks.

Finally, the Kerrville, Texas rodeo came around and as always, we went to the pens to see what bull we had. I'd drawn the big Brahmer #X. Gene said, "I saw him go a couple of times and he cracks it hard to the right at the gate, no matter what delivery."

I was out in the first section and sure enough he cracked it hard to the right. Well, I broke me my free arm so Gene cut the sleeve off my shirt and made me a sling, then sent me to the hospital to get my arm set.

I came on back to the arena with the cast on my arm because there was dance after the rodeo. When I walked into the dance hall, Gene was sitting at a table, smiling, and waving an envelope. I said, "What's that?"

He said, "Well, you can tell your grand kids about this one." I asked, "How so?" He replied, "You broke your arm and won the bull riding all in eight seconds." Gene and I went on that year, with Gene making the Finals. Gene Lyda is the finest traveling partner a guy can ask for and one hell of a man. That is my friend, Gene Lyda.

MIKE STONE
SPEEDIN' TICKETS

This is a story that I've been teased about for years, but it was not funny to me at the time. Around 1988, I was traveling from Victoria, Texas, to some rodeos around Austin, Texas. I was with a young lady that had a brand new Cadillac Seville. We had already been to three rodeos and I was ending my run on Saturday Night at a Terry Walls Rodeo in Gatesville, Texas.

My buddy Spot Stoebner needed a ride, so we made plans to pick him up in Florence, Texas, at Keith Green's house. This young lady, which we'll call Sissy, was letting me drive so we stopped and picked up Spot. Keith Green rode with us because we had plans on staying the night at his house later that night.

We were running late of course, and I had the pedal to the metal, running about eighty miles per hour down a county road with a fifty-five mph speed limit. About five miles from Gatesville, I topped a hill and there he sat, a Black and White.

I was pulled over and asked for my driver license, which I obliged. He ran my name and came back and said, "Mr. Stone, you have a warrant for an unpaid ticket in West Texas, so you're gonna have go with me and either pay the fine or go to jail."

I said, "I only have enough money for my entry fees tonight at the rodeo." He said, "Can you really ride?" I said, "Most of the time, and if I have a good one I can get the money for the fines." He said, "Oh, is that a fact?"

He said, "Wait here," and went and talked to his partner and came back and said, "We're gonna go with you and watch you ride. If you win, then you follow us to the courthouse and pay your fines, and if you don't you're going to jail. So, how does that sound?" It didn't sound very good, but it was the only option.

They followed us to the rodeo arena and I get my gear and go pay my fees. I ask Delia Walls the secretary what I had and she said, "You got that good colt, why? What's going on?" I said, "I'll tell you later," because that cop was on my tail the whole time, walkin' with me step for step. He even stood over the chute as I put my riggin' on my horse and every body was laughing and poking fun at me.

When I nodded my head, all I could think about was, "Don't miss him out." When that whistle blew, I can still hear Trent Walls sayin' as he picked me up from the ride, "Dang, that was a great ride." I won second place and almost four-hundred dollars.

When I came back to the chutes that cop said, "Good ride. Now, let's go get my money." I collected, and me and Sissy followed them to the courthouse where I paid my fines. The cop laughed and said, "If I was facing jail time, I bet I would have won some money, too."

People have said that I'm the only guy that could have ever happened to. All in all, those two Highway Patrolmen were pretty good to me for what they did, and that was the last ticket I ever got for speeding.

NED LONDO
436 MILES TO KALISPELL

One year, 1966 I think, Hugh Chambliss, Bill Smith, and I, entered the Kalispell, Montana Rodeo. We started from Cody, Wyoming, that morning and stopped at the Teepee Restaurant in Red Lodge, Montana to eat lunch. We were walking back to the car after lunch about 1 o'clock pm when someone discovered it was 436 miles to Kalispell, and the rodeo started at around 7 o'clock PM.

We had misjudged the distance and thought we had plenty of time to get there for the evening performance. Bill Smith said, "We can't get there and had better just turn out." Hugh

Chambliss said, "No, we can make it." I agreed, but Bill said he wasn't driving. So, we told him to get his Louis Lamour book and get in the back seat.

We had Hugh's car and it was a Chevrolet with a big engine so we switched off and were on our way. I don't think that speedometer ever went down to the speed limit. The roads were two-laners most of the time and we were weaving in and out of RV's, cars, and pickups, trying to get there. We even passed some on the right to be by them. When we stopped for gas, Hugh slid the car in sideways to pump. There was a guy filling up on the other side and it scared the heck out of him.

Bill was sure we were all going to get killed. Anyway, we made it to Kalispell just as the Grand Entry was on. We won first, second, and third in both go-rounds of the saddle bronc riding, and the same in the average, and didn't leave much for anyone else. Everyone was glad it was over, and we paid more attention to the maps after that.

RED DOYAL
ADVENTURES WITH CHARLIE THOMPSON

I first met Charlie Thompson at the Saturday Night winter rodeos in Lubbock, Texas, back in the early 1960's. He rode bulls and worked as a flank man for the rodeo producer, the beginning of his own life as a great producer.

After I stopped traveling, I was working for a cattle company and always kept a pen of thin bulls on feed, and would buck them for Charlie a couple of times a year. One time I had a gentle little bull that weighed about a thousand pounds and he got on the truck when we were loading.

I wasn't even going to buck him, but decided to anyway. He never moved in the chute and when we opened the gate, he just walked out. About the second or third step the bull bell clanged and he jumped about head high and turned back.

I think Charlie hauled him a couple of years before he was ever ridden. He was so small, Charlie ran him with the dogging steers and called him Pistol Pete. One time Charlie called me and wanted me to pickup at a Mexican Rodeo he was putting on in Amarillo.

I told him I didn't have a pickup horse, only ranch horses. Charlie just laughed and said, "They wouldn't ride any of 'em anyway." He was almost correct, but one guy did make the whistle. When I I rode in and took him off the bronc, he dropped down from the pickup horse and my ranch horse kicked him right in the stomach with both hind feet. Charlie never asked me to pick up for him again.

SEAN BAKER
SOUNDS

As you slide down in the chutes and your subconscious mind takes over and blocks out the conscience mind, the last few sounds you might hear could be encouragement for the other cowboys or perhaps it's the announcer calling out your name, as they play over in your head.

Then as the hair stiffens on the back of your neck, you hear and feel the snorting and stomping of the bull beneath you. He has a job to do and so do you. The two of you, each locked in your own private world. You nod your head and the gate slams open, then its silence.

Though the crowd cheers you on, you hear nothing. Cowboys shout out their encouragements, but you're unaware for the next 8 seconds. You only hear the bull under you and your own inner thoughts, each loud and confusing in their own right.

All a sudden the whistle sounds, bringing you back from your deaf limbo. You hit the ground and the sounds rush back, bringing your ride into closer focus. From the crowds you hear their approval. For the bull, a feeling of deep respect. From deep inside yourself, you hear only the call to ride again.

ROBERT DRIGGERS
JACK RUTTLE

Jack Ruttle was a Professor at NMSU, and was our faculty chaperone and a really great guy. I haven't seen him in years, but we made contact recently and are going to meet up sometime and catch up.

One time during the NIRA Finals in 1965, Jack and I were headed to Laramie, Wyoming, from the rodeo grounds in my pickup, pulling a two-horse trailer carrying my steer wrestling team.

A couple of hippies in a beat-up old car made a left turn right in front of us and we hit them head-on. We were going pretty fast and being bigger, we plowed right on through. It was a bad wreck and everything was totaled. My horse trailer came loose and jammed under my pickup.

We were not hurt, but I thought sure I'd killed my doggin' horses. When we got them out of the trailer they just went to grazing in the barrow ditch. They never even sored up, and we used them during the rodeo. The two hippies were hurt pretty bad, but both survived.

TALOONA ROSSEN McNABB
MEMORIES OF MY DAD

One time I was on a wild-ass pony and its main focus was to run like hell around the pen and try to rub me off on the corral. I would fall off and dad would pick me up, dust me off, and throw me back on with his sage advice of, "Point your toes East and West and hang on. Don't let this little horse knock you off." With dad, a few tears never worked. It was hang on at all costs.

One of the memories with dad was that I'd jump out of the car and head to the carnivals where I'd spend the whole time of the rodeo trying my luck with the ducks and fish. But, dad was a huge one on polished boots. I'd better arrive with polished boots and leave with polished boots. I knew when the bull riding was almost over I'd start running back to the chutes spit-polishing my boots. I called dad, "The Boot Nazi."

In 1963, my dad Ronnie Rossen was on his way to winning the prestigious and lucrative bull riding title at Cheyenne Frontier Days. The last weekend of the rodeo he met guitarist and entertainer Roy Clark for the first time where Clark was playing at the N.C.O Club of the Cheyenne Air Base. After the Air Force party shut down, dad and Clark carried the evening on at the Mayflower Bar and dad slipped into his motel bed about 3:00 a.m.

Two hours later there was a heavy pounding on his door. Worn out from the long night, dad opened the door and Roy Clark told him to get up. Dad related the story: "He called me Hands."

"Hands," he said, "I want you to come help me." Dad said, "What's your problem?" Clark said, "Those S.O.B's at the American Legion won't sell me a drink and I belong to it. They throwed me out of there and I want to go have a drink." Dad said, "What the hell can I do?" Clark said, "By God, you can come help me at the American Legion Club," so we went and knocked on the door.

Dad said, "A big SOB that weighed about 250, the biggest bouncer I'd seen in a hell of a long time spoke to Clark, 'You again? "You damn right," Roy said. "And, I got plenty of help." I only weighed about 150 pounds and the bouncer said, "You mean that's your help?"

"Wait a minute," I said. "Before we go any further all this guy wants is a drink. He belongs to the Legion. I'm a cowboy at the rodeo and I'm up in the bull riding today. I tried to go to my room and get some sleep, but I came down here to try and talk you into giving him a drink. All he wants is a beer."

The bouncer looked at me, then looked at Roy and said, "All right, then. Come on in. It ain't gonna hurt nothin'. I just didn't like his attitude when he came in before." Dad said, "Well, we went in and had a beer, and all made friends and drank two or three more. Then we all shook hands and I went back to the motel to get some sleep."

WES WARD
THE WRONG FERRY

One time Chuck Logue, Chuck Simonson, Shawn Frey, and I, were going to the Bremerton, Washington Rodeo. We had to get on a ferry to take our van across a big lake, or some kind of huge water way. Since we'd been in hurry all day long driving there, somehow we got on the wrong ferry that took us way north of where we needed to be.

We didn't realize it until we were out in the middle of this huge water way. Once we got on land and got the van off of the ferry, everyone wanted me to drive. I hate driving fast, but I had too. To make matters worse, this was an area of mountains, curves, hills, and no shoulders, on this two-lane highway. I was really scared of driving that fast on those roads and to add to it all, it was raining.

When we arrived at the arena the horses were already loaded in the bucking chutes, and it was bareback bronc riding time. Whew! You talk about an ordeal. But, Praise the Lord, we made it. It was an ordeal, because we didn't pay attention to what ferry we needed to be on.

TY RENALDO
JOHN SHEY, MY RODEO BUDDY

John Shea and I were entered in Ft Worth together, just a few days before he was killed in Guthrie in a car accident. After we rode our first bull in Fort Worth, we were in a hurry to get back to Colorado to see his wife, and my girlfriend. We had been on the road for a couple of weeks and we both missed home.

We got in the rental car to speed home, but John couldn't get the thing in gear. It was a small automatic car and John was about to rip that shifter off the console. He told me to get out and rock the car back and forth to try and get the transmission to engage. He jerked, pushed, pulled, and cussed while I was behind the car, trying to get it to move.

Johnny stomped on the brake because now I had another guy helping me rock that sucker back and forth and John thought we were going to push him out into the street. As soon as he hit the brake, that poor little car gently slid into drive.

A new safety law had been implemented to have the brake on before it would shift into gear. We laughed about it and made record time getting back to Colorado. John's Rental Car Motto was, "Drive 'em like they own 'em."

Miss you buddy…………..Ty.

REDBOY SCHILDT
SURPRISE

I have heard strange and wild tales of hardship and greatness all over the rodeo world. Top to bottom it's about riding and winning, or some weird thing. One year in Montana, I was working labor on a road job to pay my fees. I found I had drawn a top bareback horse and was up on a Friday afternoon, a good six hour drive away.

I'd seen the horse buck the week before and they'd won the short go on him. I was mounted in a big paying show up north. Problem was, I had to travel with a guy who wasn't up 'till Saturday and we only had one car. On top of that, we didn't get paid 'till Friday evening.

I borrowed some money and a car and gave up a few hours of work to get an early start so I could hit the road Thursday night. I left that evening in a good mood and headed across the Canadian line as darkness set in. When I got to Lethbridge, Alberta, I ran into road construction, took a wrong turn, and ended up lost in central Alberta. No road signs, all dirt roads, and no lights....I was lost.

Luckily, I had a full tank of gas and drove in circles most of the night and started getting tired. Finally at daybreak I saw a guy who was duck hunting. I waved him over and he told me I was 100 miles east of the road I should have been on. I thanked him and bent 'er west. Now I was tired and needed help driving. The dirt road dust was flying behind me at 60 mph.

That 1100 lb bronc was waiting for me and he'd be fresh. I called a girl I'd met earlier that summer from a truck stop and asked if she'd be interested in helping me drive. She said she would meet me right outside Calgary. I finally got to Calgary and waited for her. I was so tired I was almost falling asleep at the wheel, but I figured I could sleep on the way to the rodeo.

Good thing she'd join me and besides she was good looking. Pretty soon a van pulls up plumb full of people. My fantasy blew up before my eyes when I saw her and 5 small kids head for my car. She never told me she had so many kids. I was in a rush though, and figured, oh well, I guess they want to go, too.

Those kids fought and screamed for two hundred miles and I never did sleep. They had to do rest stops, buy candy, pop, and chips. I asked God what I did wrong to deserve this…..he said nothing.

Holy cow…it's rodeo time. We were running late, my horse was in the chute, and the rodeo had started by the time we got there. I had started taping and prepping my gear as we cruised along at a good old family safe pace....ugh, the pain. I hit the ground running, chaps and spurs flying, from the arena gate to the arena fence with a gate ticket taker chasing me. My car load was laughing. Those kids thought that was really funny.

Just as I got to the fence I saw that big black horse leaving the arena, turned out. When I got behind the chutes I pleaded my case with the chute boss who had no sympathy. By now, security was looking for me.

The chute boss was an old hand who just said, "When you draw that good, be here the night before and sleep at the arena." I was too embarrassed to try and explain what had happened and why I hadn't slept, but I had a whole bunch of kids and a lovely family. Don't you just love a surprise?

JOHN L. SLOAN
TRUCK FISHING

It was hot in Iowa. It was even hotter in Texas, but we were done in Iowa so it was time to head for Sherman, Texas. Some of these names may be familiar, some not so much. And to be brutal honest, old as I am I may have some of 'em dead wrong. But, best I recall it happened this way.

Somehow I got shanghaied. I had to travel with three saddle bronc riders and all that crap they have to carry with them. Truth be told, I can't remember what town we were at in Iowa. Even worse, I can't remember why I wasn't in my car or even where it was. Anyway, here is how it came to be. We got arrested for fishing from a truck.

Tom Oar, the TV Mountain Man had this old, blue truck with a raggedy, plywood camper on it. Buddy Altman, a big ol' saddle bronc rider from Alabama wanted to drive. He allowed if Tom didn't let him drive he would swallow the keys. Buddy was a B-I-G guy for a pedal pusher so he commenced drivin' while Tom navigated and smoked.

Me and Tonto George, whose real name was Harland, was in the back. He was a pedal pusher, too. I was the only one who looked like a cowboy, but hot as it was, pretty soon I had skinned down to skivvies and sweatin'.

Long about noon we're in Texas and to tell the truth, I was glad of it. Kinda sudden-like, the truck came to a halt. I kicked open the back door, me in my Hanes boxer briefs, and we are in a roadside park and a family of about six are at a table, eatin.'

Buddy ran over to the table and started shakin' hands and howdyin' and sayin' how glad he was that could all get together and boy didn't that chicken look good and could he just have a couple pieces. I have no idea how we got out of there, but I can tell you it was pretty fast 'cause best I recall, the daddy of that clan had him a Ruger Single Six stuck in the front of his bibs.

So, we motored on. Did I mention it was hot? I left the back door open on that ragged camper and that helped. I'm sittin there lookin' around for a beer that ain't been drank when I come up with a fishing rod with black line on it and an idea come to me.

I bent an empty beer can just enough so it would stay tied to the line. I made my first cast out the back door of the camper and let out about 50-feet of line. See, I was trolling. Well, we go on a bit and it was getting' kinda funny, that can bouncin' around and cars passin' us and runnin' off the road and all.

Then I see this car comin' up fast with its red lights and a siren on. I have to reel my can in cause there is one big sumbuck in a white Resistol lookin' right in may face. Ole Tonto George, he was so shook his eyes come unfocused.

Well, the man gets us all out and for some reason asks me, "Just what in the Tomball hell do you think you are doing?"

I put on my most sincere face and said, "Well officer, I was trollin'. I know I don't have a Texas license, but in Louisiana if you don't get in the barrow ditches, it's legal. Did I do something wrong?"

I swear he almost wet down his leg he was laughin' so hard and danged if he didn't let us go. He also came to the rodeo and it turns out he was a former bulldogger, back before it became steer wrestling. Of course, that was after I got Mr. Washington, the Porter at the Holiday Inn to take me over to a house where a man could buy some clear liquor…cheap. But that's another story.

RANDY MAGERS
INDIANAPOLIS

Jerome Robinson, Gene Bightol, and I, were at a Bob Barnes Rodeo in Indianapolis, on the race track, and the portable rest rooms were right behind the bucking chutes. When they started running the bulls in, I realized I needed to make a run to the John, so I climbed over the fence and hurried over to them.

When I opened the door on the men's restroom it was dirty, so since no one was around, I looked in the women's and it was empty and a lot cleaner. I had to go and my bull was in the chute so I stepped in and got down to business.

About that time three girls came by and started to open the door which had no latch on it. I was holding on to it and trying to get my clothes up at the same time. Two of the girls got hold of the handle and started pulling real hard so I yelled out real loud. "Y'all better get out of here!"

One of the girls screamed, "Oh, my God! There's a man in there!" and they took off running and yelling. I jumped up and got out of there before they could go find their parents and accuse me of being some kind of weirdo.

I hurried back over the fence where Jerome and Gene already had my rope on my bull and climbed down on him, nodded for the gate, and won first place.

RHONDA FOSCALINA
MY FIRST BULL RIDE

I was a 15 year old, 90-pound, bell-bottom wearing, bad mamajama with sandy blond hair, twinkling brown eyes, and an intense urge to ride a bull. With a cocky, Joe Foscalina grin, I could just imagine myself on a mound of pure muscle with big horns, flying snot, and pounding hooves of sheer power underneath me that only I, could conquer in eight seconds.

Hiking up my extra slim britches, I was kicking the dust up all over Northern California riding steers and cows at all the Junior Rodeos in the early 70's, finding my love of the sport with every rope that tightened around every mound of muscle I could get my hands on, and always dreaming of bigger, tougher beasts.

I could see myself sliding slowly down into the chute on top of those rippling muscles covered with hair, and seeing my hand slip into the handle of that bull rope. I could hear the clanging of the metal gate as the bull moved, waiting for its moment to throw me off. Then I'd yell, "Let's go boys," and out of the chute we would fly for the ride of my life.

It was a great summer sport. Rodeos almost every weekend and I had big plans to enter them all. However, there were two rodeos that summer I was drooling for. The wild bull riding for ages 15-18. Oh, yes, one way or another I was going to end up on a couple bulls.

With sweaty palms I rehearsed conversation after conversation over and over in my head about how to approach my parents with my career bull riding plans and how it would benefit the world, feed the hungry, and clothe the poor. Yanking my pants up one last time before the big conversation, I climbed those steps to my home with confidence.

I just knew one day they would be pointing at me from those stands and yelling, "That's my son." In reality they said, "No," and to forget about it. They decided 90 pounds was too small to ride bulls. The direct order was, "No bulls until you grow a little."

But I was not deterred. Plan B was hatching by the end of the, "No, not-on-your-life," conversation I received from my parents. The Lake Camacho Junior Rodeo was just five weeks away and I was going to ride a bull there, no matter what. So, with Plan B in full swing I pulled my older sister aside and begged her to sign the entry form.

After our debating, and "What's in it for me?" sibling bartering done, the deal was made. The forged entry form was stamped and placed in the capable hands of the United States Post Office.

My friends, the Allmon Family, also went to every rodeo and camped out. I had gone with them to rodeos for years. I would just jump in with them and go. Perfect for my Plan B. That was until Mr. Allmon mentioned to my dad about Lake Camache Rodeo having bulls. With dad eagle eyeing me, I could feel my perfect Plan B was just about to crumble. I was in a tight spot, but surprisingly my parents let me go anyway.

When that Saturday came, the Lake Camache Rodeo was finally here. My own version of, 'The Christmas Story,' was unfolding and I was holding the Red Rider BB gun. All the bull riders that were entered would ride one time, then the top 10 riders would compete in a finals.

My bull was beautiful. He was a big, grey Brahma bull with accessories of a large hump and horns. I could hear his hooves pounding through the dirt as he moved through the chutes toward mine, his massive bulk rubbing the metal and his wild crazed eyes darting back and forth.

Then the gate closed behind him with a loud clang and my reality set in along with the smell of dung. As I gazed down into my chute, I allowed a small smile to tug at the corner of my mouth. I was finally here, just me and my very first bull. Taking a deep breath, the rope was secured and I slid my small frame onto a parent's worst nightmare.

Slipping my hand into the handle I gave a tight nod to the gate men, letting them know I was ready. The gate flew open and suddenly we were in a world of our own. Just me and my first bull ride. The tossing and bucking was incredible. My dream was now my own reality. The buzzer sounded and the dance was over. My best eight second memory was in that ride…my first bull ride.

MIKE JONES
THE FLYING U HORSES

In 1988, I was just four months out of my first year of high school rodeo, riding bareback horses. I was at the Twin Falls County Fair and Rodeo in Filer, Idaho, and as I was standing above the bucking chutes while they loaded the bareback horses, Cotton Rosser rode up and asked me where Bruce Ford was.

I told him I haven't seen him yet, so he asked me to tell Bruce where his horse was when I saw him. Then he asked me where my riggin' was. I was kinda surprised and wondered how he knew I rode bareback horses. I told him it was at home, that I didn't think I was going to need it.

He smiled and said, "That's a hell of a place for it. Bring it tomorrow night." So the next night I took my riggin' bag with me. Cotton found me and pointed to a horse and said, "Put your riggin' on him when he's loaded."

I was more than happy to do it because after all, it was a Flying U Rodeo. I get all set and nodded my head, but the horse made short work of me. As I was on my way back to the chutes, Cotton told me to get on any horse that was not mounted.

Once again I'm setting my riggin' on another horse, and once again I nod my head, and this time I made a nice ride. When I hit the ground, Cotton told me to get on another one. I kinda looked at him thinking, "This is the greatest day of my life."

When the bareback riding was over and they loaded the saddle broncs, Cotton pointed out two horses that had been turned out and told me to mount both of them. I was thinking, "Is this a one day NFR, or what?"

Being a young kid who's dream was to ride bucking horses and win a gold buckle, I was more than happy to get on again. I felt rested and ready and after those two were done, I was told to get on what would have been my sixth horse. I was setting my riggin' when I heard some one yell out, "Where's my horse?" It was Denny Hay from Canada. I was kinda relieved he showed up as my body had about more than it could handle by that time.

There is an irony in the sport of rodeo. The first bareback horse I got on in a PRCA Rodeo was from the Flying U String, and the last bareback horse I got on was also from the Flying U String. My first PRCA Rodeo was in Filer, Idaho, and my last PRCA Rodeo was right back where it all started...Filer, Idaho.

SCOTT FLETCHER
RIDIN' BRONCS IN THE DARK

We were at Seminole, Oklahoma, one night at a David Bailey Rodeo, and the weather was kind of threatening, to say the least. It didn't ever rain though. Anyway while the calf roping was going on, the saddle broncs had been loaded and most everyone entered that night already had their saddles on.

About halfway through the calf roping, the lights went out. Not just some of the lights, but all of 'em. However after a little while, a few lights came back on. David Bailey was at the buckin' chute end of the arena and when this happened he screamed out, "OK, we'll ride broncs now."

So we did. Yes, it was pretty dark, but we managed somehow and even won a little money. David Bailey is a Rodeo man and I guess he knows how to handle a bad situation, at our expense. Praise God we lived to tell this story.

Scott Fletcher, "Bareback." [Tom Woods photo]

JOE FOSCALINA
HOW FOUR COWBOYS BECAME FRIENDS

The year was 1972, at the Livermore California Professional Rodeo. Two young brothers Jay and Joe Foscalina had just moved to a small ranch in the Livermore hills. We were city boys, but we wanted very much to be involved in the rodeo scene. So Saturday, when the rodeo was about to start, we climbed over the fence on the contestant's side of the rodeo grounds and started watching the show.

But, this was not enough for me and Jay. We decided to climb one more fence that put us right behind the bucking chutes where the riders were. Earlier that day two other little cowboys had jumped the same fence. Their names were well known in the town of Livermore. In fact, they were well known as the best Junior Rodeo Riders.

I better tell you their names before I finish the story it was Russell Davis and Kirk Allmon. These tough little guys had just been caught by a big fat security guard and he was dragging them our way. The rent-a-cop hollered at Jay and I to fellow him to the gate. This was the very first time all four of us boys had met.

Joe Foscalina, "Tuff Kids!"

The back gate to the bucking chute was opened and the rent-a-cop warned us to stay out, so we departed with our tails tucked between our legs. This rodeo stuff was new to Jay and I, but the other two boys were a bit pissed off and blamed us for messing up their little deal.

So, they decided they were going to set us straight. Kirk Allmon was doing a little strong arm talking by telling me he'd take his pocket knife and cut my hair long. Russell Davis had his chest poked out and when Kirk's warning speech was over, Russell spit his soda ice in Jay's face.

Well, city boys might not be real cowboys, but they will fight. So after spitting the ice, Russell grinned. I stepped in front of Jay and socked Russell and then it was on. Kirk, Russell, Jay, and I went to the ground. Two real large ladies had a hard time slowing us down. So that is how we all became best rodeo friends… for the past 45 years.

RICHARD MURRAY
STUPID IS, AS STUPID DOES

In the summer of 2000, my traveling partner and I were entered up that weekend at the Yerington, Nevada Rodeo that started on Sunday where my dad had some bulls. We were also entered up that Saturday at a two header in Fresno, California, with the Hartbar Rodeo Company.

I ended up winning it and my traveling partner ended up second so we had a nice pot between us in the car. Later that night we followed a friend of ours who worked for Hartbar Rodeo Company to his second job where he worked as security at a Club, promising us free drinks.

That was all fine and dandy as long as we got to my dad's bull riding by three o'clock on Sunday. After all, it was only a five hour trip so we could make it. I was telling myself to go ahead and have a few, get a nap, then get on the road.

We met at the Club and the drinks were a pitcher of Kamakazie which were really good by the glass, but here they were served by the pitcher. We downed two pitchers in less then 30 minutes, it was 90 degree weather at 9 o'clock at night, we had lots of money, the adrenaline was still pumpin', and we were feeling really good.

About an hour later, it was decided that the place was not our cup of tea so we decided to turn our attention elsewhere.

My traveling partner wanted me to drive even though I insisted I didn't do well in big cities and didn't want to. Looking back, I don't know how I let myself get talked into it.

We went back and forth with me saying no and him saying he'd guide me. But, off we went and the drinks hit me like a truck. I was gassed and kept telling my traveling partner I was not fit to drive.

He'd say, "No, you're fine. I'll guide you." Yeah, right. I was so gassed that the last thing I remember hearing was, "No, Richard, don't!" I had jumped a concrete flower bed, the ones they divide the road, and we flew up like the Dukes of Hazard.

We came down on all four tires, blowing out all the tires but one and finally slid to a stop. I was laughing so hard at my partner who was screaming in my ear about how stupid I was. I laughed and said, "I told you I didn't want to drive." He kept on and on about how stupid I was, so I wandered off to a pay phone and called a cab.

My traveling partner had followed me to the phone, continuing to yap in my ear. Next thing I realize I'm on the phone and I have him in a head lock trying to give directions to cabby. I told him to calm down, but he gets mad drives the car off across the street where I watched him get out and start ranting and raving and kicking the tires.

In a few minutes he comes back again and starts in again about the time the cops show up and we get the alternative go to jail, or get a cab and a room to sleep it off. Somehow we made it to a motel and the next morning was a hazy, dehydrating type of morning.

Our first thought was, "Where are we and where's our car?" I got on the phone called a friend who lived in Fresno to come get us. We drove around all morning looking for the car and it was almost 11 o'clock before we found it. Well, we could still make Yerington because all we had to do is change tires and we're off. Right? Nope.

Besides the five hundred dollars for tires, the two hundred that the cabby took us for, the hundred fifty for one night of partying, then giving my buddy a hundred bucks for helping us get the tires put on, come to find out, my traveling partner got mad the night before a threw the keys away.

So now we had to pay a locksmith. When he showed up and saw what we were up against, he took us for another two hundred. That left us with about forty or fifty bucks to get home o and we still had to barrow money for gas to make it to my drive way. On top of all that, we never made it to the Yerington, Nevada Rodeo. So the moral is, stupid is, as stupid does.

RICK McCUMBER
RODEO AND SONG WRITING AIN'T FOR SISSIES

For most of us, rodeo is not only a passion it is a way of life. When the time comes to let go of something so dear to us it is a moving experience, a decision we often agonize over and reluctantly step back, a day we remember forever. If we're lucky we get to make the decision for ourselves and if we're not, the doctors sometimes make it for us.

In my case, I knew the decision was made when I came home one afternoon to find my wife leading my little girl through the pole pattern on my knot head roan heel horse. A Driftwood Ike horse, he was all of 16 years old and definitely not kid broke. A few simple rules for survival around him, never swing a rope on his left side, never touch his ears, and certainly never hang a rope bag off the horn from either side and expect him to carry it to the arena for you.

Here he was with hair 'thingees' in his mane and tail and my little girl was climbing up his front leg to get on. He was patiently walking the poles as if he had been doing it his entire life and he sure didn't seem to mind the newfound attention from my little girl. At the far end of the arena was her big brother with a neck rope on his heel horse, popping the horse in the chest and slowly circling the arena backwards in a valiant effort to teach him to work a rope.

This young man, with eyes set on a gold buckle someday would go on to become a very talented roper in his own right. He certainly went on to win more than his share and then some, while my daughter was given a full ride by Wharton Junior College, and then on to Sam Houston State, earning a Bachelor's degree and finally a Masters, all based upon her ability to swing a rope.

One summer afternoon in Casper, Wyoming, the National Intercollegiate Rodeo Association declared her the third best breakaway roper in the nation for the year. My retirement from rodeoing in exchange for seeing their success is a trade I would make every time.

Along the rodeo road I had started a side business Silver Smithing. You know, trophy buckles, bracelets, money clips, necklaces and such, and as my rodeo career wound down I decided to ramp up my efforts and try to make a go of it as a full time gig. My wife would always bring a briefcase full of silver to the youth rodeos and high school rodeos and pro rodeos to show prospective clients and take orders.

Lots of good times and great friends were made during these family weekends on the road, and there are tons of great memories. One of my favorite memories doesn't involve my kids, but Buddy and George Strait's boys. The year was 1999 and we were at the Texas High School Finals in Abilene.

There had been a full week of eliminating team ropers and the short go found the Strait boys, cousins Trey and George Jr., with Bubba at the top of the heap. High call back to the short go means one nice run could secure the win for them as the best high school team ropers in the Lone Star state, definitely not an honor to be taken lightly.

The steers for the Finals were a nice pen of steers, but some could have used a little more horn as the horn wraps bulked out their head. Bubba and Trey had drawn a nice steer, but he had the smaller horns. Trey pushed the barrier as he rode hard to the hip and drug a knot off of the steer and carefully drew his slack tight.

Going left, Trey looked back as Bubba swung over the steer's back before giving it to the steer and pulling back on two on a short rope. Trey was looking right at Bubba when the ropes came tight and the flag dropped, clean run, new State Champions about to be crowned and on to the National Finals to represent Texas, when at that very second the head rope popped off those short horns.

The judge waved it off, giving the Strait boys a no time. At most rodeos or ropings this is when the fireworks start, but not this day, not for the Strait boys or their fathers. They went to the official and asked for an explanation and then they moved on, clearing the arena and heading to their trailers, truly the classy thing to do and in hindsight, the best thing they could have possibly done.

That's what I remember most about the THSRA Finals of 1999. Well, that and writing a song for George Strait. High school rodeo in Texas is divided into ten regions. Most states have one. The Strait kids and the McCumber kids competed in Region 8, south of San Antonio to the Rio Grande valley. The Straits, Buddy and George, were raised around this part of Texas and some folks can remember when George was going to get up a band and see if he could make it in the music business.

The point I'm making is that George could be among us and his fans would not disrupt the function. Norma and George had many of the kids under the shade of their RV lots of the time. Just regular folks, and they still are. Now, George's older brother John Buddy Strait and I spent a lot of time together just killing time whilst waiting on our kids to compete.

If you have ever youth rodeo'ed you know all too well how the events can drag on all day and into the night. Well, Buddy

Chimp Robertson

and I did our very best to entertain each other while we waited. One night in particular, along about the spring of 1999, we got to laughing about the Wild Horse Dance Club on TNN. Before the weekend was over we had hatched a fictional plan of putting together a dance group, practicing up, and heading for Nashville to get on TV and winning that coveted line dancing trophy.

We even planned out our outfits with t-shirts and bandanas, white boots, and of course, no hats, so that everyone could marvel at our mullets. We're out hitting up other parents to join the McStrait Strutters and of course, those that knew us well just shook their heads and walked on. Others just plain walked on. We found a nice lady that agreed to be our choreographer as she had a dance studio and was a real dancer.

When she asked my wife in a soft whisper if we were serious, well now, that just made our day. One weekend, unbeknownst to each other, we both went to our respective homes, Buddy and I, and we locked the gate, the door, and pulled down the blinds and watched the Wild Horse Saloon, and we practiced. So the next rodeo we show up with a few new moves, you know, not much, just a little something, a step left, spin to the right, stomp and clap. You get the idea.

We went on late into the night, sitting on the bottom steps of the bleachers planning our next move. Now, George just happens by and sits down to visit. We start right in, and putting up a hand he says, "Stop right there. I don't want to hear about the McStrait Stompers." I then asked if we might use his tour bus and driver to get us to the Saloon.

Now, I know what those words meant when he said them, but I can't repeat them. I do recall a statement from George about a new contract that forbid any of his music being played in a line dance joint or something to that effect. I told George that his new song, 'I Can Still Make Cheyenne,' might replace, 'Amarillo by Morning' in my all time favorites of his.

He thanked me and made the comment that the original, written by Aaron Baker and Erv Woolsey, had some odd Nashville phrases in it that George had been allowed to change to more proper rodeo terms, a privilege he hadn't had in the beginning of his career.

Meanwhile, the announcer at the high school rodeo droned on, "Whitney you're up. Carly be ready. Samantha, you're in the hole." As we watched, I thought to myself that these kids just don't realize that they are around George Strait weekly, and how special that was. I had an idea, "What if you made a music video about rodeo, using these little girls and boys and our teenage boys and girls? They'd always have something very special from you to remember these times together."

George said he thought it was a great idea and that he was in. Then he asked, "Just where will we get a song?" Now, that's something that at that time I didn't realize was a problem. "Why, you're George Strait. Just write one." Chuckling, he said he'd tried to write songs over the years, and had actually written a few that sounded fantastic at midnight, but were awful the next day.

Song writers and song singers are rarely the same person. Pondering again, I said, "Hmmmm, but you're George Strait. Surely you know someone that could write it."

Chuckle number 2. "Song writers have no idea what we are doing here. Chances are I couldn't edit that song enough to be something that we would want our kids associated with, let alone make it good."

"Ok then, I'll write one," I said, certain that I was onto something big. "If you write one that I like, I will record it." Wow!! King George singing my song. In a Kasey Kasem voice, "The next song was written because of a chance late night chat between George Strait and a one time hit song writer while their youngsters raced the barrels and busted broncos."

Monday morning of the next week found all of us parents loading the trucks and trailers and going to the 1999 THSRA Fnals. I had a booth each year that we went and tried to offset some of the expenses by selling buckles and bracelets and money clips while my kids competed.

When all was loaded and checked and double checked I got in and said, "I don't want to hear any radio or talking until I get that song on paper. Just don't distract me for awhile. This is our big chance."

It is 331 miles from Live Oak County, Texas to Abilene, Texas, a drive of about 5 hours or so. I was out of paper by San Antonio and a yellow stream of wadded up papers fell out of the truck at the Dollar Store where I bought a Big Chief tablet. But, by the time we rolled into Taylor County I had two verses and chorus down pat. I felt the pentameter beat was great and of course, the last word in each line even rhymed, something us songwriters knew.

Thursday morning, during the first slack I was manning the booth when George slipped in. He was incognito. That means he put on a Cactus Rope cap. The public couldn't find him in a cap, it seems. I found my tablet where I had hid it. No one was going to get that work from me.

"Well, here it is, the song, the one that will change everything." He grinned. I didn't know why because I was very serious. With great anticipation I watched George Strait get out his cheaters, unfold the valuable piece of paper and slowly read. My thoughts were that he was already humming it in his head, "Lets hear it for the good kids."

George hands the song back, takes off his cheaters, puts them in his pocket, clasps my shoulder and says, "Rick, I'll stay out of buckles. You stay out of music." Looking back now, it was an awful song. Turns out, it's not as easy as I thought. But, I have since moved on. Buddy Strait passed away a few years back and we all miss him. So, Buddy, if you read this find out if there is line dancing up there and put in a good word for me.

R J PRESTON
THE ARENA PASS

I was entered in the Denver National Western, back in the seventies and always traveled with my pit bull/blue heeler cross named Hitch. His name implied where he came from. I had bought him from Cotton Furnish at the Hitch Ranch.

At any rate, I was going into the coliseum with Hitch and the security guards said, "No dogs, no way." I argued my case, but to no avail. So I turned around to take him back out to the truck and on the way to the truck I saw a bull rider friend of mine on crutches going the same way.

I asked him what happened and he said he broke his ankle and was going home to Nebraska. I asked him if I could have his arena pass and he gave it to me. I put it on Hitch's collar and went back to the arena, going to another entrance.

The security guards there did the same thing, "No dogs, no way." I said, "He's with the specialty act and pointed out he even had an arena pass.

One of the security guards looked at his collar and said, "Yep, he has an arena pass so he's OK." So, me and Hitch got a coke and headed behind the chutes.

I was sitting there, the Grand Entry was starting, and Jiggs Beutler came back behind the chutes and saw me and said. "Howdy, RJ. What are you getting on?" Before I could answer he said, "How in the hell did you get that dog in here?"

I said, "Not a problem Jiggs. He has an arena pass." Jiggs looked at the pass, then looked at me again, then shook his head and smiled and walked off. The collar arena pass worked for the duration of the National Western.

MIKE DUPLISSEY
THOSE WILD DAYS

I'm motivated to set the record straight with my and Jacky Maroney's harmless afternoon of horseback entertainment for all to enjoy. It was a combination of the signs of the time, not only in the rodeo world, but in America. It was in July, a week or so after the Fourth of July and it had been a real dry run for me and my crew.

I hadn't placed in five or six shows in a row and had ended the run at a Sunday afternoon in Virginia at one of those throw up arenas. I had just started dating Marilyn and it seemed that most all of timed event and rough stock riders had decided to have their own combined party down close to the chutes while waiting for the pay off.

The night before, Gary Hiner had streaked across the arena on foot and disappeared on down the road. Well, Jacky would always instigate anything that would be entertaining for all. There must have been fifteen or so of us partying just outside arena and we were passing the whiskey round.

Out of the blue, Jacky suggested we should streak at the end of the rodeo on horseback. That's all I needed, and my now brother-in-law Don Smith says "I got ol' Spooks saddled and tied to trailer." So, we take one more good pull on the half gallon of booze and off we go in search of ol' Spooks.

We jumped in the camper and shucked 'em off, and all we had on was our hats and boots. Jacky was ridin' in front with me behind with jug in my hand as we whip and ride into the arena. Low and behold, Marilyn was our first victim and she squealed as we headed around arena and right on through the party.

Amongst all the cheering, one roper sails his hat under ol' Spooks and he breaks into with the local Rodeo Chairman hot on our trail. I tell Jacky if I hit the ground he's going too, so I dropped jug and got a death grip round his round his waist because we would go to jail if we got caught. He says not to worry because he had a dally.

We rode ol' Spooks through the crowd just as the rodeo ended and the people were flooding out of the stands. We weaved our way through the crowd amongst cheers, and made the circle back to Smith's trailer. We jumped ol' Spooks in trailer and got rid of our hats, slipped into our clothes, slicked our hair back from the water bucket, and joined the crowd looking for us.

We got smuggled out by our feller brothers on down the road, thinking everything was cool. Well, when that Rodeo Chairman raised so much hell with the Administration of the IRA that we were to blacklisted for life. Thank the Lord we had allies on the board.

Lecile Harris, Ron Martin, and Shorty Woods explained that we had sold more tickets in fifteen minutes to the next rodeos and that we should get a reward. Not so easy though, as we got fined a grand. Marilyn and her sister Susan Smith took up a collection and paid our fines. Oh, what a family we all belonged to during those wild days.

ED LeTOURNEAU
BULL FIGHTIN BULL RIDER

In 1956 and 1957, while riding bulls at amateur rodeos I also worked as a bull fighter. At a rodeo in Susanville, California, I drew the Brahma bull #12. He was a good spinning bull you could win first on, but there was one problem. He liked to make you pay for putting the steel to his ribs.

When the whistle blew, he would stop and wait for you to get off and usually no matter how you worked it he would get you. I was working the rodeo with another bull fighter named Buzz. We made the arrangement that when the bull stopped, Buzz would get him going, then I would get away clean.

So it happened that when I rode him and he stopped, Buzz got his attention and got him going after him. Buzz threw his red cape at him which hit him on the head. #12 stopped and flipped the cape up in the air and it landed on me just as I jumped off. I tripped and fell and #12 was all over me.

It seemed like an eternity, but Buzz finally got him off of me and I was safe, but dazed. I picked up my bull rope and headed back to the chutes. On the way back while passing the stands someone yelled, "That's the best act I've ever seen. I'm coming back tomorrow to see it again."

Rodeo Stories III

"Flalshin' Spurs" © Roger Langford

PART 5

1. Everett Campbell...Stomp On The Breaks
2. Don Mellgren...Me And Pat Russell
3. Don Graham...Last 4th Of July Run
4. David Hardage...Sand Springs
5. Brent Futch...Two Buffalo Calves
6. Bret Corley...My First Buckle
7. Russ Shook...Mount St. Helens
8. Steve Roy Ballentine...Lucky 13
9. Richard Flechsig...The Referee Got Arrested
10. Ned Londo...Happy To Leave
11. Red Doyle...Ill-Fated Road Trips
12. Mick Roughan...From City Kid To Cowboy
13. Jon Vick...The Night Baby Huey Caught Fire
14. Greg Doering...Road Trip To Montana With A. J. Swaim
15. Jim Liles...Flyin' High
16. Joe Bob Nunez...Three Rodeos That Day
17. John Sloan...The Drug Lords
18. Joe Foscalina...History Of The Bull Rope
19. Allan Howard...Pushin' Seventy
20. Darryl Davis-Wanting To Be A Rodeo Clown
21. Chimp Robertson...He Went That-A-Way
22. Terri Abrahamsen...Crooked Nose
23. Todd Gaudin-D. J. Gaudin (The Kajun Kid)
24. Ed LeTourneau...The Timex Watch
25. Rome Wager...The Hockey Rink Wall

EVERETT CAMPBELL
STOMP ON THE BREAKS

In July of 1979 my father co-signed for me a brand new F-150 Ford pick up truck. My brother Glenn Campbell had been a member of the International Professional Rodeo Association for around two years, winning the Rookie of the Year in 1978, and his first trip to the Finals in the bull riding. I was a member of the Mid-States Rodeo Association.

One day during my third year there, Glenn comes up to me and our cousin John Reek and says, "You guys need to join the IPRA and come with me." At first, I was flattered he thought I was good enough to make this jump when I was only riding 50% of my bulls at that time, and John felt the same way.

I told him I'd give it some thought. Also at the time, I was trucking hay and straw for our dad and didn't want to leave him short on help and drivers. The thought of dad getting older and slowing down with his hay hook, scared me. Our dad Elwood Campbell was a master of all trades, a super mechanic, raised horses and cattle, and was former bull rider in his day. But, if there was something he couldn't fix or figure out, he always went to his buddy Bill Marshall who had a garage in town.

One day, we had to take one of our trucks to Bill's garage and I'd got to looking around the property. I noticed a black Ford van setting off to the side and took a look. It was in new condition inside and out, the motor, a six popper, was clean as a whistle and I wondered why Ol' Bill had it setting there.

I soon asked him about the van and he tells me a college girl had wrecked it with only fender damage that he'd already fixed, but she didn't want it anymore so he bought it. The wheels in my head begin to turn. I thought, "Well, Glenn's been wanting me to go with him and we're gonna need something to travel in, and since Rob McDonald and Bobby Gillis were using vans I figured, why not.

I also had the thought of a total black van. What are people gonna think of us? A few days later Glenn calls home and I told him of my find and he says, "Prefect." I said, "Well, what's people gonna think about a wild bunch of teenage cowboys with the radio blasting AC-DC out the windows?" He says, "Well, they can get own AC-DC," so I said, "Good enough for me."

So, I asked my dad if I can talk Ol'Bill into it would it be OK to trade him my truck for his van, even trade. Also, that I would not hit the road until he had help and drivers to take my place when I'm gone rodeoing. He told me he'd seen the look in my eyes when Glenn and I were talking about it and after me spotting the van, he made some phone calls and had arranged things, and to go see the world.

I'd had my van only a few days when Glenn walks outta the house and says, "We're all entered in IPRA Rodeos in Illinois, Iowa and also in Missouri . I don't remember in what order, only that Illinois was the last on that week. I didn't have enough money to fix up the van the way we wanted to travel, but it had nice big comfortable Captains chairs in the front with only a mattress in the back.

It had a three speed shift on the column that everybody had to get use to driving. After several jerks and bucks and after letting out on the clutch, it ran like an 80 mph sewing machine.

The day we set off on 'Blacks' maiden voyage, there was Glenn and I, Cousin John Reek, and Phil Modisett. We all rode in Wild West Shows, High School, and Mid-States, and many open rodeos together. Last and certainly not least was our very good friend and hand, Jack Ebberts.

Jack was the oldest of the group and was our mentor, teacher, and most important, the only one old enough to buy beer. He was a fantastic bareback and bull rider, with a trip or two to the National

Finals Rodeo under his belt. Now, this took place 30 years ago so I don't remember all the rides we had at those rodeos.

But, I do remember we were on our way home from one of the shows and it was around two o'clock Sunday Morning when I heard Jack, who'd been driving a long time say, "Someone's gotta drive. I can't make another mile." We always took turns driving to make sure everyone got to sleep during these long hard rides so we'd be able to ride when we got there.

It was Phil's turn to drive so I woke him up. Well, Phil started whining that he was too tired to drive. I'd just driven right before Jack did and we were all exhausted. That, plus the fact that it was 22 degrees outside and way too cold to pull over to rest because we didn't have enough gas to just sit and idle.

John, being the Marine his dad was said, "I'll drive if you'll stay up with me." So, we're flyin' down I-70 East with Bob Seger playing, and after a few cigarettes I looked over at John and he's wide awake, nodding to the rhythm on the stereo. I felt my head nod and woke myself up. I looked over and John's doing good so I nod out again.

All of a sudden I feel myself bouncing in my seat with my head hitting the ceiling. I open my eyes and see nothing but green. I realized we're not on the road, but in the median, mowing down all the bushes the state had planted there when they built the highway.

I looked over at John and hands are on the steering wheel at the old 2 and 10 o'clock position we were taught in Diver's Ed. The difference being, his head was tilted and resting on the driver's side door and his eyes shut and he was sound asleep. At the same time I noticed the speedometer needle was buried at 100 mph.

I thought, "We gotta get outta this jungle in the middle on the highway quick before we hit an overpass bridge and get killed." I grabbed John by his right arm and screamed, "Get this son-of-a-bitch on the road."

Bad mistake, because John suddenly woke up and not knowing what to do, gave the steering wheel a giant turn to the right. I felt the end of the van turn like it was chasing its own tail as it started doing 80-90 mph donuts down the middle of the highway. I heard nothing but screams from the back, "Get under the mattress."

At that time, I laid my head against the seat asked the Lord to forgive me and all of us in this van. It was pitch black outside and I can only see the dim of the headlights and the green from all the bushes we are mowing down. I grabbed the arm rest on the seat, squeezing with all my strength, closed my eyes and braced myself for what ever we were about to crash in to.

The van goes up over the highway still spinning in donuts and is doing the same thing on the right side of the interstate. Feeling like I'm one of the pilots at the end of a space mission for NASA, spinning about and getting ready to plunge into the ocean. I'm yelling out orders to John to push the clutch in and stomp on the brakes.

Thru all the commotion and noise he finally heard me and the van suddenly slows down, brings itself up outta the ditch and perfectly parks on the berm of the highway. Houston, we have landed! Total silence and not a word was said for a good five minutes.

A trucker stopped and asked if we were alright and John said, "Yeah, we blew the air outta the left front tire." Then, another trucker pulls over, asking the same thing. All of a sudden there's trucks pulled off and over to the sides of the highway with Iowa State Troopers telling us they had heard of horrific crash.

Thank God there weren't any bridges or overpasses to crash into along that 1.5 miles of five foot high solid bushes. I honestly believe at the speed we were traveling and the spinning that van was doing, it would have killed us all.

DON MELLGREN
PAT RUSSELL AND I

In 1962, Pat Russell and I entered the rodeo at Panguitch, Utah. We got to town a few days early so we slept at the rodeo grounds in our sleeping bags and showered at a local motel in rooms people had already checked out of. They always gave us clean towels and wouldn't take any money. They were really great people. Also, we bucked hay for a local rancher at 3 cents a bale that was stacked in the barn. We were up Friday night. Pat was sitting 2nd in the bareback riding and I was splitting 2nd and 3rd in the bull riding. We waited around until the last performance on Saturday night to get any checks we might have coming.

The Saturday rodeo was just about to start when in drives a red pickup with a plywood camper on it and out steps a young guy with his very young wife and little baby. I remember loving the shape of his hat. This kid was entered in all three riding events. He had drawn a big, strong, bareback horse named Tipperary and was all over him.

He came back to the chutes and I said, "Pretty strong horse?" He was mad and said, "Yeah, I really tried him, didn't I?" I don't remember what he did on his saddle bronc horse, but in the bull riding he spurred the heck out of a really good bull. After that ride I wasn't splitting end and 3rd anymore, I was splitting 3rd and 4th.

That kid was Larry Mahan and I remember thinking, "Wow, goin' down the rodeo road with a young wife and little baby. That is really confidence and chasing his dreams." He became my hero right then and there, and he still is. A local kid named Carl Yardley was in the bull riding. I don't remember what he did on his bull, but he was a nice guy. His folks owned the best steakhouse in town. We got our checks and went straight to the steakhouse.

Carl Yardly's folks cashed our checks and we had the best steaks money could buy. To this day that is the best steak I've have ever had. I still have those programs and I don't know why, but I am glad I do now. Glory Days. Those were some very happy times.

DON GRAHAM
LAST FORTH OF JULY RUN

If my memory serves me right, my last Forth of July run was in 1977. With Sandy Kirby and his brother Kaye, Pete Gay, and Jim Mc Reynolds, we made twenty-one rodeos in twelve days. Everyone had to enter two events, the bareback riding and the bull riding, and some of us made it to all twenty-one of 'em.

We flew out of Regina, Saskatchewan to Williams Lake, British Columbia to the afternoon performance, and entered Lehi, Utah, that night. We run into a headwind and barely made it in time to compete so I'd already put on my chaps and spurs before the cab even got to the airport to pick us up.

The rodeo had already started so the cabbie drove as fast as he could to get us to the arena. I bailed out of the cab and ran for the contestant's entrance, jumped up on the back of the chute, climbed down on my horse, and they opened the gate. I paid my fees and went back to the cab. Killer and Jim McReynolds rode their horses then we hauled ass to Lehi, Utah.

As luck would have it we got hung up at Customs in Seattle, having to wait on them to get back from lunch. We finally got through just in time for me to miss my bareback horse. But, because I'm up in the slack they let me get on my bull and I scored seventy-seven points, leaving there splitting first place.

Come to find out, we had landed at the wrong airport so the rodeo committee came out and shined their head lights down the runway so we can depart. We flew off into the night and made it time to ride at Spooner, Wisconsin the next morning, then made it in time to compete in Springdale, Arkansas that night.

That's only part of it. Even though we used a lot of rosin and a lot of Bute, there were an awful lot of laughs along the way. And I don't want to forget our good friend Danny Whitely, the Police Chief in Poplar Bluff, Missouri, who not only served as our co-pilot, but also worked the steer wrestling and the bull riding.

DAVID HARDAGE
SAND SPRINGS

Allen Dickerson was the stock contractor at the Sand Springs, Oklahoma NYRA Rodeo for the sixteen to nineteen age group in a rodeo arena that I helped build at ten years of age. My dad Bill Hardage was the announcer at the rodeo. He was the youngest man to ever qualify for the IFR in the early 1960's.

I had drawn a bull called Lemon Drop and he was trash. He was the hardest bull to ride, but scored the least amount of points and I was riding horrible at the time. My dad, with the microphone in his hand said to my home town crowd, "If he bucks off this bull he's his momma's boy. But, if he rides him he's my son."

Terry Don West pulled my rope and when I nodded for the gate and he came out, bullfighter Mark Burgess slapped him on the nose. Old Lemon Drop turned back and bucked like he never had before.

I rode him like a pro, all the while hearing my dad yelling thru the speakers, "Sit up! Sit up! Sit up!" I did, and it is one of the, if not the best, bull ride I ever made. It is my most special memory of twenty-five years of riding, and that's my memory to the tee.

BRENT FUTCH
TWO BUFFALO CALVES

Around 1981 or so, a handful of cowboys and I were in my van headed out on Interstate Ten to the Circuit Finals at Matt Dryden's in Marianna, Florida. I was drivin' and pulled off on an exit near Tallahassee or somewhere like that, to fuel up at a truck stop.

After completing the task and upon return from the restroom to resume our travels, I found one of the cowboys I was travelin' with sittin' behind the wheel in my place. "Let me drive!" he says.

Now, since I didn't ask his permission to share this story with the rest of the world I'll just call him Bill. I know you've all heard the phrase, "Some names have been changed to protect the innocent." Well, I changed this one to protect the guilty.

The ensuing events always makes me think of a joke some of you may have heard about an old Indian Chief who was waitin' on a plane in an airport when he spied a hippy with a thick, bushy beard and long, shaggy brown hair.

Directly, the hippy sees the old Indian starin' at him and after a few minutes of this he begins to grow a little uncomfortable. Soon the hippy can't stand it any longer so he looks at the old Indian and hollers, "Hey man! Stop staring at me! Why do you keep staring me?"

The old Indian chief replied, "Sorry, I have no intention of offending you. But, many moons ago on dark night out on prairie I had affair with buffalo cow. Think maybe you be my son."

Ever since I first heard that joke, probably 40 years or so ago, someone with a thick bushy beard and long shaggy hair has been known to me and the circle of folks Bill and I ran with, as a buffalo calf.

Meanwhile back at the truck stop on Interstate Ten, I shrugged my shoulders and loaded up in the van's shotgun seat, decidin' to go ahead and let Bill drive without protest. As we moved from the loadin' ramp onto the Interstate, we saw two buffalo calves loungin' on a bunch of bags and such with their thumbs sticking up in the air, wantin' to hitch a ride.

As we got a little closer I notice Bill began to steer my van in their direction and I yelled, "What are you doin'?" Bill, as you can imagine, is a little on the ornery side and he said, "Watch this." He stomped on the gas petal and that Ford Econoline went, Wooo-woooo! I yelled, "Bill you'll kill 'em!" Bill looked straight ahead with a wild look in his eyes and yelled back, "They'll move!" Then he hung his head out of the window and yelled, "Move, Buffalo!"

Well, I guess those guys must've soiled their britches as their eyes bulged out from under all that hair and made some fast tracks as they lit a shuck gettin' out of the right-of-way of that brown van. Just as they cleared their pile of trappins', Bill plowed through that stuff and crap went flyin' everywhere.

I thought somethin' was dragging under the chassis, but Bill just kept on laughin' and lookin' in the rearview mirror at that pair of buffalo calves standin' on the side of the road, shakin' their fists at a van full of cowboys headin' on down the highway.

BRET CORLEY
MY FIRST BUCKLE

In 1985 I was entered in Homestead, Florida rodeo in the bull riding for Friday night so I called the secretary on Thursday to see if I could swap out for the Saturday afternoon performance. She said it would be alright, but I would have to find someone to swap with. I called a few of my buddies and finally found someone who said they were willing to swap with me.

When I got to the rodeo, my buddy that I swapped with had the same bull drawn on Friday night that I had on Saturday. I knew this bull and he was a good one, but he told me that he just kinda hopped down the pen during the performance and also in the slack.

While I was setting my bull rope, David Morgan, the stock contractor came over to flank the bull and he told me, we'll, I can't say what he said about the bull, but he did say, "He's gonna buck tonight or go to the meat house tomorrow."

I pulled a tight rope and nodded my head and David Morgan was right about him bucking because I left there winning the round that night, but still had to sweat Sundays performance.

I couldn't make it to Sunday's performance, but my brother did and I sweated the next four hours and did a lot of praying. My brother called me from Homestead and said, "Hey, I got your money."

I asked him where I placed and he said, "Oh, by the way, you won it, I have your buckle, too." That turned out to be the only buckle I ever won and I'm still proud of it to this day, and wear it proudly when I'm Announcing rodeos and bull ridings.

RUSS SHOOK
MOUNT SAINT HELENS

Neal Camarillo and I entered a very amateur rodeo in Union Gap, Washington, over the weekend of May 17 and 18 back in 1980. Some of our friends lived close by and they put us and the horses up at their home. We roped our first steer during the performance on Saturday and had a fine time at our friends' house that Saturday night.

We were at the arena the next morning for slack at 8:00. Everybody was warming up when I heard a helluva noise off to the West. The blackest cloud I'd ever saw was headed our way. I thought we were in for an epic thunderstorm. The announcer had his radio on and screamed in the microphone, "Mt. St. Helens just blew and the fallout should be here in a couple of hours. Get out, or it will kill the horses."

Bravery has never been one of my long suits so I thought, "If it's gonna kill the horses......what about me?" I loaded my horse in the trailer and looked frantically around for Neal. He came wandering up and I yelled, "Get him in the (^(*&%^(^ trailer!"

The fallout didn't take two hours. It was more like 45 minutes, and pulling out I had to reach out the window to help the windshield wipers. Ash was coming down that fast. We went the few miles to our friends' place, but they were still in church. When we parked in their yard, the ash cloud completely enveloped us and it went black.

Neal, who couldn't have cared less, and just dozed off. I was listening to the local A.M. radio station and this idiot DJ had the ear of everybody in the Yakima Valley. Neal woke up long enough to ask me if I thought we were gonna have to throw away the bale of hay in the back of the pickup. That's when I stopped talking to Neal and directed the rest of my conversation to my dog.

The DJ said, "I've got unconfirmed reports that the whole Cascade Range is blowing." By now, I'm picturing flaming boulders as big as horse trailers raining out of the sky. Then he exclaimed, "Oh My God!" I thought, "That's it, the radio station has been covered up by magma." A minute later he said, "Oooops, I dropped the phone in the waste basket."

The only thing I knew about volcanoes came from old black and white movies where Native people were running as fast as they could to get away from the magma flows. My imagination was running wild, sitting there in the dark listening to Neal snore. By noon or so, my friends pulled in, back from church and we went inside.

Unbelievably, the power was still on so we watched the news and calmed down a little when we saw an aerial view of the ash cloud. It was fairly localized and we were directly under it. I'm pretty sure we were the first ones out of the area early the next morning. Thirty miles or so, and we were out of the worst of it.

I had to get rid of that rig because the brakes were ruined and every time you turned on the air conditioning, it formed another ash cloud inside the cab. The horses coughed for a good 60 days after that, but recovered fully. Neal and I often call each other on our, "Anniversary," of May 18th. I'm sure it affected me much more than him, but anyway it's quite a memory.

STEVE ROY BLALLENTINE
LUCKY 13

Back in 1991, I was entered in two rodeos one weekend in May. The first one was the Myrtle Creek, Oregon, night performance. On Friday the 13th.it was a CCPRA/IPRA/NPRA Rodeo, so the first thing I did was check the draw sheet. I found my name and followed the line across the sheet to where the bulls were listed and found that my bull was the only bull without a name, only a fire brand nine eleven.

The stock contractor was the Howell Rodeo Company. I didn't know any of the bulls in their pen so I started asking around about my mount. I asked everyone I could find, "Does anyone know that nine eleven bull?" But, no one knew which bull he was, let alone how he was, and there were no bulls in the pens with those numbers on their hips or ear tags.

I was getting a bit worried until Howell's bull fighter finally figured out the deal. He said, "That aint nine eleven, that's nine, one, one." To my dismay 911 was the most evil Satan looking Brahma I'd ever seen in my life. And to top it off, he was a chute fightin', flat spinnin', ass hookin', welly, no good SOB.

The bullfighter said, "Which ever chap he sees first is the direction he'll spin, so when you get off I hope you land on your feet or we're both gonna take a hookin."

"Dang," I thought. "Could it get any worse?"

I was traveling alone and had driven way up there trying to get some points ahead. I thought, "What a dumb ass idea this was.

I drove all the way up here and I'm sure the grim reaper is close by." It was Friday the 13th and I'd drawn The Devil's Bovine named "9-1-1 Emergency.................I just knew I was gonna die.

Of course, I was first out and felt like puking by the time I got strapped to that POS. He came out and never kicked higher than a beer can, just roll-n-rock, belly kickin', and cuttin' a trail. He didn't even turn back, just headed straight across the arena to the fence and proceeded to scrape me off.

When the buzzer sounded I grabbed the tail of my rope and unwrapped, then grabbed both hand's full of fence and got off of him. In doing so I spurred myself along my shinbone on my right leg. It ripped my britches and my leg wide open, plus getting plenty of Oregon dirt mixed in.

I scored sixty-seven Championship points, loaded my gear in the car and burned rubber, thankful I was still alive. I drove to Gardnerville, Nevada, to the CCPRA Rodeo, and back around familiar folks. I scored eighty-five points and split first and second which was about eleven hundred bucks and got back home with my pockets full.

I got a phone call on Wednesday of that next week from Jerry Howell. "Is this Steve Ballentine?"

"Yes Sir" I said.

"Well," he said. "We need an address to mail your check."

I was confused so I asked, "Check for what?"

He said, "You were the only qualified ride of all three performances."

I had won the average and the ground money, and got another check that Friday for $1800.00. From then on out my lucky day has been Friday 13th. I consider 13 to be "Lucky 13" for me, although I still won't put my hat on the bed, or wear a yellow shirt.

RICHARD FLECHSIG
THE REFEREE GOT ARRESTED

I judged the Lauderdale, Mississippi Rodeo for several years back in about 1995 or 1996. While driving on State Highway 45, I saw blue lights flashing so I pulled over turned off the truck. I looked in the mirror and saw a rather large black officer coming my way.

He explained that I was exceeding the speed limit. I, of course, said I hadn't realized I was going that fast so he requested to see my license. He wrote out the ticket and seeing that I was wearing a cowboy hat, asked if I was going to the rodeo. I also had my Judge's vest hanging in the back and commented that I was a rodeo judge.

Paying tickets always makes me feel like I'm giving money away. I commented to a couple of people at the rodeo about getting stopped and someone said, "Talk to Ralph Morgan. He's connected in Lauderdale County."

As most know, the rodeo was at Ralph's Ranch, and of course Harper-Morgan was the contractor. I really hate do things like that, but what the heck. So, that night we were down at the timed event end for the dogging and I was working the line. Ralph was down there, too, so I said, "Ralph, I got a speeding ticket on the way over here this evening. Do you think you could help?" Ralph took the ticket put it in his shirt pocket and I kind of forgot about it.

The next evening I was back down at the dogging box when Ralph walked over said, "You'll never guess who was at my house this morning." I said, "Who?" He said, "That Highway Patrol Officer. He said, 'Mr. Ralph. I arrested one of your referee's last night and I decided I don't want to give that boy a ticket, so if you could get it back I'd tear it up.' As Garth Brooks sang, "I got friends in high places." Sorry, Garth, I changed it a bit.

NED LONDO
HAPPY TO LEAVE

Chuck Swanson, Bill Smith, Hugh Chambliss, and I, went back to Chicago to a rodeo in 1966. It was at Soldier Stadium and we stayed at a hotel close to the stadium. While we were there, there was a race war going on with drive-by shootings, and cars driving by with bullet holes in them.

The hotel we were staying at was robbed and several blocks away a guy named Richard Speck had broken into a nurse's dormitory and tied up seven nurses and killed them. He was still at large when we left.

Chuck only left the hotel when we would go to the rodeo. He just ate out of the vending machines. We were all ready to get back to Montana and Wyoming, and Chuck drove all the way, he was so happy to leave.

RED DOYLE
ILL FATED ROAD TRIPS

The Fort Worth and El Paso Rodeos always overlapped so we would make a run to El Paso each year. One year I was up in El Paso one night, but due back in Fort Worth for the 10 am slack the next morning.

The fact that I had drawn a high horned hooker in the slack at Fort Worth, but wouldn't have to pay turn out fees for slack, I decided to stay in El Paso and enjoy the good times across the river and turn out in Fort Worth the next morning.

We loaded up and crossed the river and the last thing I remember was a two-foot high stack of shot glasses on the table. There was a group of college girls from Lubbock that were partying with us, and the next morning I woke up in the back seat of a car feeling like warmed-over death.

The two girls in the front seat were driving like a race car. When they saw I was awake they excitedly told me they were going to get me to Fort Worth in time to get on my bull. They put me in a position of havin' to get on that hooker with a giant hangover, so I cowboyed up and took my hookin.' Friends like that are hard to find.

MICK ROUGHAN
FROM CITY KID TO COWBOY

I still remember the first time I saw someone ride a bull as vividly as it was yesterday. I was 12 years old when our family had just gone through the turmoil of Mum and Dad splitting up. Mum had taken us kids from Brisbane City back to Mount Isa, her home town where she had family for support. I was a skinny city kid who was not the most confident kid getting around. In fact, I lacked any self belief what so ever.

But here I was, suddenly in yet another strange town trying to come to grips with starting another new school with no friends. This scenario was repeated many times through my childhood as my father was in the army and we would get transferred to a different place every two or three years. Mount Isa is a mining town in North West Queensland, Australia. It boasts one of the largest, richest, and longest running rodeos in the country.

Not long after we settled into the town, my Aunty decided to take us to a little rodeo just out of town called Wook-a-Took. The whole scenario was something quite foreign to me so I sat there wide eyed and excited to see broncs bucking and cowboys leaping from horses onto steers to wrestle them to ground.

The sounds and smells were all very exciting to see for a young city kid, but something life changing was about to happen. As with most rodeos, the bull riding was the last event on the program. Straight away I sensed the energy in the air around me change, the sight and sound of huge bulls battering their way through the ally and into the chutes had me fixated.

Cowboys dressed in brightly colored chaps standing over the chutes, putting their ropes on their bulls with a look of confidence, and mixed with nervous energy as if they were about go to battle. It was as if the world around me had gone silent and the only thing that existed was there before my eyes.

When the first bull left the chute, it blew up high in the air, turned back hard and slammed the cowboy head first into the ground. Tough as nails, he got up and dusted himself off, retreating to the back of the chutes.

My spirit began to stir. I don't think I took my eyes off the chutes or spoke to anyone while the bull riding was on. As the chutes were emptied and the cowboys seemed to be losing the odds against the bulls, next up was a local Aboriginal Cowboy who was a bit of an All-Around hand.

His name was Johnny Craigey, if I remember right. He had drawn a big, white Brahma that had a reputation as a bucker. When that chute gate flew open, the bull did not disappoint. He turned back hard, right there in the chute, before swapping directions.

Johnny was grabbing fresh holds with his spurs and making all the right moves. When the whistle blew, he bailed off and the crowd stood and cheered. Somehow, someway, I think I got a small dose of the adrenaline rush Johnny Craigey must have felt that day, because it was right there in that very moment something clicked in my spirit and I knew I wanted to be a bull rider.

By chance, my uncle was involved with the Mount Isa Rodeo. He and a bunch of mates would run the stock in the back yards. Back in those days the rodeo committee had their own famous herd of broncs that they would run in every year.

When the rodeo came to town I asked Mum to enter me in the calf riding. I was so excited. I had spent all my energy trying to find out as much as I could about rodeo. I even remember the way my class at school all laughed when we were asked to talk about what we wanted to do when we grew up.

I said, "I want to be a Rodeo Cowboy." Slightly embarrassed, but undeterred, I was sticking to my guns. I had bought myself a hat and some elastic side riding boots, popular with Aussie Ringers and station hands, so when the day came to get on my first calf I was up early and dressed way ahead of time.

When the time came for the calf riding, all the kids who had entered were gathered nervously to be let in behind the chutes with the real cowboys. That was rock star status to me. I could walk right by all the Champs of the day, and watch them prepare for their rides. How cool was I.

In a loud gruff voice, the chute boss called my name, "Mick Roughan, Yellow Chute." I hurried down to the chute to see a big, grey, Brahma calf rattling back and forth. Things suddenly got real and I sheepishly clambered up and over the chute, my uncle sliding down inside the chute to help block the calf from lurching forward.

As I stood straddled above the calf, my shaking legs rattled the heavy wooden chute gate, I was shaking that hard. With no gear to my name, I used a flank rope for a bull rope, and I had no riding glove or spurs. As I put my hand under the rope and they pulled it tight, it seemed like a million instructions were being shouted at me as I slid up on my rope.

Before I knew it, the chute gate swung open and we lurched into the arena. I really don't remember much of the actual ride, but I remember vividly I was still there when the horn sounded. Picking myself up in the middle of the giant Mount Isa arena, I dusted myself off and strutted back to the chutes proud as punch.

The feeling so good I could have easily shed tears of joy, but I was trying to put on the brave cowboy act. There were lots of pats on the back and, "Good on you mate," from people around the chutes, and it was the best feeling I had ever experienced in my young life.

Now, Mount Isa was notorious for attracting huge numbers of entries so I had a long wait before I would find out if my score would see me place. The smile on my face nearly split my cheeks when I placed second at my very first rodeo. I was hooked. From that day forward, my every thought revolved around rodeo, I got jobs in feed stores, fruit barns, and at the race track, to save money for buying gear and entry fees.

As I grew up I progressed through steer, and bullock riding, into bull riding. The winter months would see the Australian Rough Riders Association Northern Run start, which was our favorite time of the year as we got to go to seven or eight rodeos on consecutive weekends.

When I left school and started working in the mines at Mount Isa, it opened up a whole new world as I could drive myself and my younger brother to rodeos and also to practice days at a friends place who lived a short four hour drive away. Where I grew up is very remote so that was considered a short drive.

Once I had finished my apprenticeship in the mines, there was no holding me back. I saved hard and eventually quit work and hit the rodeo road full time. Driving out of my home town that day never felt so good. I was about to start living what was a childhood dream.

Now, as you all know, the rodeo road can be a tough one, but I loved every minute of it. So many rich memories are engraved in my mind. I wasted a lot of opportunities to cover good bulls in the early days due to a lack of confidence, but I kept going.

Whilst my home is not adorned with lots of trophy buckles and saddles, I never won a title, which in some ways haunts me. However I'm proud to say that I was never thrown before the whistle at my home town rodeo from the first time I entered in 1975, right through to the last time I rode there in 1991. Yet, I only won money there four times.

I rode some real good bulls and held my head up high, the way I conducted myself and treated other people. The cowboy way is entrenched in my very soul. It is, and will always, be part of who I am. It taught me much about myself and a whole lot about other people. It taught me to deal with fear, to believe in myself, and brought life into perspective for me.

Some of the friendships I made have endured all the years and tribulations that have past, solid bonds built on cowboy principles and support of each other that will never die.

Whilst my rodeo career may have passed by many without much notice, it really doesn't bother me, for I was there for more than 18 years chasing the dream and I know in my heart I gave it a good shot. It has made me the man I am today. I conducted myself with honor, integrity and dignity, which is more than I can say for a few of the so called 'elite' of my era.

I still follow the PBR and even get to an event once in a while, but it just makes me wish I could do it all again. And knowing that the road would be paved with hardship and pain, along with incredible highs and life long memories, I would do it all again in an instant if I could step into a time machine.

Rodeo led me into my current career as a successful stuntman and stunt rigger who works globally on some of the biggest films made over the last 25 years. Much of my life experience as a cowboy has somehow helped me in my film career. I guess we look at life and situations a little different than regular people. You take a cowboy out of rodeo, but you'll never take rodeo out of a cowboy.

JON VICK
THE NIGHT BABY HUEY CAUGHT FIRE

At the beginning of summer in 1982, I had just graduated from high school. As we often did, Chris Moore, Kevin Taylor and I, headed out to Steiner's old arena by Mansfield Dam, Texas. Tommy Steiner would often buck his best bulls such as Savage Seven, Black Six, etc., as well as some old rangy bulls that had been wondering the hill country without human contact for some while.

When we arrived at our destination there was quite a large crowd of spectators gathered around. Tommy bucked out some bareback broncs first and I ended up getting on a few head. Another friend whom we called Baby Huey, whose real name was R. C. Glover had showed up and also rode a few broncs.

I kept noticing, as did others, how stiff and ridged Baby's chaps were. They simply didn't flap when he walked. None of us asked about them and went on about our business. Later that day when Tommy started bucking some bulls, I was standing there in my chaps and spurs with my bull rope in hand when Leon Coffee walked up. He started a conversation with Chris Moore and I noticed he was looking my way and pointing.

Leon walked over to me and said, "So you want to be a bullfighter? Well, come on."

I looked at Chris and he laughed and said, "Who could say no, to Leon Coffee?"

Suffice it to say, I received a crash course in Bullfighting 101 in a pair of borrowed tennis shoes. Leon was a great teacher and his first words were, "Charge the bull. Go to him. I want you to get hooked." We had quite an evening, spending around three hours fighting bull after bull.

When it got dark, they built a fire to smoke some meat on. It seems like everyone at the after-party, including Baby Huey, had gravitated towards the fire, standing around shooting the bull.

Suddenly, Chris yelled, "Huey, your chaps on fire?"

I looked over and sure enough, a blaze was burning fast up Baby's legs. He took off running which only made it worse, but a bystander and a few others tackled him rolled him around on the ground, throwing dirt on him. With the fire out and Baby Huey unharmed, we eventually got back to the after-party.

Huey, with no chaps, said, "I guess I'll half to make me another pair."

We looked puzzled, so Baby Huey said, "It's easy, come look."

We followed him over to his old jalopy and he opened the door and out of the rear seat covers were cut the perfect shape of chap leggings. Huey had cut and made his chaps out of his car seats which were made of Naugahyde. Needless to say, I don't think we ever laughed as hard as on the night Baby Huey Caught Fire.

GREG DOERING
ROAD TRIP TO MONTANA WITH A.J. SWAIM

A.J. Swaim and I grew up around the rodeo trail in the Pacific Northwest. AJ's dad Bob, was a top all-around hand and my dad Karl, was a world renowned clown and bull fighter. We became good friends with desires to follow the family tradition in the rodeo arena. We ended up attending Eastern Oregon State University together. My Intercollegiate rodeo career lasted for four years while AJ's was a bit shorter, as the lure of the PRCA-NFR was too strong.

Our road trip started at the Umpqua Valley Round Up in Roseburg, Oregon on Father's Day weekend 1972. It was my hometown rodeo that my dad Karl Doering and mom Kay Doering had both served as President. At the time it was the third largest rodeo in Oregon and attracted many top cowboys. Winners coveted the 30-30 Winchester trophy rifles that were awarded.

Another big attraction was being the home of the first four, Cowboy Clown Reunions. The Christensen Brothers Ranch also hosted a very popular party with live music and various entertainments that lasted to the wee hours of the morning. You could probably write a book about stories from that party.

After finishing up in Roseburg we headed to Bozeman, Montana to the NIRA (National Intercollegiate Rodeo Association) National Finals Rodeo. I was the Northwest Regional Student Director so I had to be there a couple days early for summer board meetings. Some of my close friends on the board included Bud Munroe from Montana, and Jimmie Gibbs from Texas, who would later marry.

With extra time on our hands, we hung out and played pool at the Holiday Inn with several members of the Cal Poly Rodeo Team whose members included Lee Rosser, Tom Ferguson, Dave Clark, John McDonald, and Colleen Semas. Somehow A. J. and I pretty much controlled the pool table. Fortunately, A. J. was a skilled player.

He probably made 90% of the shots. I made a cripple or two, but the general strategy would be for me to follow his advice and hide the cue ball leaving them with nearly impossible shots. It was a fun afternoon of swapping stories, drinking a beer or two, and getting ready for the rodeo.

We knew several Montana State University cowboys including Bob Schall, Jim Jacobson, and Cleve Loney so they showed us some of the finer spots around town. There was the little hole in the wall diner called Manny's that only had a counter and a few bar stools. For $3.99 you got steak, eggs and hash browns that filled two large platters. Truly a great find for a couple of less than prosperous college students.

Then, there was the night life. Montana's drinking age was nineteen so we were legal. The American Legion Hall and another club had live music every night. With college cowboys and cowgirls from all over the U.S., plus much local talent the night life was fun. You could even carry your drink down the street between bars. I wasn't much of a beer drinker and didn't have money to buy top of the line whiskey so I eased into whiskey sours as the drink of choice.

Oh, by the way, Montana State put on a great rodeo. Their men's team dominated and won the Team Championship. The Northwest region competed well with three and four National Champions between the boy's and girl's teams. There were a couple young timed event cowboys that looked like they might be pretty good: Tom and Larry Ferguson, and Dave Brock.

Reg Kesler was the main stock contractor and ran the show, and his bulls and broncs really fired. Many cowboys got the first taste of NFR stock. It was always fun to see some Midwest and Southern cowboys being introduced to Reg's often loud, brash encouragement, to get on and get out of the chute.

It was an especially good rodeo for A.J. as he finished 3rd. in the world for bareback riding and 2nd. in his favorite event, bull riding. As we wrapped up finals night in Bozeman it was time to move on for a one day rodeo at Augusta Montana. At least one of us were up in the early morning slack Sunday morning so we drove on over to Augusta, a thriving metropolis of about 300 people.

We arrived just as the lone bar and street dance was shutting down. The main drag was congested with 100's of partiers. It took us a good half hour to ease through town to the rodeo grounds. Of course, there were no available motel rooms so we slept a few hours in the car before 8:00 o'clock slack. At least we tried to sleep, but the parties carried on most of the night.

What a marked contrast from a Reg Kesler production and a Sonny Linger rodeo, Sonny was a calm, even mannered, excellent stockman that ran a smooth rodeo without getting too excited. As I recall, we had a great sunny day and an enthusiastic crowd who cheered loudly for their Montana cowboys.

As the afternoon continued, the beer stands continued to do a thriving business. All of a sudden during the first section of bull riding, one whole section of bleachers collapsed, sending the crowd tumbling to the ground. Sonny calmly held up the rodeo while security and paramedics quickly evaluated the situation.

Luckily there were no serious injuries, probably largely due to the alcohol content. The rodeo was back in full swing in a few minutes. Soon, the champions were crowned, crowds faded off into the sunset, and we headed back west with all kinds of stories to relive on our way back to Oregon.

A. J. soon hooked up with Denny Flynn, Randy Magers, and Guy Barth, and went down the rodeo trail hard and made several NFR appearances in the bull riding. Upon retirement, he started a successful construction company in Canby, Oregon. He now gives back to the community and rodeo by serving on the Canby Rodeo Committee.

I took a more local route. I did go to the winter rodeos as a bull rider twice, and once as a steer wrestler, and barrel horse groom. I rodeoed primarily in the northwest and Canada, competing in my two events, steer wrestling and bull riding, plus clowning and bull fighting.

As a gold card member I enjoy seeing the opportunities that today's cowboys have. I usually go to four or five rodeos each year and to the Rodeo Clown Rreunions every other year. I do arboriculture sales and consulting and live in Tualatin, Oregon.

JIM LILES
FLYIN' HIGH

Now and then we had a chance, to leave the truck at home
To rodeo without the drive that wears you to the bone
It's not so hard to complete this feat if your nerves are made of steel
But, boys listen to this tale before ya make that leap
We know a guy who's name was Jeff and he wanted so to fly
But, lessons for a private plane, why they were just too high
But, with his friendly bankers help within a month or so
He had his license firm in hand and he was set to go
He looked for ways to log some hours and that's where we came in
Seems a local flyin' club was just plum broke back then
No money for the maintenance fee and friends that ain't no joke
There are lots of things they didn't do and things we didn't know

To rent that plane for a couple a days was a very nominal fee
Why, we jumped in with both front feet. How scary could it be
We headed for the airport with our new pilot close in tow
He could log some needed hours and we could rodeo
The plane was gassed and set to go, so we loaded her to the hilt
Three cowboys and a pilot and a ton of rodeo gear
We all jumped in and fastened down, smilin' from ear to ear
We were all set to go. Let's get this thing in gear
He checked and checked, hell I was so impressed by the list that he checked clear
Now, he tried to start the thing and it just went click, click
It seems the battery was a little low and our hearts sank in a pit
But Jeff said, "Not to worry. A jump is what we'll get
I'll call for an APU and we'll soon be on our way
Sure 'nuff we got her started and got her in the air
And that's when things got interesting and Brad he got plum scared
The trim tabs are that tricky part that makes the plane fly straight
You know, level out flat with its nose not in the air
It seems those silly things don't work and the pilot he don't care
So Jeff he says, "Not to fear. We'll make it there just fine
But, Brad, well he's just not real sure our pilots wrapped real tight
So I asked Jeff, "Now tell me son. What other things don't work
He says the gas gauge has a glitch. Shucks, I thought it was a joke
He has a little kitchen timer set up there on the dash
When it goes off he switches tanks to balance out the gas
By the time we get to Folsom, old Brad why he's scared stiff
He'd just as soon walk back home than climb in that plane with Jeff
An APU was what it took to get us in the air
And Brad, he kicked and screamed and yelled. He wanted to just stay there

Soon we had to land for gas just where I'm not real sure
We landed and we fueled the plane, but Brad he wasn't there
He'd wandered off and found a lounge and that was where he sat
A beer, he said, "Then I'll call a cab, or a bus I will take on back"
It took two hours and a bunch of beer to get Brad on that plane
All we heard the whole way back was Brad as he complained
We made it back all safe and sound and another trip was planned
Except for Brad who said, "Hell no, I'll never fly again."

JOE BOB NUNEZ
THREE RODEOS THAT DAY

One year me and Riley Henson were entered in some rodeos in Southern California. I think we flew into Orange County and rented the car. We had three rodeos that day and went to the first one at Rancho Santa Margarita. We had one at eleven o'clock that morning, and one at two o'clock that afternoon, then one later that night.

We also had another rodeo the next day. Anyway, Riley got knocked out at the first rodeo. When they brought the ambulance in for him I ran out and said, "Riley, you got to get up. We have two more rodeos today." LOL.

Needless to say, they hauled him out and I had to leave him with a guy named Calvin Nez who took care of him and got him back to New Mexico. I hated to leave him, but I think he forgave me. I won two rodeos that day so it turned out better for me than it did for ol' Riley.

JOHN SLOAN
THE DRUG LORDS

In the mid 1960's, Rodeos Incorporated had a series of rodeos in the Midwest. One of them was at a dude ranch in Hudson, Wisconsin, owned by a guy named John Rauchnot. I had come to that rodeo straight from a Barnes Rodeo in Cherokee, Iowa, and traveling with me was Tom Gentry, a saddle bronc rider from Clint, Texas.

My regular traveling partner, a bronc and bull rider from Illinois, Larry Spurgeon, had just left the Mayo Clinic where he had his nose rebuilt. Larry joined us in Hudson and you can imagine what he looked like after a nose job.

The night before the rodeo started the three of us partook of several adult beverages at one of the local watering holes then repaired to our hotel room. About 10:00 the next morning we are at the arena just visiting and waiting, and in pulls two police cars.

With very little ceremony, four deputies tell Tom, Larry, and I, to get in our vehicles and follow them to the police station. We knew we had not broken any laws so we do as they asked. Tom and Larry were in his truck and I was in my car. When we got to the station we are separated and taken to interrogation rooms.

A young detective walked in my room and introduced himself. Nice guy. We chat. And in the course of that he says, "Please roll up your shirt sleeves." I had seen enough up shows to know what he is looking for. I comply-no needle tracks. He says, "Tell me about your partners."

I know we have done nothing, but stupid I, decided to "play" along and said, "Which one?" He replies, "Well, tell me about Larry. What happened to his nose?" I kinda hang my head and say, "I'm not supposed to talk about it, but you being the law and all, I guess it's okay.

He is in the witness protection program and is changing the way he looks." The guy about jumped out his chair. Well," says I, "Tommy, is from Clint, Texas, and he got caught selling 1,000 baby chickens for $50 dollars over the radio. But, he don't have no chickens so he is just hit the road."

By then the cop caught on that his leg was being slightly pulled so I told him the truth. He wanted to know where we had been before coming to Hudson and I told him Cherokee, Iowa. And he wants to know why Tom has so much Maalox and I say because he has ulcers. And he leaves the room.

He comes back in a minute and says we are all free to go. Turns out, a drug store had been broken into the night before and they just figured it had to be cowboys since we had been seen in town. He checked in Cherokee and there'd been no drug store burglaries there, so they turn us lose after searching our vehicles and belongings.

Back at the arena, John Snow, the announcer and part owner of Rodeos Inc. is some mad. A few minutes before the Grand Entry he gets me in the arena with a hand-held microphone and we do an interview in which I tell my, by then, a somewhat embellished tale of police harassment. The crowd is immediately on my side and by the time I am done they all love me and Tom and Larry.

Tom and I are competing, and when we ride, the crowd goes wild. By the end of the first performance I am sitting first in the bares, and splitting the bull riding-thanks to crowd approval. Tom, as he often did, got bucked off. But the crowd loved him, anyway.

Now Larry, Tom, and I had moved from the downtown motel to the dude ranch. Somehow that night, well after closing time, another bronc rider Ken Badger and I find ourselves still sitting in the bar, even though there is no bartender.

We are hungry so Ken goes in the kitchen and starts browsing through the big refrigerator and says, "How about we cook a couple of these big T-bones with some fried potatoes?" I think that is a splendid idea and immediately fire up the big grill. Well, to cut to the chase, we dine on perfect steaks, potatoes, salad, and wash it all down with Old Charter.

Says Kenny, "Reckon what we owe?"

I reply, "Five should do it."

Thinking five dollars each, Kenny puts a five under a spatula and says, "I got it, let's get some sleep."

Next morning the four of us are at breakfast and the waitress is mad as a smashed cat about something. Keeps mumbling, "Comes in my kitchen, steals my steaks, leaves a mess, and just a five dollar tip. Wish I could get my hands on whoever did it."

And in walks Gene and Bobby Clark and their pet chimp dressed in human clothes. They plop down in a booth across from us and I say to the waitress, "There they are. The little one is the cook." The waitress storms over to their booth like a battleship coming into dock.

Before she can say a word, the chimp grabs her and kisses her like a chimp will do, then lets out a screech and that big chimp grinned with 30 yards of gum showing. I cannot in words, describe the following scene. The waitress goes flying out the door, order pad going one way, her apron another, and issuing about as foul a screamed sentence as I have ever heard.

The Clarks are looking stunned, having no idea what went on, and the four of us are about to soil ourselves from laughing. Just as it all subsides Gene Clark says, "What in the hell got into her? You'd think somebody stole her tip jar or something." That was a great time to be rodeoin' and bein' on the road.

JOE FOSCALINA
HISTORY OF THE BULL ROPE

The night before the Oakdale, California Professional Rodeo is when this story started about the year 1979. A young, cocky, up-and-coming Champion Circuit Bull Rider from a well-known rodeo family had just broke the wear strip on his bull rope.

This young man was in his third year as a professional and had already conquered the great and famous bucking bull #16. That number was well-known to all the riders. If a bull is great enough, they are honored and recognized by the number of riders they kept from making a qualified eight second ride.

Joe Foscalina

I want to tell you about one of those names to that famous #16. The bull rider was Allan Jordan and the famous bull was Oscar. Oscar was little and fast. He had thrown hundreds riders and was ridden only a handful of times.

Bob Cook was a stock contractor from the West Coast and he was the proud owner of Oscar. Now, on the morning of the Oakdale Rodeo I ran into Allan and he said, "I need to borrow your rope. I broke mine last night."

I replied, "Wait a minute Allan. You don't want to use my rope because you ride left handed and my rope is right handed."

Well, if you know Allan, what he said next won't surprise you. "Joe," he said. "If you can ride bulls, you can ride 'em with a gate rope." I smiled, shook my head and said, "OK, Allan." Allan laughed and said, "Joe, I'm only getting on Oscar."

Well, the story ends good because my friend Allan Jordan went on to ride Oscar that day. The rest of that season, every time we were up in the same performance we shared that rope. My dad kept that old worn out rope and hung it in the barn and proudly told the story about the rope that rode Oscar, every chance he had. This is a picture of that old rope and those precious memories that are attached.

ALLAN HOWARD
PUSHIN' SEVENTY

One summer during the middle of July, it had rained a lot and it was hotter than all hell. I had my cows and calves in a pasture along the Sheyenne River and the brush and trees were really thick due to the amount of rain we'd had. My cows were getting foot rot faster than I could treat them, so Duane and I decided to corral them and move them to another pasture on higher ground.

We set up the corral and caught all but one pair that we couldn't find. We treated what was lame and hauled the cow/calf pairs to the other pasture. It was getting late in the day so I told Duane that I would get up early the next morning and take the saddle horse and the dogs and go find that missing pair.

In the pasture there was a small island and you had to cross a wide boggy spot to get to it. I got across okay, and rode 'till the dogs found the cow. It was so thick, if it wasn't for the dogs I would have ridden right past her and her calf. The cow had foot rot real bad so I left her there and rode back home to call Duane to tell him that I'd found her.

When I called we talked about what to do. I told him we'd better go get her right away because she might move when it cools off and we would have to hunt for her all over again. He said he'd be there right after dinner. By the time we got going it was hot and humid. The only 2 horses I had handy were my two bull pullin' horses that I used in the arena. They were part draft so they were big and stout with wide backs. It was so hot and humid that they sweat just standing around fighting flies.

I did the chores with these horses all winter feeding cows, and they were pretty honest except the one I rode always had to hump up a little when I would get on. I told Duane we would ride bareback so our saddles and tack would not get all muddy when we crossed onto the island, like what had happened to me that morning.

We got them caught and bridled and Duane laughed about the wide back on his horse and how stout he was. I helped Duane up on his horse and I jumped on mine and of course he was wanted to hump up a little. Duane laughed at me trying get him straightened out, but it wasn't long and he was fine.

You didn't have to ride far 'till the seat of your pants were wet from the horses sweating. We headed to the island and started across that mud and water and the horses were clear to their bellies in mud. The mosquitoes and flies were so thick you could hardly stand it and it was getting hotter and hotter.

We found the cow and her calf and started them off the island. They went good and we all got across again. Duane and I got the cow and calf in the corral, treated her, and hauled her to the pasture where the rest were.

It was funny because the next evening when Duane called to see how the cows were doing I told him they were doing better in their new pasture out of that wet mess. I asked Duane how he was doing after his long bareback ride and he said he was fine except that big old sweaty, wide-backed horse had blistered his rear end.

He said, "I'm sure glad I don't have to get on one of those big, rank Calgary saddle broncs today." As I'm writing this, I still remember him telling me about it just like it was yesterday.

Duane was pushing seventy at the time and there's just no way around it, you had to like the guy. Rest in Peace, my friend.

DARRYL DAVIS
WANTING TO BE A RODEO CLOWN

I started riding bulls when I was seventeen back in the mid-seventies. I didn't stop 'till the late nineties, and all those years I had the utmost respect for the rodeo clowns. Today, their called bullfighters and I like that name better. Its fits with the job they do in protecting the cowboy when he comes off the bull. Believe me I owe all of them for getting those bulls attention while I got safely away. Even though I did not escape the wrath of the bull's punishment sometimes, does not mean those guys in those shorts and track shoes were not doing their job.

About 1979, Greg Moore and Lynn Sanford who were my running buddies, worked the First Annual Houston Police Department Mounted Patrol Rodeo. It was held in Montgomery County if my memory is right. I had the privilege of being one of the rough stock judges along with Edwin Dickman.

Watching Greg and Lynn working that show really impressed me and had me wanting to try my hand at fighting bulls. I told Greg if there was a chance, and we got invited back for next year's show, I would like to give clowning a shot. The next year we were invited back.

The Rodeo was held at the old Sam Houston Coliseum in downtown Houston, Texas. I remember going to that coliseum when I was a kid to watch the circus. Now, I would get to be on the ground floor where the Beatles, Elvis, and others had performed many years ago.

I was excited to be helping Greg and a guy named Terry. I left out his last name to not embarrass him later in this story. Terry had been doing this for a while. He brought his clown acts and his fighting barrel and any clothing that we needed. He knew

I was new at doing something like this so he insisted that during the bull riding I remain in the barrel.

I was alright with that, but I was really hoping to be able to turn a bull back out of the gate into a spin or help a fallen cowboy away from danger. Terry was a quiet guy. He didn't say much when we weren't in the arena, but he was spot on during the clown acts. One of the clown acts I was to accuse Terry of sleeping with my wife and I'd shoot him in the butt with a fake gun which sets off an explosion.

This explosion technique had to be prepared before the rodeo even starts. You poured gun powder and baby powder into a small plastic bag then run two electrical wires into that plastic bag and bury them into the gun and baby powder. You run wire from your backside to your shirt pocket and in your shirt pocket you have a battery.

To set that gun powder off, you had to touch the wires to the battery for the explosion. If all goes according to plan you touch the wires to the battery and the current goes to the gunpowder, then boom. The gunpowder goes off and with the baby powder it leaves a big cloud of white smoke.

An hour before the Grand Entry was to start Greg and I were in the dressing room with Terry. We were getting ready and painting our faces while Terry was preparing the bomb. He had a big coffee can of gunpowder and was pouring it into a measuring cup. He then proceeded to poor what was in the measuring cup into a plastic bag. He would then add a certain amount of baby powder into the plastic bag.

The whole time he was doing that his hands are shaking. I mean they were shaking where there was no way that if he was holding a glass of water that none of that water would remain in that glass. It was that bad. I asked him if he was alright and he said he was just gets a bit nervous handling gunpowder.

He then grabbed the wire with the battery and at this moment Greg and I looked at each other and decided to leave the dressing room and go get something to drink. We left Terry in the dressing room preparing the explosive device with shaky hands, hoping the dressing room would still be there when we got back.

We were to do the, 'Hey, you're sleeping with my wife act,' while they were setting up the barrels for the girls barrel race. There was a discussion about having an explosive devise go off in a covered arena before we were to start our act. The coliseum personal suggested we not do this act since it was a closed building and there was livestock everywhere.

I was disappointed because I had a big part in this act. But, we did it anyway and I got to talk and shoot someone and Terry seemed happy. You'd think he just won the rodeo. I found out later that Terry had added too much gunpowder a time or two in the past to this act and basically, had no more butt to loose. The rodeo was a success and we did the two day event and after that I never saw Terry again. That was my one and only time of being a rodeo clown.

CHIMP ROBERTSON
HE WENT THAT-A-WAY

I was entered in the bull ridin' at the famous XIT Rodeo in my hometown of Dalhart, Texas, and had drawn L. D. Ward's big, white Brahma #14. He was their fighting bull and they always bucked him last so the clown Jake Mitchell could mess with him with his tractor inner tube.

It was Saturday night and the stands were full. People were sitting on the ground in front of the bleachers, all the way down to the arena fence. It was one of the largest crowds in the rodeo's history, and the announcer made a big spill about how this bull couldn't be ridden and how this hometown cowboy was going to try to be the one to do it.

Old #14 came out jumping high and kicking back like a saddle bronc. I rode him several jumps before he jerked my arm straight out, popped my hand out of the limber rope handle, and my spurs out of his loose hide, and drove me head first into the hard-packed dirt out in the middle of the arena.

The noise from the crowd was so loud I couldn't even hear the announcer. I got up, punched the dents out of my straw hat, picked up my bull rope, and started walking back to the chutes. From somewhere way up in that crowd among all those thousands of people, I heard my uncle Ben yell, "Haaaaaaay, Chimp. He went that-a-way..."

TERRI ABRAHAMSEN
CROOKED NOSE

Here are a few memories of everybody's good friend, Mr. Harry Vold. He used to try and keep us photographers as family at the rodeos. For example at the Fort Smith, Arkansas May Rodeo, he always had us have a potluck supper behind the chutes. It was such a great way to kick back and tell tales and enjoy the fellowship, and not working while we did.

Terri Abrahamson [Terri Abrahamson photo]

The other thing was his care for all who were in the arena during his rodeos. My favorite memory of him that stands out was the first time I was blessed to photograph his good bull Crooked Nose. I was unaware of how aggressive this bull was, so at the Tulsa, Oklahoma PRCA Rodeo, Harry rode up to me just before Crooked Nose was to be ridden and told me to leave the arena.

Rodeo Producer Harry Knight, center, on chutes, Tulsa Rodeo 1983. [Terri Abrahamson photo]

I had never been told that before while taking rodeo photographs so I sort of argued with him a bit. He told me I would be in danger if I stayed so I said alright, and shot pictures of Crooked Nose from outside of the arena.

Harry had also told Bern Gregory to leave the arena when Crooked Nose bucked. With the speed that Crooked Nose had, I was so glad that he knew this bull and tried to keep even us photographers out of harms' way. Rest in Peace, Mr. Vold.

TODD GAUDIN
D. J. GAUDIN (THE KAJUN KID)

The Kajun Kidd was a rodeo clown and bullfighter during the 50's, 60's & 70's. He was a member of the PRCA Hall of Fame, the National Cowboy and Western Heritage Museum, Texas Cowboy Hall of Fame, Texas Rodeo Cowboy Hall of Fame, and the Bull Riding Hall of Fame.

These are stories I have heard more than a few times in my life, not only from my dad, but also from many of the cowboys involved. I won't swear to their accuracy, but I have tried to present them in the most accurate manner I can as they were told to me.

Bull rider Dan Willis was frequent passenger with my dad, traveling from rodeo to rodeo to help him drive. Dan was Rookie of the Year in 1965, and the Kajun Kidd was the one that gave him the nickname of, 'Rook'.

This was back before the Interstate Highway System was completed, when travel took much longer. It wasn't unusual for cowboys to team up and travel down the road together to share expenses like gas and food.

One year at Fort Worth, Dan Willis had drawn a black, muley bull of Steiner's that he said everyone seemed to ride, but him. Dan bucked off right in front of the chutes and was getting worked over pretty good.

The Kajun Kidd was in there trying to get the bull off of him, but John Routh was out of the picture. Among all the commotion, Dan said the only thing he could hear was the Kajun Kidd hollering, "John, John.... get in here and help me. He's killing my driver."

ED LeTOURNEAU
THE TIMEX WATCH

At the Yuma, Arizona Rodeo one year, I went to the rodeo office to pay my fees and see what I'd drawn. #34 meant nothing to me and I didn't recognize him. The other bull riders didn't help because no one knew him.

So, I went and looked at him in the pen and he was a young Brahma with a fresh brand. Just purchased and probably really bucks, so I knew I had drawn a good one. When they ran him in the chute and the flank man was putting the flank rope on him I asked bout him. The flank man said, "Don't worry, he's a good one."

About that time someone comes up and ties a Timex Watch on his horns. Now I now what I got, the fightin' bull. When I was getting' on him I asked the flank man," When the whistle blows, can I keep the watch if I can reach down and grab it before I get off?" and he said, "If you can do that, it's yours."

When the whistle blew we were almost all the way down the arena. I reached down for the watch and got thrown right over his head and got mauled around some before the clown rescued me.

#34 ran down the fence to the other end of the arena and I was thinking, "There went my only chance of getting anything out of this day, because it sure wasn't going to be at the pay window."

While I was trying to get myself together, I looked down toward the other end of the arena and saw several guys trying to get the Timex off the bull's horns. Suddenly he starts coming back my way. I jumped up on the fence and as he went by, I reached down and plucked the watch off his horns. My big pay for that rodeo-a Timex Watch.

ROME WAGER
THE HOCKEY RINK WALL

I was up in the Edmonton Super Rodeo in 1975, and drew Harry Vold's horse Wall Street. He'd been to the NFR a few times was known as a very good bronc. I asked Harry about the rein which was X, or known by most as average. I didn't know Harry very well, but he had a reputation as being very honest and very knowledgeable. My dad rode in Harry's rodeos back in 1950's, so I had no reason to doubt what he said.

I got on and called for him and he had a very good trip and all was going well, but boy, he was pulling on me. I was teetering every jump, but the ride was going well 'till we came to the hockey rink wall on the arena.

The previous week, I'd ridden in Calgary at Rodeo Royal in a similar situation, but I spurred over my cantle. I shot my feet straight back down to get set back down in my saddle, but instead I shot my right foot into the seat of the saddle and when he kicked, it sent me way up in the air.

I saw the hockey rink wall below me and I didn't want to fly over the wall, so I doubled up and tried to dive to the ground. I missed and instead, came down face first onto the hockey rink wall which knocked me colder than a wedge.

When I came to I felt a terrible jabbing pain and it was a doctor jabbing me in the eye brow. I said, "What are you doing?" He said, "Sewing you up, tough guy."

They said when they came out to me lying in the arena and were trying to carry me out on a stretcher that I was hollering, "My eyes, my eyes." The doctor said, "You've got your eyes. You're OK." I said, "No. I want my eyes." One of the guys figured it out and told the doctor I was talking about my glasses.

The doctor said, "Forget about your glasses. They're history. They've been busted in several pieces." But, I only had 4 inches good vision and was used to fixing my broken glasses because somebody was always punchin' me and breaking them.

They said I cussed at the doctor and said they were to go get my glasses or I was gonna whip him. Intelligence wasn't one of my strong points. So, they went and got my busted up glasses. The doctor had not given me any anesthesia so as he was yanking the knots tight on my stitches he said, "How do like that, tuff guy?"

I finally got out of the EMT area, but I didn't remember know who I'd come with. I saw a couple guys I recognized, but they said I hadn't come with them so I went outside and couldn't find my car. I was madder than a hornet, thinking someone stolen my car which was a four-hundred dollar 1962 Nash Rambler and I'd never heard of anyone stealing a junker like that. Finally, Gary Hasti, a bull riding buddy of mine from South Dakota, tracked me down and explained I'd come with him.

So, getting back to the hockey rink wall in Edmonton, it was coming at me again. I was teetering on going over his head which would have been fine, but I was thinking, "Not again." So, this time I picked my head up and jumped and I flew over the hockey rink wall and landed on my feet in the Aisle about 5 rows up, and sat down by a lady who thought it was very funny.

The next go-round I asked Harry about my horse and he held his hand out with his thumb extended to show the average rein, then stopped and looked at my 5' 2" 120 lb body and says, "No, I think maybe we'll go with two extra fingers, so how about four fingers over average."

For the next 35 plus years I started with four fingers over average when measuring my rein. Harry Knight knew better than I did about what I needed for a rein. Through all those years he was correct on the rein measurements he gave me, and that gave me the style I rode with.

"Tasmanian" © Roger Langford

PART 6

1. Darryl Davis...The Moon Roof
2. Abe Morris...Cowtown Bulls
3. Barry Adams...DeKalb County Rodeo
4. Albert Bissett...Headed Back To Texas
5. Brad Ewell...The Shirt
6. Chimp Robertson...The Hayden Rodeo
7. Dennis Merrell...My Good Friend Steve Williams
8. Fred Schwartz...What Fans Don't See After The Rodeo
9. Everett Campbell...Mid-States Rodeo Association
10. Gloria Hall...Clemente's Junior Rodeo
11. Jerry Gustafson...Portland To Chicago
12. Gary Bowden...I Didn't Even Put On My Chaps
13. Dwayne Jett...Winning Twice In One night
14. Jay Foscalina...An Amazing Career
15. Redboy Schlidt...Peaks and Valleys
16. John Sloan...Oops
17. Allan Howard...A Tough Hand
18. Wayne Decker...The Check
19. Tim Sample...Filling My Permit
20. Ronnie Allen, Sr...Tough Bulldoggers
21. Ron Warr...When I Got My Come-ups
22. David Hardage...Jim and Marvin Paul
23. Ed LeTourneau..."Punch" Rossen
24. Tom Ray...Me and 011 Buster
25. Abe Morris...Dustin Young

DARRYL W. DAVIS
THE MOON ROOF

Back in the early 1980s I purchased my older sister's car from her, a 1975 Mercury Ford Cougar 2- door with power windows and a moon roof. It had a cold AC for those long summer drives and a good heater in case one of those Texas cold fronts came through. It was the best transportation I ever had at the time. Everything worked and it had new tires.

Lynn Sanford, Ronny Ashley, and I headed up to Mansfield, Texas from Houston, to ride at the Kowbell Rodeo arena on a Saturday night. We took my car, had the old AC going and listening to Chris LeDoux on the 8 track and four hours later we pulled into Mansfield.

We decided to get some hamburgers at one of the dinners then drive on over to the Kowbell Rodeo parking lot and relax a little before check in. The weather was nice so we rolled down the windows and opened the moon roof.

Check in time came so I rolled the windows up and we headed in. After we rode, it was maybe around 10:30 pm so we decided to take off and head to Fort Worth area and see about checking out one of the night clubs. When we got in the car, the dash, seats, and floor had dust all over them. I realized I'd forgoten to close the moon roof.

We got most of the dust out by rolling the windows down and blowing it out while driving. We got to the dance hall and I know these people have seen rodeo cowboys before, but I think they thought we were from some cattle drive. We had dust all over us and it was even in our ears and noses. We went to the restroom and washed our faces and came out and ordered a few beers.

While we were in the club enjoying conversation with others, talking about rodeo and the weather, and by the way not one of us had checked the weather, a Texas Blue Northern came through. The temperature dropped from 70 to 30 in less than an hour. Lynn, Ronny, and I didn't bring any winter gear, only some light jackets, but that was it.

We came out of the club and it was cold and wet, and crap I'd left the moon roof open again. The cloth seats were wet and there was water on the dash. I started the car and turned on the heater and tried to shut the moon roof, but it wouldn't work. I checked fuse and it was OK. I had to get a crow bar out of the trunk and force that thing shut. We lacked an inch to it being completely closed.

One of the guys was able to round up some plastic garbage bags to put over the seats so our butts would not get wet. We decided to head back to Houston since more bad weather was on the way. I drove for over an hour with the heater going full blast which made me very sleepy. I must have dozed off because I was rudely awakened by my car running over those reflector posts that are along the road shoulder.

I just held the car straight and finally maneuvered it back up on to the road. I was a little shaken, but when I looked over at my buddies they were still asleep. I felt bad because I could have killed us all. I drove a little ways further and saw a rest stop and pulled in there to take a nap. I left the car running and the heater blowing and fell fast asleep.

I woke up later when Ronny asked, "Where are we?" I said, "At a rest stop." Lynn said, "Good Lord, its cold." He was right because you could see our breath. Apparently the heater wasn't working anymore and it was freezing outside. It was raining and the water was coming through the one inch crack of the moon roof.

To make matters worse, Ronny must have accidentally rolled his window down half way and we couldn't get it back up. We pulled and pulled, but it wouldn't budge. I guess with me leaving the moon roof open earlier when the rain came through, it must have shorted out some of the electronics.

We drove to a store and got something to eat and some coffee to warm us up and to talk about how to cover up the gap in the moon roof and the half open window. Can we make it back home driving my car that has turned into a refrigerator on four wheels? We had no choice. We stuffed clothes into the one inch crack of the moon roof and covered window with Ronny's sleeping bag.

We put on dry clothes and gave Ronny our light jackets. Lynn crawled into his sleeping bag in the back seat. I took my sleeping bag and opened the bottom part of it so my feet could push the gas pedal and brake. While standing outside the car I slipped the sleeping bag up to my chest and got in the driver's seat.

While we are doing this, several people were looking at us and wondering just what the heck we were doing. I was ready and warm so here we go. Three rodeo cowboys heading down the road in a freezing drizzle with foggy windows, clothes flapping on the roof, and half a sleeping bag flapping in the wind on the side of the car. We made it home very cold and a very wet. The next day the window worked, but the moon roof was no more. We finally got it shut all the way and it was never thought of again.

ABE MORRIS
COWTOWN BULLS

Retired Texas bull rider Kelly Riley who spent the entire summer competing at the Cowtown Rodeo in Woodstown, New Jersey in July 1972 was working for Howard Harris III. Back then the RCA allowed local entries without having a permit and the Cowtown Rodeo accepted local entries on a regular basis. A best-selling book titled, "Future Shock," written by Alvin Toffler had been published in 1970 made mention of the Cowtown Rodeo.

Until then, I'm sure city slickers from Philadelphia and New York City had never even heard of the Cowtown Rodeo, but wanted to be thrill seekers and find out what a taste of the Wild

West would be like. Philadelphia was only 30 miles away and it was about 100 miles to New York City.

Two young aspiring wanna be bull riders in their mid 20's entered the bull riding event. They'd probably gone to some saddle shop and purchased some riding equipment before venturing down to the Cowtown Rodeo. This was about the same time that Bobby DelVecchio from the Bronx, New York also got the itch to someday become a professional bull rider, but that is another story.

Back in the 1970's Howard Harris III had one of the best pen of bucking bulls in the nation. His bulls were well-fed, mean and rank. It was certainly not a place for the feint of heart to risk their lives, discovering if they were cut out to be bull riders.

Growing up in Woodstown, New Jersey with my first cousins Gene, David, Jimmy Lee, and Willie Ed Walker, we referred to the rodeo arena as *Cape Cowtown*. It honestly was a launching pad for those rank Harris bulls. We theorized that if anyone could successfully ride Cowtown bulls, they could go anywhere in the nation and be successful in Professional Rodeo.

One of the young adventurous guys drew #4-40 Punt. He was a big, black and white spotted bull that was selected to go to the National Finals Rodeo in 1972. He originally had great long horns, but he was so mean that Howard Harris chopped them way down and they ended up short and thick. The markings on Punt reminded me of the great bucking bull Mr. T that was owned by Pete and Hal Burns from Laramie, Wyoming.

The first wanna be cowboy nodded his head and Punt disposed of him in no time flat. He'd also whacked him upside the head and knocked him unconscious before he hit the ground. Very few people ever got safely away from Punt because he was a headhunter. As soon as a fallen bull rider moved to get away he would be on them in a flash.

Because the guy was knocked out cold, there was an immediate hush over the crowd. Punt was looking around for his would-be target, but couldn't find him because the guy never moved. Howard Harris remarked that, "It was deep, dark, and lonely, wherever that guy was currently at."

It was so quiet that one could hear a pin drop. Even though the guy was lying face first with his head in the dirt, his legs were violently quivering due to muscles spasms of being unconscious. He was wearing a pair of cheap riding spurs and the rowels were loose.

Because it was so quiet in that arena his spurs were making a jingle, jingle, jingle sound. It was the weirdest thing I ever witnessed during my entire rodeo career. They got Punt out of the arena so he never hooked the poor unconscious guy. He finally came to and didn't have to go to the hospital, but did need assistance leaving the arena.

His traveling buddy was still on the back of the bucking chutes awaiting his turn to compete and watched the whole thing take place. He immediately reached down and jerked his rope off of the bull and exclaimed that he was getting the heck out of dodge. He left the rodeo with his partner and they were never seen again. Their very brief bull riding careers had come to a sudden and grinding halt.

BARRY ADAMS
DeKALB COUNTY RODEO

Me, John Clark, Davey (DJ) Pruder, Joe Lero, Ricky White, Carl Fiorito, and a few others entered the DeKalb County Rodeo in Alanta, Georgia. I was in the bareback riding, Joe was in the bronc riding, and DJ was entered in the bull riding. Not sure as to how they did because I wasn't around to watch the other events.

During the bareback riding I had a big grey horse and was doing alright when I heard a loud pop. At the time, I though my rigging had broken. I came off the horse and landed on my feet and started walking to the contestants gate when Ricky White said, "Barry, I think your arm is broken."

I looked down and part of my forearm was going east, but my hand was pointing north. A man at the gate placed a program under my arm which helped stabilize it, and a young police officer who wanted to play medic, started wrapping it with ace bandage. That didn't make my day any better as the bandage pushed together the broken bones, and I passed out.

They placed me in an ambulance and carried me to the local hospital. This happened on a Saturday and surgery was scheduled on a Monday. DJ and Joe stopped by to check on me and I told them to take my truck and go on home and come back Friday and pick me up.

Interestingly, I had a gentleman in the bed next to me who had broken his leg while taking his first sky diving trip and his family took care of me. I had the opportunity to meet him and his son about five years later. DJ cracked his hip during the bull riding at Stone Mountain, Georgia and we went to the same hospital. I ran into that same family in the emergency room.

When I was released on Friday, DJ and Joe picked me up in my truck and away we went, me in a long arm splint with two plates holding my arm together. Our first Rodeo was in Michigan where I met a couple of bulldoggers who were pulling a two horse trailer loaded with Coors instead of horses.

They had been west of the Mississippi, the only place you could buy Coors back then. We left Michigan and headed to another show in Waconda, Illinois and then on to Alex Martinez's house. We stayed there for a week before heading on to the next show in Paducah, Kentucky, the first IRA Rodeo to be held in this small town.

The trip there was interesting when the second adventure began. We left Chicago and headed to Kentucky with DJ and Joe in the camper sleeping, due to over indulgence. Carl Fiorito was sleeping in the passenger seat while I drove with my left arm in a soft cast. It was raining, and with four bald tires I was utilizing all the lanes available.

How we made it to Paducah was a miracle. We found the rodeo grounds and after fixing one flat tire we were greeted by one John Clark. Clark wanted to know if I would judge the show since he was supposed to, but instead wanted to enter the bull riding. I said I would because we were just about broke.

DJ and Joe had enough money to enter the rodeo with a bit left over while Carl and I judged the show. DJ and Joe tried to find another tire since our spare was flat and believe it or not, not one cowboy or cowgirl had a tire we could borrow that late at night. One interesting fact was I had an old 8 track tape machine and a copy of, 'Paint Your Wagon.'

That night John Clark sat on the ground in the passenger door and listened to, 'Wandering Star,' until it was totally worn out. The rodeo went well even though DJ, Joe, and John thought they were sneaking off to a show that no one would be at. Well, surprise, surprise, as the top fifteen cowboys showed up. We did have a couple of our boys ride into the Grand Entry with their boots and hats on and that was all.

Well, it was a great trip, yeah, broken arm and all. Upon arriving home we parked the truck and went to bed, and the next morning we woke up and when we went out to the truck it had three flat tires. What a trip. Since I wasn't able to ride until the plates came out of my arm, I picked up a camera…and that started my Rodeo Photography Career.

ALBERT BISSETT
HEADED BACK TO TEXAS

I have participated in the sport of rodeo for as far back as I can remember, but I don't believe I'll ever be able put in words, the fun, the emotions of winning, and of course the feeling of losing, and I did a lot of both. One of the stories that still makes me laugh out loud to this day, was the time me and my buddy Carl Larsen decided to hit the rodeo trail one summer.

Al Bissett

We figured we'd make a run up through North Texas, Oklahoma, and on into Colorado. Right before we left, one of our friends Johnny Vasbinder, asked if he could go with us. Carl rode barebacks, and I roped, bulldogged, and rode saddle broncs. Johnny didn't rodeo, but we figured what the hell, he offered to pay half the gas so you bet he could go.

Well, we took off on a Tuesday and made it to some friend's house near Amarillo. We had a soft bed and lots of good food, something we were not going to experience for a while, little did we know. We were traveling in Carl's El Camino. This car was fast and beautiful. It was red with a white stripe, just what two cowboys needed.

Carl and I would sleep in the truck bed in sleeping bags, but Johnny had to sleep on an army cot outside on the ground. Our friend let us know that night at dinner that a bear had mauled a man a couple of weeks before in Colorado. Well, the next day we made it to Lamar, Colorado.

We were up in the performance that night and luckily we drew good stock and Carl and I both placed. We headed to the mountains and found a nice park to camp at. I went to the store for groceries and came back with two heads of lettuce and a case of beanie weenies. No one said much, but I kinda got the idea they were not crazy about my shopping abilities.

We built a camp fire and fell asleep. Along about 1 or 2 o'clock in the morning we heard Johnny hollering that a bear had him. Carl being the brave one, reached down and grabbed the tailgate and shut it in about a half of a second, and Johnny was still hollering.

We couldn't see what was going on, but we could hear a lot of noise. I told Carl that I thought he was just dreaming. Carl was a little leary, but he dropped the tailgate and stepped out and sure enough, Johnny was having one heck of a dream. We finally got him awake and he explained about a huge bear at the foot of his cot that was trying to steal his boots. We really got to rib him the rest of the trip.

Well, I got mine later. We were out looking for wood a day or so later, and Johnny snuck up behind me and latched one of those devils claws on the back of my leg. I jumped about 6 feet high and screamed that a snake had bit me and wouldn't let go. It didn't take me long to figure out it was a prank, since Carl and Johnny were bent over laughing their butts off at me.

We made the rodeo at Colorado Springs, but didn't make any money. We drew horses that were a lot ranker than what we were used to getting on down in Texas, plus Carl's hand had swollen up about twice its normal size. I didn't mention that after bucking off my saddle bronc that I had to use baling wire for my halter to fit him, he had around spun and threw me against the chute gate and in a split second, kicked me right below the belt buckle.

They carried me out of the arena and set me on my riggin bag. Carl was sitting there rubbing his sore hand and I'm hunched over there thinking I'm dying. After a minute or so I said, "Carl and Johnny. We've been rodeoing and roughing it for a couple of weeks now. You know, if we head home right now, we got just enough money to rent a motel room, eat a big steak dinner, and barely have enough gas money to make it back to Texas?"

They never said a word. Carl just stood up and grabbed his riggin' bag, while Johnny helped me up and grabbed mine. We headed to the nearest motel, had the biggest steak, and headed back to Texas the next morning. It was an adventure I will never forget.

BRAD EWELL
THE SHIRT

I knew Billy Bob Cleveland back in the late seventies. He was killed at the Mesquite Rodeo in the early eighties. After that, I met his younger brother Colt and we ran into each other from time to time at rodeos at Northside, especially in the Cadillac bar at the Stockyards.

In 1999 I was coming out of the Cadillac about 11 o'clock one night and Colt and a friend of his were coming up the sidewalk so we stopped and have a nice long chat. He knew I was there when his brother was killed so we talked about that quite a bit. I had on a starched white Wrangler shirt that had Wrangler on the collar and back, and down the sleeves.

Colt said, "Brad, I've got two good bulls drawn tomorrow night and man, I'd like to ride in that shirt." So, being the good cowboy I am I just unbuttoned it and stripped it off and handed it to him. When he thanked me I said, "Well I'm gonna need a shirt to wear the rest of the way home." So he took his off shirt and we made the exchange right out there on the sidewalk in front of the Cadillac at 11 o'clock at night and the looks we got from some of those people, wow.

Then as lots of cowboys do, I didn't see Colt again for a long time. We eventually became friends on Facebook and hooked up again. We went to some WSPRO (World Senior Pro Bull Ridings) together, helping our friend Bryan Ely and other people, just doing the cowboy thing and having a good time.

When Colt gave me his shirt that night, when I got home I took it to the cleaners and had it starched and pressed and hung it in my closet and eighteen years later it was still hanging there. I told Colt at Lake Worth when Bryan Ely was up in the bull riding that I still had that shirt he looked at me and said, "Really!" I said, "Yeah, it's starched and hanging in my closet and has been since 1999."

I said, "I don't suppose you still have the shirt I gave you do you?" and he answered, "I don't know. I'll have to look." A few weeks went by and since I worked out in the Weatherford area, Colt was on his way through Weatherford and called me and invited me to lunch.

When he pulled up in the parking lot he said, "I've got something for you." I could not believe my eyes when he handed me the 1999 shirt I'd loaned him. He'd found it, so now we have each other shirts back. Colt and I have become really close friends, not just because of me knowing his brother, but because we just love each other as brothers and that's just the way it is.

CHIMP ROBERTSON
THE HAYDEN RODEO

The Hayden, New Mexico rodeo was a favorite of a lot of good cowboys. It was open to the world and held in an old hog wire fence arena with wood chutes, way out in the middle of a pasture, miles from any town. I've ridden over there with rank beginners, cowboys on college rodeo teams, and some who left when the rodeo was over and headed straight to a PRCA Rodeo somewhere across the country.

Chimp Robertson

Hayden held two rodeos a year, one on Memorial Day, and one on Labor Day. They'd have so many contestants that once in a while the bull riding wouldn't be over until three or four o'clock in the morning. In all the years I rode at Hayden, I never bucked off a single bull. I was proud of it because my dad competed at that rodeo long before my time. And later, after I hung up my rope, my son Bryan rode over there when he started rodeoing.

The Labor Day rodeo was a two-header, and between the go-rounds they'd have matched horse racing and a big Bar-B-Q, making it well after dark by the time the second go-round got started. About two o'clock one morning I was just getting down on my bull when all of a sudden above the noise of the crowd and the announcer, I heard someone yelling, "CHIMPY! CHIMPY!"

No one except my family ever heard me called that. I was a long way from home and didn't know anybody in that part of the country. My dad's nickname was Chimp, and since I'm a junior, when I was growing up they called him Chimp and called me Chimpy.

I glanced over my shoulder and there was my grandmother with her arm stuck through the fence waiving a big, white scarf and yelling at the top of her voice, "CHIMPY! CHIMPY!"

It embarrassed the heck out of me when all my rodeo buddies started laughing and yelling, "CHIMPY! CHIMPY!" It took the wind right out of my sails when I looked up at the announcer Richard Mausby from Clayton, and he was grinning. I shook my head no, but he cranked up the microphone and announced, "Okay folks, out of chute number two is CHIMPYYYYYYYY ROBERTSON!"

It shouldn't have bothered me because I hadn't seen my grandmother in years. But, I completely lost my concentration and that old, black bull drove my head in the ground right out in front of the chutes. My first ever buck off at the Hayden Rodeo and all I could think of as I picked myself up out of the dirt was, "Dadgum it, grandmother..."

DENNIS MERRELL
MY GOOD FRIEND STEVE WILLIMAS

I'll follow up on the story with Steve Williams as I hate to leave him swinging in the breeze. Fast forward from Louisville, Kentucky to the Minnesota State Fair Rodeo on August 31, 1978, during the last performance where I drew one to win some money on, G 103, a bad hombre. I think Barnes had bought him from Neal.

I had been sick with strep throat, treating it cowboy style with Jambalaya and Jack Daniels, but sick or not I was riding. I slid up and nodded and #103 did his usual high jump with a kick. About seven seconds into the ride I'm thinking, "I got this."

The very next jump he got me into my hand and slung me right under him. When I hit the ground it felt like a bomb exploded in my chest. Steve Williams pulled the bull off of me and I got up and ran about forty yards and dropped right in the alley way.

Steve ran up and asked if I was hurt, but I had no air, so I nodded yes. He asked, "Are you hurt bad?" and I nodded yes, again. There were no EMT's, just two volunteers so they backed in with a funeral home ambulance and took me to St. Paul Ramsey to trauma surgery.

I had two collapsed lungs and eight ribs fractured in twenty-four places, the result of being stomped on without a vest. Steve Williams picked my wife up at the airport the next morning and arranged for her to stay with a local cowgirl. After several days in ICU they let me fly to Texas and check in with my own doctor.

Two weeks later while I was at home recuperating, Steve drove all the way from Minnesota to check on me. As usual, his jokes had me rolling. All of a sudden I felt a sharp pain in my left chest that left me speechless. It passed just as quick, but about three minutes later another one hit the same spot, only lasting longer.

I called my doctor and as I was talking to him the third one hit and I passed out. I came to just as Steve was scooping me up off the floor. He'd gotten the doctor on the phone who told him to get me to the nearest hospital. He told him not to stop even if a cop tried to pull him over and said he'd take care of everything.

During the twenty minutes to the hospital the pain became excruciating and constant, so Steve headed straight to the emergency door. When I came to I heard a doctor yelling at everyone. They were all thinking heart attack so the doctor ripped open my shirt to give me a shot in the heart. Luckily, he saw where the tubes had been.

About that time my own doctor came in and took over. He told me later, that less than five percent survive a pulmonary embolism. All is good now, but a bullfighter saved my life that day. Thank you, Steve Williams. Rest in Peace, my good friend.

FRED SCHWARTZ
WHAT FANS DON'T SEE AFTER RODEOS

Back in the late 70's I had come back to Florida from fighting bulls at the Cowtown Professional Rodeo of the late Howard Harris for his rodeos and road show. I came to back to Florida for the winter to fight bulls for the Pat Hansle Rodeo Company. Pat had hired me to work his run of winter Rodeos.

He had a good pen of bulls and was always on the hunt for a good fighting bull to throw at you to show your bull fighting skills to the fans. My mom lived in Florida and she would find an apartment that my wife and I could that we cold rent by the month. Mom would travel all over Florida to watch me fight bulls and even though she didn't like what I did, she still always supported me.

I went to work a rodeo in Deland, Florida and mom said she would be there to watch, not knowing what lay ahead. Pat had a spotted, cross-breed Brahma that he called Indian Chief. He was

Rodeo Stories III

pretty proud of this bull and used him in the draw because he'd turn back right in the gate. He also used him as a fighting bull.

The first performance he didn't have him in the draw and just used him for me to fight after all the other bulls had been bucked. I'd fought him before at several of his other rodeos and he would sure eye you the minute you nodded to turn him out on you.

He wasted no time coming right to you and you needed to make short fast moves to get around him. We got it on for about a minute and all went wild and fast and the crowd and the kids enjoyed it.

The following night Pat had him in the draw to buck. A young fellow with a permit had him drawn. The guy had come to me before the rodeo and said he hadn't been on many bulls of this speed, or as rank and mean as what he had drawn. I could see and feel the nervous sensations he was going through.

He asked if I would look out for him. I could tell he was scared so I told him that if there happens to be a wreck that we would go through it together and to just think about riding him. I was hoping it would help him put his mind where it needed to be. I could tell he had drawn a bull way above his riding level, but he didn't turn him out. He was going to cowboy up and get on and try.

As the young fellow was getting on, I could see the sweat running down the side of his face so I hollered at him, "Keep your head down. Watch the bull and use those feet. I'm right here for you."

Indian chief was in a right hand delivery and I stood at the opening of the chute so I would be real close. The fellow nodded and when they opened the gate Indian Chief turned back in the gate and almost threw him off into me. When the guy hit the ground that bull was on target, but I was able to push him behind me as he was trying to get to his feet.

By then Indian Chief's head was at my elbow and I knew I'd been had. He hit me in my rib cage and threw me into the pipe chute gate behind me. As I started to get up he hit me again, this time with a horn in the calf of my leg which was up against the pipe.

I got to my feet, but he was still on me so a cowboy reached down and pulled me up over the back of the chute. I knew something was bad wrong. I sat on the cat-walk behind the chutes and ran my hands about half way under my knee and my finger slipped into a hole in the calf of my leg all the way up to my knuckle.

By then, my mom was behind the chutes and I could see the fear in her face. I told her I was OK, but she knew different. They helped me to the ambulance and gave me some oxygen while they cleaned it out the best they could. I was young and dumb and refused to go to the hospital. As I was leaving to go back to the hotel the young man that had gotten on Indian Chief came up to me and thanked me for the save. I even got a hug from his mom.

Back at the hotel I tried to wash the grit and dirt out of the hole in my leg and realized it was a lot deeper then I thought so I poured it full of Peroxide. I told my wife to get my crutches because we were going to go have a drink at the rodeo dance. They all thought I was in the hospital. Pat Hansle and his wife shared a bottle of Lord Calvert with me which I commenced to take part in. Later, they helped me out to our car and I went back to the hotel feeling a little better.

The next morning, my leg was not looking good so we headed out on the three and a half hour drive back home. My leg had swollen so big the outer skin was starting to crack and my foot was turning blue. I knew things were not good so I went to the hospital. The doctor said there was hardly any blood flow through my calf and foot. He also said my leg was full of blood clots and that I shouldn't be moving around.

I didn't want to stay in the hospital, but a man in the next bed said he had blood clot one time and wound up having open heart surgery to save his life so I decided to stay. They put three IV's in me to thin my blood and try to dissolve the clots. They said I might lose my leg if they couldn't dissolve the clots, and suddenly I became a model patient.

It took several months for the hole in my leg to heal. I was very grateful my mom. That's moms are for, to take care of their dumb, young sons. She always hugged me and cried, knowing what I did. Her son was a rodeo bull fighter.

EVERETT CAMPBELL
MID-STATES RODEO FINALS

On a Saturday night in November 1977, the Mid-States Rodeo Association Finals Awards and Banquet had ended the night before and my brother Glenn Campbell was the new Champion Bull Rider. That Sunday morning, we said our good-byes to fellow riders, friends, our dad, and to my girlfriend because we were entered in the bi-weekly rodeo in Rochelle, Illinois.

The rodeo started at one o'clock and we had 4 hours to make a 250 mile trip. Pulling out of the Days Inn parking lot, there were two other bareback riders with us, Myron Wilson and Adam Tinch, both seasoned riders.

The bad part about this ride was my 1969 Ford pick-up with a screaming 390 engine with over-drive and camper shell. I'd been hunting with my coon dogs in it and forgot to clean out the mess they had left, so that caused the four of us to ride in the cab.

As country and rock and roll 8 track tapes played, we spun the tires getting up on Interstate toll road 80-90, leaving Toledo, Ohio. The windshield wipers keeping time with fast rock songs playing tells you how hard it was raining at 9 o'clock that morning.

I was tired and my brother Glenn knew it, so he said he'd drive. Two miles down the road I pulled over and we traded places and I was asleep before my head hit his shoulders in that cramped cab. I was asleep maybe a half hour when I felt a nudge at my ribs with Glenn's voice saying we were about to get pulled over.

Glenn, being only fourteen at the time, we couldn't allow this to happen so as he slid the truck to a halt and we all jumped out, racing around, bumping into one another, and switching seats.

Thank God for the fog that morning because the officer didn't see a thing. He walked up to the driver's door and asked me for my license so I said, "Sure Officer. What seems to be the problem?" The officer said you were doing 85 mph in a 55mph zone. I look over at Glenn and said, "Really? I was going that fast?" The cop said, "Just set tight and I'll be right back."

Everybody had a big laugh because of the speed Glenn was doing until the Officer comes back to my truck and said, "You have an Ohio driver's license. Do you know you're in Indiana?" I said, "Yeah, I crossed the line a few miles back." He said, "With you having an Ohio drivers license and this being Indiana, you need to fellow me to the State Trooper Post in Ft. Wayne."

So, on the way I'm saying, "I'm going to jail!" I'd just turned eighteen and had never been in any trouble before and I'm going to jail. Oh, my God! We got to the State Trooper's Post and he asked about our comings and goings and why we are late. He asked me, "Well, if you have $185.00 you can be on your way."

I said, "Hell no, I ain't got that much money. Why do you think I'm going to this rodeo for?" He said, "Well, I'm gonna have to arrest you if you can't pay this ticket." I swear I was so scared I could hardly speak. I told the officer that I don't have the money, but to let me talk to my brother and our friends about this. We emptied out our pockets and come up with $150.00 collars so I said, "Sir, this is all we have."

After a short story of where we'd been and where you're headed, I believe he felt a little sorry for us so he said, "Well maybe you were only going 75 instead of 85 so that knocks the fine down to $150.00." Later in life I often thought about that and all I can come up with was that the officer must have needed the money.

Back on the trail, Glenn talks me into letting him drive and guns Ole Green again. Not 15 miles later, Glenn's nudging me saying, "They got me again." My eyes shot open and all I can think about is, "I'm going to jail because we surly ain't got money for this ticket." I said, "You're getting this ticket." After a few other comments, I climbed over him and got in the driver's seat.

We figured it would be the same cop, but it instead it was a female officer. She said I was traveling at a speed of 90 mph in a 55 mph zone. It had stopped raining, but we couldn't get the wipers to stop and that was another thing she inquired about. Praying she wouldn't arrest me, I explained our situation and that we were late.

Now, this was before computers and she didn't know that Glenn and I had just received a similar ticket. So after running my licenses and plates she comes to my door with a speeding ticket and tells me to appear in court at the date marked and said, "Slow it down, and have a nice day." I wanted to kiss her.

I eased Ole Green back on the Interstate looked over at Glenn with the grin on my face told him not to even look at the steering wheel. Through all this we never realized that we're gonna need more gas and we are out of money. That's when I reminded everyone, "If we're gonna make it to the rodeo we need money for gas."

I looked at the last exit sign for Ft. Wayne and it hit me. Glenn and I had an Aunt who lived there although we hadn't seen her in years. We found her number in the pone book and called her. I told her our story and she gave me directions to her house and to get right over there.

We arrived at our Aunt Betty's home, keeping our minds on the clock and what we needed to do. I walked in and there is this big lay out of food. Aunt Betty is a kisser and if you don't give her a kiss she'll pin you down 'til you do, plus our family are great cooks, and it'll piss 'em off if you don't eat.

We told her what happened and that we were late and couldn't stay…..hmm, well OK, but just for a minute, and we ate as fast as we could. Aunt Betty bagged up a giant to-go bag then handed us $200.00 and said, "Go get 'em and no more speeding tickets, Everett."

We're off once more, gassing it around Chicago to the state routes to Rochelle. Glenn is rosining up our bull ropes as I'm driving like he did and we finally made it. With no time to waste, the rodeo was indoors and we slid up and blocked the main door, grabbed our gear bags and ran towards the chutes.

As I'm entering the arena I heard the announcer, whose was Joe Copeland's father saying, "That's the end of the show," and giving thanks to all who attended. We're runnin' and hollerin' as we cross the arena for them to hold up because, "We're here, we're here!"

I saw the chute men turn out one of two bulls that were left, and we got to the chutes just as they're getting ready to let the last bull out. Joe Copeland's Father jumped up and said, "Well, hold on folks. We have one last bull rider." It was my bull that had gotten turned out and now it was all up to Glenn.

Our great friend Cecile Davis was winning the bull riding and was showing his friendship to Glenn by pulling his rope for him. Glenn made a fantastic ride and won the bull riding. He also won my trust to let him drive home. I'll never forget the day I received two speeding within twenty miles, while sleeping.

GLORIA HALL
CLEMENTE'S JUNIOR RODEO

I was at Clemente's Junior Rodeo when I started riding steers and was up on Saturday. I covered my steer that day, but tore up my left hand and was hit in my left ear by the steer's horn. Come Sunday, it was down to me and Joe Foscalina.

It's been forty plus years since Joe and I rode against each other. It was Joe and Jay Foscalina, Kirk Allmon, Russell Davis, and of course Jimmy Donnell, and we started a life-long friendship.

This brings back a lot of memories. I knew it way back then at the Woodside Junior Rodeo when a young cowboy walking toward me and I said, "You must be a Foscalina." Rodeo is the best place to meet friends and I am looking forward to seeing all of them at Joe and Rhonda's wedding.

JERRY GUSTAFSON
PORTLAND TO CHICAGO

In the winter of 1973, we had just finished the rodeo in North Portland, Oregon on Sunday Night and were headed out of town, towing our twenty-five foot travel trailer. When we got about fifty miles east of Portland we ran into a blizzard. A highway patrolman stopped us and said the Interstate was closed. He told us there was a truck stop about 25 miles down the road and that we should pull off there.

Well, we didn't stop. About twenty miles past the truck stop, another patrolman stopped us and said we had to pull off the Interstate and should take the next exit. We didn't exit there either. About fifty miles further, another patrolman stopped us and said it was obvious we weren't going to stop, so to take it easy.

The roads would be snow-packed for about 3 miles, then just wet for two miles. I kept getting out of the truck to put chains on or take chains off. I finally gave up and just left the chains on. The Interstate was under construction near Pendleton and we had to use a two-lane road through the mountains to detour around the construction.

At one point, one of the tire chains started coming off so I pulled over to the shoulder, which had no guard rail and a steep drop off. As I got to the back of the truck, the truck and trailer started sliding backwards because of the slick conditions. I was able to jump back in the truck and keep it on the road. I ended up burning through 2 brand new sets of chains.

We struggled on to Denver and dropped our travel trailer with some friends, then continued on to Chicago and spent 8 nights in a Motel. Our gross sales at the rodeo ??? $58.00.

GARY BOWDEN
I DIDN'T EVEN PUT ON MY CHAPS

There was this odd little bull weighing only about 1200 pounds, short, wide, and long bodied, and sorta looked like a hog. He had a very unorthodox way of bucking that was almost freakish and would push you down over his head.

Although I'd been on the bull twice before and had won money both times, the third time I had him he clicked my heels, slammed me, and then ran over me. The next week I had him again and was not happy about it. I just knew he was gonna do his weird move and thump me again.

I was so dejected that I didn't even put on my chaps. I've never competed before without wearing my chaps and tightening down my spurs. I also had never gotten on a bull believing he was gonna buck me off, but that night I felt as if I had no hope.

None the less, I got on him anyway and nodded my head. Somewhere in those first two jumps I got squared away, and 8 seconds later I had won the bull riding.

DWAYNE JETT
WINNING TWICE IN ONE NIGHT

July 5th, 1985 was my rookie year and I was entered at the Mesquite Championship Rodeo. My wife and 5 children stayed at home because my wife was pregnant and due with our 6th child. As I pulled onto the rodeo grounds and was driving across the parking lot, 'Amarillo by Morning' by George Strait, came on the radio. I thought to myself, "This would be a great night to win the bull riding."

I had drawn a bull named Flipper of Rafter G's. I didn't know anything about him because he was a new bull. As I got ready to get down on him, Jim Gay told me not to sit all the way down on him because he had a tendency to rare up and flip over on a cowboy, hence the name Flipper.

Dwayne Jett

Pete gay was standin' in the arena in front of the chute. He had a flank strap that was twisted around the bull's horns to keep him from flipping over, that he would release when I nodded for the gate.

I crossed the back of the chute and had my feet in the slats where I could set my rope and take my wrap while I stayed about 6 inches above the bulls back. I got my hand in my rope and had my brother Bob pull it up tight, as I was standing above the bull. I called for the gate and as it opened, I dropped down on his back.

He jumped out of the chute and didn't spin, but jumped high in the air. I didn't notice at the time, but the flank strap that was around his horns had also wrapped around my free arm. The bull jumped, kicked, and blew up right in front of the bucking chutes.

When I heard the whistle I jumped off and had just won the Mesquite Championship Rodeo, a lifelong dream that I had had since I was about 5 years old. The pride in my heart was so extreme I could hardly swallow.

I left the arena and drove to Parkland Hospital where my wife had just had our 6th child, April Dawn Jett. We didn't know if it was gonna be a boy or girl. I had chosen the name Jim Bob Jett if it was a boy because I thought that would sound pretty rodeo if he ever became a bull rider.

But, it was a beautiful little girl so we named her April Dawn. I call her April Jim Bob in fun and she even has Jim Bob on her Face book profile as her nickname. So, on July 5th, 1985 I was a two time winner that night, winning the Mesquite Championship Rodeo and also having my little April Jim Bob. It doesn't get any better.

JAY FOSCALINA
AN AMAZING CAREER

The local news station used to do a short segment about the Cow Palace Junior Grand National Rodeo a couple of days before it started. They wanted around a minute's worth of film footage to advertise the upcoming event. They said they would contact our NHSRA local district to send a couple of contestants to the Cow Palace to ride some bulls and broncs for the TV cameras.

The building was empty except for Cotton Rosser, a few cowboys, and the camera crew. The bull I got on was flying U Patches. There were no bull fighters present at that time, at least not yet. One of the guys with us was named Rob Smets who had no previous bull fighting experience at the time.

So, I got on my bull and he jumped out and started turning back kind of flat and fast. He dropped me down in the well and began hooking me. Without hesitation, Rob rushes in and fends the bull off like he'd been doing it all his life. And so, began an amazing career, not mine but Rob's who went on to win several World Championships in bull fighting.

REDBOY SCHILDT
PEAKS AND VALLEYS

Back in the mid 80's, I was on a run after the 4th of July. I'd been struggling with my bareback riding for a while and just kept having problems missing horses out. It cost me a lot of money the year. During that summer we went to 5-10 rodeos after the 4th of July, traveling 24/7, from Edmonton, Alberta to the Cody, Wyoming Night Rodeo.

Along the way we entered NRA, Indian, Open Rodeos, and also jackpots. My traveling partner was riding bulls, steer wrestling, and roping calves. The only rule I could apply was, "If you rode yourself into a slump, you must ride yourself out of one." It was frustrating, to say the least.

A few days before I had the bronc Tanya Tucker, who had helped cowboys win a lot of money at the Calgary Stampede and I missed her out, but rode good. Misery. In Dodson, Montana, I had drawn the horse of the year, Geers-Bar Maid. She was a decent sized mare, about 1250 lbs.

It was a night show and about 78 degrees on a windless day. I paid my fees and set my mind to get it right this time. She stood fine until I started to pull my rigging. Then the old bay mare decided to squat. She knew it was time, and every time I started to run my hand in my handhold she'd lay down or lay against the backside of the chute as soon as she heard rosin and leather.

There ain't much you can do when the old campaigners start doing this stuff. They just know how to give you misery so they can try to throw you off. She was fine if you could get out clean, but getting out clean on her was not in the books that night. We tried everything we could to get her to stand up, but she would just lean against the backside of the chute.

Finally I just said, "I'm gonna take her laying down," and asked the judge to take her squatting into consideration. It's been a while, but seems like he asked me if I'd take a re-ride or take the mare. I wanted the mare. Finally I just took the best seat I could and nodded.

She shot out of there like a rocket and was much stronger than I figured. I blew my feet bad, and if not for my bind I would have gone out the back door. It seemed like her jumps were high, long, and in slow motion. I could feel her drop and kick. Just couldn't get my feet set.

I went about three more jumps with my feet waving over my head until I heard the rosin squawk from my handhold. I did about two and a half summersaults out the back door and hit squarely on my neck and head. Lucky for me, the dirt was nice and deep or I'd have a broken neck.

It's embarrassing enough to have that happen, but worse when you can hear the timed event guys laughing half arena away. I heard one guy yell, "Kinda missed 'er out, didn't he." It was nothing new for my luck streak at the time. After my traveling partner rode his bull, we just bailed in and kept going. Dodson is about 320 miles, 5 hours and 18 minutes from Cody, and I thought about that mare all the way there.

We left Dodson about 10 o'clock that night and got to Cody the next morning about 5 o'clock. We slept on the city park lawn for a while, then went and got some coffee. The night rodeo didn't start until 8 o'clock that night. Eight has always been my lucky number so I decided that was a good thing.

My partner wanted to rope some practice calves near Cody, so we called a guy out of town and headed for a practice pen. The trip, the practice pen, and the horse care, took us longer than we thought that day. We got a late start back to town and just barely made the rodeo performance.

My horse was already loaded in the chute when we got there and producer Ike Sankey was half way through the event when I got my riggin' on a big, piebald paint. No time for anything and it seemed like I got there, set my rig, and nodded, in less than five minutes. I won the rodeo, so I guess that's what happens when you just ride and don't think yourself into messing up. It's called mental. "Get outta your way and ride and win."

JOHN SLOAN
Ooops

Coach Dale 'Daddy Dale" Stiles was drivin,' with bull riders Charlie Winters and Doug Wilson, bareback riders Scotty Platts and me, and timed event gunsel, Dave Brock as passengers. . We were headed north somewhere between Cheyenne and Casper, tooling down the Interstate, heading home from Pueblo. It was flat, ugly, sage and dirt prairie. Earlier, we had stopped to eat, and most of us had some sort of Mexican food.

Says Doug Wilson, "Coach, I need to stop." No answer. Couple minutes later. "Coach, really, I need to stop. I mean like, right now." No answer.

Pipes up Charlie Winters. "Coach, I think he does need to stop." No answer. Says Doug, a few minutes later, "Ooops!"

Says Dave Brock, "What is that?" Says me, "Coach, stop now or I'm going to puke." Car comes to a screeching halt right on the side of the Interstate. Wilson goes hobbling out through the sage in a bandy-legged shuffle we all have known at one time or another. While he is gone, searching for a tree or some sort for cover and maybe a little water, the conversation is as follows, but I don't remember who said what.

"God! Open the doors let some air in." "Coach, I told you he needed to stop." "By gadfries," Coach said, "I'm gonna kill that little sumbuck. From now on, he can find his own ride to the rodoes." And finally, the one word that would crack us up for years, "Ooops!" At that point we all dissolved in laughter.

In 1995 at a testimonial dinner honoring Coach Dale Edward Stiles at Casper College, as Master of Ceremonies I began my after dinner talk by simply saying, "Ooops!" It got a standing ovation.

ALLAN HOWARD
A TOUGH HAND

Several years ago my Cousin Duane and I decided to go to Spearfish, South Dakota to a horse sale. I was working on horse teeth at the time, so we planned to leave early and work on horse in New Salem, North Dakota. The people that we going to work for had running Quarter Horses, and we'd been friends for some time. The guy had done some work for me so I was going to work these horses in return. The horse sale was on Sunday and I had planned on buying some mares.

We left early Saturday morning around 6:00 o'clock and got to the people's ranch around 9:30. We worked on the horses 'till about 9:00 p.m. and packed up and headed out. Duane said Bowman, North Dakota had a place we could stay so we got a room. By this time it almost midnight and I was worn out and sore from working on those horses so I went straight to bed.

I woke up the next morning around 5:30 and I heard Duane huffing and puffing. I looked over at his bed, but nobody was in it. More huffing and puffing so I listened, trying to figure out what was going on. The first thing I thought was he was still in the damn bath tub.

The sound seemed like it was coming from the foot of my bed so I sat up and there was Duane doing his push-ups. I was so relieved that he wasn't still in the bath tub. He was 70 years old at the time and I thought, here I am sore and tired and he's 70 years and doing push-ups at 5:30 in the morning. Duane stood up and said, "Allan, we better get going. The sale starts at 12:00 o'clock."

We loaded up and headed for Spearfish and on the way I was realized that Duane hadn't had his hearing aids in, and that why he was huffing and puffing so loud and I had to laugh to myself. I bought four mares and by the time the sale was over it was getting late. I settled up with the sale barn and told Duane I was going to buy some hay, and that we'd better get a room and stay over being it was already 9:30 p.m.

Duane had a different idea and thought we should load up and head for home. So, we fueled up and drove all the way back to Sheyenne, North Dakota, stopping only one time for fuel. We got home about 4:30 a.m. and Duane had driven almost all the way.

I was so tired and worn out from working those horses and driving off and on, I was thinking to myself, "How damn tough is this guy? He's 30 years older than me and look at him go." I guess he had to be tough to ride bulls and do what he did all his life. Rest if Peace, Duane.

WAYNE DECKER
THE CHECK

There might be some rodeo stories that probably shouldn't be made public, but here's a 'safe' one. Around 1979, three of us were traveling together. My two buddies, I'll call them Bill & Dave, got entered up in 3 rodeos one weekend and I could only get entered up in two because the books filled up fast in the bull riding, back then.

I rode some good ones at the two rodeos I went to, but at the second rodeo my traveling partner Bill, broke his collar bone so we spent part of the night at the ER. Bill said, "I guess I'll have to draw out tomorrow." I said "No, I'll just be you for that rodeo. They probably won't even notice."

Well, he had a good one drawn so when I sat down on him to get ready that night I looked up at Bill and whispered, "This is gonna be the best ride you ever made." After the dust settled, it was his highest marked ride, too. I also remember arguing over the check.

TIM SAMPLE
FILLIN' MY PERMIT

I remember when I got my permit, I borrowed my Mom's car to go to the local rodeo in Bryan, Texas, and me and the guys I was rodeoin' with entered three events and we all won day money.

Since I had my Mom's car, I was told not to leave town in it, but I did anyway. We went to Leesville, Louisiana. Me and Milton Allen, and Robbie Byers, all won day money there too, so we headed for Bonifay, Florida, where Milton and Robbie won day money at that rodeo.

On our way back to Texas we were stopped by a State Trooper because our feet were sticking out of the windows of Mom's 1974 VW. He told us that he'd stopped us just to laugh at us then sent us on our way. We headed on down the road and my Mom never knew we'd even let town. Two of us filled our permits in those three days. Those were amazing times.

RONNIE ALLEN
TOUGH BULL DOGGERS

I'm not very good at this, but here goes. I rode for thirty-five years. In about 1983 or 1984, I went to ninety-five rodeos and only bucked off three times. I won Madison Square Garden in 1981, won the Florida Cowboys Association six times, the American Cowboy Association seven times, the Professional Cowboys Association one time, the Southern Cowboys Association two times, and the IRPA World Championship, and the average winner in 1986.

On of my funniest stories is when we were at a Longhorn Rodeo in Lexington, Kentucky. We got to the arena early that morning and went to the locker room. Jack Wiseman and some bulldoggers where in there and they'd had the hell beat out of them.

I said, "Jack, what happened to y'all?"

He said, "We were at a bar playing pool and got into argument with the bouncer."

I said, "Well, how big was he?"

Jack said, "About five feet tall."

I said, "He was only five feet tall and he beat the hell out of all five of you?"

Jack said, "Well, he had a rope with two sticks on the end of it."

That was in the early 1980's and we all know what numb chucks are.

Later that day, when more of Jack's buddies got to the arena, they said, "Let's go get him," but Jack said, "Hell no. I ain't goin' nowhere near that place."

I thought it was so damn funny I laughed my ass off, but I didn't let Jack see me.

RONN WARR
WHEN I GOT MY 'COME-UPINS'

I got my start riding broncs and bulls when I was sixteen years old in Littleton, Colorado, which at that time was the home of the Little Britches Rodeos. I got started on a "dare" from a guy that was a year ahead of me in high school. He had been riding for a few years and asked me if I wanted to try riding his practice bareback bronc. I said, "Yeah," and the rest is history.

I started riding barebacks and bulls in Little Britches Rodeos, amateur rodeos, and jackpots in the area. I didn't start riding saddle broncs until I was seventeen. My first one was at a Little Britches Rodeo in Wakeeney, Kansas. Having never been on a saddle bronc before, meant I never had any equipment, but the stock contractor had a few extra association saddles, bronc halters, and reins.

I had no real idea how to set my stirrups or measure my rein, but I sort of figured it out. I had a good horse under me and won third place. I really thought that was pretty good so I bought a bronc saddle and rein and had a saddle maker friend make me a bronc halter.

I rode for another year in Little Britches until I was eighteen and then the age limit kicked in. I had been riding in a number of jackpots and amateur rodeos also, and was winning and placing in a lot of them. I thought I was doing pretty well and decided to turn professional and join the PRCA, at that time it was the RCA.

The RCA headquarters at that time was in Denver so I went up and applied for my RCA permit. I got my permit and was going to go 'down the rodeo road' and make my mark, and the first RCA rodeo I entered was in Castle Rock, Colorado.

The bronc riding was a two-head go. I ended up drawing two National Finals horses and they both threw my butt down hard in the dirt after about four jumps. I guessed then that maybe

I wasn't quite as good as I thought I was. That's when I got my "Come-upins".

But, I didn't let it discourage me and kept on riding and eventually got better. It was a great twenty-two years, winning some saddle bronc and bareback ridings along the way. I won't even go into my bull riding career - that was not my forte, but I did manage to get some "covered" over that time period. That's another story for another time.

DAVID HARDAGE
JIM AND MARVIN PAUL

In was about 1985 and I was notified that Jim and Marvin Paul Shoulders were bringing a truck load of green bulls every weekend to Tulsa to try out, and wanted me to get a bunch of riders ready.

We met on Sundays for a month solid. After I saw the bulls he brought and how crazy they were, I knew it was a jackpot and I was judging. I didn't need no practice getting the tar beat out of me in the chutes by them bug eyed bulls he brought.

We bucked and we bucked and afterwards, I would get watermelons and cantaloupes and cut them up and we would sit underneath the shade trees and visit for hours.

I was honored to be sitting on the tailgate of that Ford truck during that hot summer with 16 times World Champion Cowboy Jim Shoulders and his family, spitting seeds and wiping sweat.

ED LeTOURNEAU
"PUNCH" ROSSEN

Ronnie "Punch" Rossen was getting on his bull at Cheyenne and had just taken his wrap and was sliding up on his rope and about to ask for the gate. He always used his right hand to help slid up, by grabbing the top chute rail and pulling himself forward.

The bull slung his head back and his horn smashed Ronnie's thumb. When Ronnie looked at his thumb, blood was spurting in his face. He just pointed it the other way and said, "Open the gate." He bailed off after the whistle blew, grabbed his thumb and ran behind the chutes to find Benny Reynold's gear bag.

I said, "You won't find any Band Aid's in there." Ronnie pulls out a half pint of whiskey and takes a swig and says, "Beats Band Aids, don't it?" I miss those good ol' days.

TOM RAY
ME AND #011 BUSTER

I grew up watching the Forth of July Rodeo in Belton, Texas, and counted down the years untill I could enter. In 1968, I was old enough so I got my permit in March. I had success at high school rodeos, and local rodeos, and I was ready to try my skills at the big time.

I didn't know how to phone in, so I went in person and waited full of dreams for my debut in frot of my home town crowd. When the draw was posted I was there and found my name. When I went across with my finger to my draw, my heart sank. I'd drawn #011 Buster. Could it be worse?

He was high-horned Brindle who could hook the flies off his back. I'd never seen anyone get on him, but I had seen him attack the clown's barrel and toss it at least fifteen feet into the air. Was this to be my fate?

While standing at pens looking at him, the flank man Wilbur asked, "What'd you draw?" I told him, and with no change in expression he said, "I'll flank him so you can place on him."

That evening when I got home my dad asked, "Did you get a good one?" I said, "Yeah, #011 Buster." Dad said, "What's he?" With great detail I explained all of the dangers and that I wouldn't place on him either. His response was, "He can't hook you while you're ridin' him." Hell, that made sense.

Well, it was finally the Forth of July, and here I was behind bucking chutes. It seemed like being at the NFR with all of greats and me. Looking in pens I thought, "#011 Buster's horns must be three feet high straight up into the air. But, he can't hook me while I'm ridin' him."

Finally, they're loading the bulls. The first six loaded and bucked. Then Buster is in the chute and I'm ready. When I put my rope on him he turned his head around and tried bite my foot. We are chute one, the furthest from let out gate. John Farris said, "You're last."

When they bucked the fifth bull, I slid down on him and he's standing prefect. As I started pulling as my rope, the tighter it gets, the higher he raises his head. When I slid up, his horns almost touched my chest. He's gonna buck, or so I was told.

We're both ready, so a nod from me and the gate flew open. #O11 Buster made a huge jump and a 90 degree turn to left. The front of chutes are clear with only me and him and the clowns in the arena. As we pass by each chute, his horns are slashing in front of me only an inch away.

When we got to the corner he's spinning flat as table top, waiting for me to get on the ground. The eight seconds are over so now what? If bail off, there will a hooking. Each round I see the arena fence. Can I get there before he gets me? I dived for the cable.

A half round and we meet again. I'm hanging on fence like wet shirt on a clothesline. The good news was, he's beside me and not behind me. With one horn between me and the fence, he crashes into it like a freight train and flips me into the air. Still holding the cable the force breaks my hold, and that's what saved me from what would have been a terrible hooking.

I was thrown over the box seats and into the second row, landing on the fans like a sack of potatoes thrown off of a four-story building. Soft drinks and popcorn flew into the air. The only harm was that some of the fans lost their concessions. I was bruised and battered, but OK.

When I climbed back into the arena and picked up my bull rope, my dad asked if I was OK. I answered, "Yeah, but you said he couldn't hook me?" Half smiling, dad said, "Not while your riding him." When I'm asked by some of the cowboys if I'd ever get on #011 Buster again, I always reply, "Yep. He can't hook me while I am riding him."

ABE MORRIS
DUSTIN YOUNG

Dustin Young started riding calves in the Idaho Junior Rodeo Association and by the age of thirteen he was riding junior bulls and was going to a lot of amateur rodeos and had great deal of success at this level.

He won the rookie of the year title in the Eastern Idaho Rodeo Association. His junior and senior years in high school, he qualified and competed at the National High School Finals. During Dustin's senior year in high school he won the state titles in the bull riding, bareback riding, and also topped it off with the All-Around title.

Dustin attended Central Wyoming College in Riverton on a rodeo scholarship. He won the Central Rocky Mountain Regional Title of the National Intercollegiate Rodeo Association in the bull riding each of the two years that he attended CWC.

While he was still in college he purchased his PRCA permit and set his sights on a potential NFR qualification just like everyone else out there on the rodeo trail. It took Dustin about a year to fill his permit. He won first at Evanston, Wyoming and that was enough to put him over the top. He was the 1990 PRCA Wilderness Circuit Champion and also won the average twice at the circuit finals in 1992 and 1993. Dustin qualified three times for the Dodge National Circuit Finals Rodeo in Pocatello, Idaho.

Most bull riders experience a scary situation in the arena during their career, but Dustin's happened outside of the arena. He was traveling with Butch Kuhn and Jessie Allred on their way from Rapid City, South Dakota to Fort Worth.

They pulled into a Comfort Inn motel to get a room and left the pick up running while they went in to get a room. Dustin was asleep in the camper when all of the sudden the truck jumped forward then stalled. Dustin yelled, "Hey, you got the emergency brake on," but there was no response as the driver restarted the engine and gunned it.

When he sat up he was surprised to see a man sitting in the driver's seat. Suddenly guy sped out of the parking lot and headed down the Interstate at 120 mils per hour, using all four lanes. Dustin realized the guy was drunk and he was afraid he'd wreck the truck and kill both of them.

It was 3 o'clock in the morning and there was hardly anyone else on the Interstate. The guy told Dustin he was going to kill him, but finally decided to stop let him out. Dustin made sure he grabbed his wallet when the guy pulled over and jumped out the back and ran toward the nearest exit. No one would stop for him so he ran to a motel and called 911.

All three guys flew back to their respective states – Dustin to Idaho, Jessie to Utah and Butch to California, and about a month later the guy was arrested and their pickup truck was recovered. Their clothes were gone, but luckily, the rodeo gear bags were left behind.

Dustin qualified for the PBR Finals in Vegas in 1994, and also competed in BRO events. He hung up his bull rope in 1997, but judged a few PBR Built Ford Tough events, as well as a few Touring Pro events.

At age forty-five Dustin Young and his wife Georgia live in Pocatello, Idaho. He is a Senior Inspector with a Construction

Management background and works with his brother Jimmy for Horrocks Engineers. Dustin is grateful for the things that did happen, and those that didn't, and is especially grateful for where his life is today.

Abe Morris' books, "Justin: A Father's Fight for His Son," and, "My Cowboy Hat Still Fits," can be ordered directly from: Abe Morris, P.O. Box 470404, Aurora, Colorado 80047. email hamskaber@hotmail.com

"Whirlwind" © Roger Langford

PART 7

1. Richard Flechsig…Just Give Me Second
2. Brent Futch…Young Florida Cowboys
3. Don Endsley…My Good Friend, Keith Chapman
4. Clark Rossi…The Sadalia Story
5. Chimp Robertson…The XIT Rodeo
6. Charlie Finely…Tommy Steiner, World Class Rodeo Producer and Showman Extraordinaire
7. Dudley Barker…Escape Plan Gone Wrong
8. Ken Judge…The First Ride
9. Charlie Finley…Broncs, Bulls, and Guitars All in One Night
10. Brent Futch…Some Old Rodeo Cowboys
11. Tait Cortez…They Thought I was Just a Rookie
12, Wayne Stringfellow…Life With the Wild West Shows, By Tom Oar
13. Lance Anderson…His Name Was Aspro
14. Tom Ray…Popped My Balloon
15. John Clark…Out of the Dark Came Ol' John Clark

RICHARD FLECHSIG
JUST GIVE ME SECOND

Back in the late 1980's, Charley Lowery put on a rodeo at a large paper mill in South Alabama. The rodeo was for the employees and their families. The night shift attended the afternoon performance, and the day shift attended the morning performance.

During the afternoon performance we had a bad rain storm just before the bull riding, and we still had some calf roping slack after the performance. During the slack, one of the last couple of ropers to go was Ernie Theriot. He made a heck of a run in some really bad conditions. I was flagging and after the tie was complete and approved, I rode back to get in position for the next roper.

Wanda Lowery leaned out of the announcers stand and said, "Dick we didn't get Ernie's time."

I said, "Wanda, please tell me you're kidding."

She said, "No. I hate it, but we missed getting Ernie's time."

I yelled for them to hold up then rode back down to the roping box and told Ernie they had missed his time.

He just laughed and said, "That's alright. Just give me second place."

I said, "I wish I could, but you'll have to run an extra calf because right about here the ropers are going to come untracked and start raising hell about it."

Ernie said, "Ok," and went and got a dry rope.

We ran the calf of the last roper, then Ernie rode into the box. I'm thinking, "Man, I sure hope he catches and makes a good run."

Ernie Theroit, the Pro that he was, did make that extra run and roped and tied his calf faster than his first run, the mark of a true cowboy. When the six seconds on the tie was approved they announced Ernie's time and guess what, he won second. I rode over to Ernie and thanked him for the way he handled the problem and added, "You're a hell of hand, Pard."

BRENT FUTCH
YOUNG FLORIDA COWBOYS

When I graduated from high school in 1975, I loaded up in the back of a camper topped 3/4 ton Ford pickup truck with 4 other rodeo cowboys from Florida, and headed to the heartland and hit the rodeo trail.

Bottom row, L to R: Ricky Rumore (SB), Brent Futch (SB), L. C. Lawrence (BR); Standing, L to R: Carson Futch (BR), Doug Abbiatti (BB), Curtis Davis (BB).

Those four cowboys were my cousin Carson Futch from Plant City, Curtis Davis from Cocoa, LC Lawrence from Bowling Green, and Ricky Rumore from Plant City. Our first stop was Doug Abbiatti's parents' place in Carthage, Missouri where Doug loaded up with us.

We would go to three to five rodeos every week in Missouri, Iowa, Kansas, and a few in Oklahoma and Arkansas, for pretty much the entire summer, and then gravitate back to Carthage between runs when leisurely activities like the one picturing Doug and Ricky above often took place.

Melvin and Baeulah, Doug's parents were good to us and in later years, they came to be like second parents to me after I moved to Carthage. We met some really great people at those rodeos up there and had a blast. A couple of guys who stand out in my mind are Louie Ochsenbein and David Clinkenbeard, but there were many others

DON ENDSLEY
MY GOOD FRIEND, KEITH CHAPMAN

I announced the big Tops N' Texas Steiner Rodeo in Jacksonville, Texas for 21 years every July. One year a bad bull jumped out of the pen behind the chutes and ran through the parking lot, missing every car except one. That car had been purposely and carefully parked in the far back corner away from everything so it would not be subject to even the littlest door ding.

As the pick-up men chased the bull, we heard a loud bang and metal crashing off in the distance. Yes, the raging bull had managed to miss all the other cars and zeroed in on the one brand new Mercedes in the back corner. The driver had just taken delivery that day and it was his first trip in his new shinny car, a real beauty for sure.

I didn't know whos car it was until after the rodeo when the driver told me it was his. That lucky cowboy was my good friend and great saddle bronc rider Keith Chapman. As with his nature and good guy attitude, he was smiling all the while he was telling me about the night's experiences.

Keith is one of the good, happy go lucky guys, always has been and always will be. I don't remember how his ride turned out that night, but I know he was smiling either way, win, lose, or draw.

L to R: Sharon Endsley, Don Endsley, Terry Chapman, Keith Chapman, and Jackie Hoforth.

Don Endsley; NFR Announcer
Texas Rodeo Cowboy Hall of Fame Inductee 2011

CLARK ROSSI
THE SADALIA STORY

At Sedalia Missouri in 1980, I was 24 years old and getting on Harry Vold's great bucking horse #26 Necktie. This was such a cool place to rodeo. It was in an old wooden building, enclosed, and internally reinforced with steel. I remember the first time I pulled into town. There must have been about fifteen or twenty thousand people.

We are driving along and came to a block where when you could look in both directions and there was nothing as far as you could see. Weird, right? That's exactly what I thought, too. When we finally arrived at the arena I asked someone what was up and the guy told me that about two weeks earlier a tornado had come through Sadalia and that was all that was left of the town.

Well, let me tell you that made quite an impression on this South Texas boy. I had heard about those things, but had never seen anything like it in my life. Needless to say, from that point on, I couldn't wait to get the heck out of there.

Clark Rossi

I rode Necktie that night, but didn't place on him. I don't remember what my haulin' partner at the time, Gene Coquat did. Anyway, we pulled out of Sadalia right the rodeo and headed for Cherokee, Iowa, to a Barnes Rodeo. We hit some more rodeos on the way back to Texas, and I can still see all that in my minds eye thirty-seven years later, just like it was yesterday.

CHIMP ROBERTSON
THE XIT RODEO

Alton Robertson, The XIT Rodeo, Dalhart, Texas, 1938 – the year he won the calf roping.

Back in the 1930's when the Famous XIT Rodeo first started up in the panhandle town of Dalhart, Texas, the arena was down by the canyon near the rail road bridge on west Highway 54. At those early rodeos, cars parked in a long oval served as the arena fence. My dad Alton Robertson entered the bareback riding, calf roping, and the bull riding.

He made the eight seconds in the bareback riding and when the horn sounded the horse threw his head up and took off running. He headed straight toward the line of cars and the pickup men couldn't catch up with him. The old bronc never slowed down a bit. He jumped over the hood of a car and headed off down the canyon in a dead run.

The pickup men didn't even try to come after him and he knew the longer he stayed on, the farther he'd have to walk back. The runaway bronc was tearing out across the sage brush so dad bailed off and landed on his shoulder. After tumbling end over end a few times, he got up and started walking back, but couldn't raise his arm and figured his shoulder was broken.

By the time the calf roping started he'd gotten a little feeling back and was in the money. When the bull riding started he had a little more feeling in his arm and went on to make a successful ride. According to family and friends who witnessed the ride, the bull he'd drawn had high horns and he waived 'em right under dad's nose the whole ride, but he set up and made a good ride.

When they built the arena out by the lake, dad won the calf roping at the 1938 XIT Rodeo, competing with tough rodeo cowboys like Jiggs Burke, Berry Pettigrew, and Clyde Burke. He was just a forty dollar a month ranch hand, but he was a cowboy. He didn't just rope cattle and ride buckin' horses at rodeos, he did it every day.

CHARLIE FINELY
TOMMY STEINER, WORLD CLASS RODEO PRODUCER AND SHOWMAN EXTRAORDINAIRE

It was the middle of the first full week of December, 1989, and my wife Debbie and I had decided to attend the National Finals Rodeo. We booked our flight and drove to the Austin Municipal Airport to board a Southwest Airlines flight to Las Vegas. There was a group from Waco going as well and we gathered at the departing gate, all excited about going to the year end Finals for the Professional Rodeo Cowboys Association.

Just before the call to board, I noticed famed Austin Texas Rodeo Producer Tommy Steiner was checking with the gate attendant about the flight. He was alone and dressed as you'd always see him, in pressed slacks, a colorful western cut sport coat and tie, along with his silver belly hat.

His only apparent luggage was an oversized, high end, department store shopping bag. I had been competing at his rodeos for several years and got to know him and his bucking bulls pretty well. I went over to say hello, and he was pleased to see me as we began to catch up.

He asked if we were going to the Finals and I said we were. He said he was too, because he had to take Benny his hat. I didn't know what he was referring to so when I asked, he spread open the shopping bag and all I could see was a felt hat inside. He said that that several weeks earlier Benny Binion had stopped by his ranch just outside of Austin on his way to Houston for cancer treatment. They'd stayed up late reminiscing into the night and when Benny left the next day, he had forgotten to take his hat.

Tommy's wife Beverly had recently passed away and Tommy said he just didn't have the interest in going to the NFR without her. They had taken over the Steiner Rodeo Company with the famous XS brand from his dad Buck, in 1945, and she had been an integral part of the colorful production with deep Texas roots and rodeo tradition.

Tommy said he noticed that Benny had left his twenty-five hundred dollar hat up on the mantel at the ranch house and what with the NFR going on, why Benny needed his hat. So, he took the felt hat put it in an available shopping bag, put on a coat and tie, and headed for the airport. Nothing else, just Benny's hat in a bag.

Tommy fell in with our group as we heard the boarding call. Back then on a lot of airlines, there were usually two rows of seats facing each other near or right behind the wing in the middle of the long cabin. We all chose to sit in that section and it wasn't long before Tommy was holding court.

The flight had originated in Houston with other rodeo fans headed to Vegas, and they had gotten a head start on the partying and drinking. As we flew west across New Mexico and Arizona, headed for our brief stop in Phoenix, Tommy told us stories of producing rodeos all over the country and having meetings with folks like Fidel Castro, Lyndon Johnson, and John Kennedy, to name a few.

Everyone around us was listening to the stories he would spin off one right after the other, so much so that two of the stewardesses just stood in the aisle so they could listen in. He was clearly enjoying himself and as we pulled into the gate at Sky Harbor Airport. He leaned over to my wife and asked where we were staying and when she told him he said, "How are you going to get to your hotel?"

Debbie replied that we would do like everyone else does, take a cab, or share a ride. He then asked if she'd ever ridden in a limousine. She said that she had, to which he responded, "Have you ever ridden in a BIG limousine?" She said she hadn't, so he said, "Well, let me call Benny from here in Phoenix, and I'll get him to have us a ride ready when we arrive at the airport in Vegas."

After landing at McCarran International airport we all headed to the baggage claim area to retrieve our luggage and Tommy stayed with us as we went to gather up our belongings. We then joined the crush of travelers like at any busy airport, and headed out the front entrance to begin looking for our rides, cabs, and significant others.

As we exited the front of the terminal, sure enough, parked across the street right in front of us was a long, white, stretch limousine with the chauffeur-driver standing at attention outside the driver's door. Tommy motioned for us to follow and we rushed across the street in the cold, but clear Nevada night.

The driver came around, popped open the trunk, and loaded our bags as Tommy lit up his trademark cigar. We were standing on the sidewalk on the passenger's side of the limo, and after closing the trunk, the driver came around and opened the rear passenger door for us.

As my wife started to step into the huge back seat, Tommy reached out and grabbed her by the arm and said, "Hold on just a minute." Debbie quickly looked back at me and I shrugged like, "I don't know what's going on." My first thought was that there was someone else he was waiting on to share the ride with us.

At that moment Tommy steps out into the middle of the street, almost as if he's going back across to the terminal. There were still quite a lot of people hurriedly exiting the building, and even more still milling at the opposite curb, hailing cabs, or getting into their rides.

Tommy stops right between us and them and with a big wave of his hand, yells out, "Welcome to Vegas everyone. See you at the Rodeo." Almost everyone paused for a moment and looked at the big, well-dressed Cowboy greeting them.

Well, Debbie, the limo driver, and I, were just standing by the car wide eyed at what we just witnessed, as Tommy hurriedly comes back over and quietly says, "Now get in." With everyone across the street staring at us, we quickly entered and settled back in the plush leather seats with Tommy across from us, his back to the driver.

All was quiet for a few minutes as we took in all the exquisite furnishings and features of this beautiful ride. However, I'm thinking, "What the hell did we just see?" As we pulled away from the curb in that long white stretch limousine and with the crowd watching, Tommy leaned back, took a long pull on his cigar, blew the smoke up into the air and said, "Ya know, it sure is a shame to get into a car like this when there's no one around to see ya do it."

Those airline travelers that cold night in Las Vegas had no clue who the well-dressed cowboy was greeting them from the middle of the street. But, as most people in Vegas do at National Finals Rodeo and its related events, chances are you would see him again. Even though you didn't know who he was you 'knew' he was somebody. That bigger than life presence is what Tommy Steiner possessed, and it showed whether he was in the rodeo arena directing the action or passing you on the street.

Getting ready to ride one of his bulls and looking out through the slats in the bucking chute, I can still see Tommy Steiner sitting on a magnificent mount in the center of the arena during one of his rodeos. You 'knew' who the arena director was, and who was Boss of the Rodeo.

I'll always remember the matching parade horses, the long openings, and Grand Entries, the color and pageantry, along with trick riders, actual rodeo bands, and world class bucking stock. I don't recall ever seeing him without his pressed slacks, colored sport coat, of which he had a different color for each day, and tie, crisp felt hat, and boots.

Benny Binion passed away a few weeks after the NFR that year. Tommy Steiner left us in 1999, after fifty-four years of producing Professional Rodeo all across the U.S. I enjoyed entering his rodeos. He was always good to me as I was attempting to ride his rank bucking bulls. I'll be forever grateful to have shared that flight with him, and am honored to have known Tommy Steiner of the XS Rodeo brand.

DUDLEY BARKER
ESCAPE PLAN GONE WRONG

Back in the day when doing the San Angelo Texas rodeo, I spotted a Cervi bull that was bad to hook, plus they kept running him up in the chutes. A little history on that arena, it has a solid concrete wall with a pipe rail above your head to grab hold to, and a board about chest high. With me being so short, I added a 2x4 driven in the ground to help me climb up to the next level.

John Hester, the Justin Sports Medicine guy was next to the wall, plus several cowboys, including the judge. When I spotted the bull go in the chute I warned John that he was bad to hook. John asked to use my 'step-up board.' I said, "OK, but be up and out of the way if I need it."

When they snapped the latch on that bad bull he came straight down the wall and John is gazing around. I'm getting anxious so I yelled, "John, hurry and get up—NOW." He did, but in the process he pushed my 2x4 step down and I had no place to go. Everyone else had gone up to the next higher spot.

Well, to say the least I made a good target and he still had the cowboy on his back when he tore into me. The bull hooked my hat off and mashed me around before the bull fighters came in and distracted him, but he left shit on me as he left. I gathered up my hat and cussed John, but still felt pretty lucky.

KEN JUDGE
THE FIRST RIDE

I was always into sports growing up. I played baseball, football, and ran track, but all that all changed when I turned fifteen. Some good friends invited me to go to a local buck out that was held every Wednesday Night, so I decided to take 'em up on the offer.

Little did I know what to expect, but it ended up being a life changing event for me.

My buddies had a plan and that was to dare me to get on a bull. Me, being the dare devil that I was anyway, took the dare. I had ridden a horse or two, but they were gentle riding horses. Never had I crawled down on a bull. So I borrowed some equipment and picked out the one I was gonna get on.

I was totally inexperienced, but I did have some athletic ability. So, my bull was getting loaded in the chute and I took the borrowed gear and climbed up on the gate to put my rope on, with all my buddies cheering me on.

There was a cowboy on the backside of the chute that started helping me. He had experience in his voice, and very calmly talked me down on the bull and pulled my rope. It was the coolest thing that I'd ever done up to this time. I scooted up on the rope and took a deep breath and said, "Let's go boys."

Ken Judge [Dudley photo]

When the chute gate opened I couldn't hear anything. It was just me and the bull, and it seemed like everything was in slow motion. I had me a grip and I wasn't turnin loose. I had also done some gymnastics and had pretty good balance.

It seemed like I was on the bull for a full minute when I heard a whistle blow and voices hollerin' for me to get off. So, I let go and came down on my feet. It was nothing like I had ever in my life experienced before. I had actually ridden my first bull the full eight seconds, and I was totally hooked from that point on.

I ate, slept, and breathed, riding bulls. The cowboy that helped me down on my first bull ended up being one of my good friends. His name was Marty Honey. He hauled me to several rodeos for several years and would even pay my fees, for a split of my winnings.

I won my first open bull riding when I was only fifteen. I ended up competing for twenty-eight years in several different associations such as the NTHSRA, AJRA, PRCA, OTRCA, and TSPRA. Thanks to my buddies David Lynch, Clifford and Benny Doty for daring me to get on a bull. It changed my life, and I will always cherish all the memories.

CHARLIE FINLEY
BRONCS, BULLS, AND GUITARS ALL IN ONE NIGHT

In April 1977, I had only been in Waco, Texas, for about eighteen months. I was attending college at TSTI (now TSTC) majoring in Ag and Livestock Management and going to rodeos on weekends.

During that spring of 1977, there were a lot of rodeos around central Texas. When I had left my hometown of Gonzales, Texas, all I had with me was my suitcase, rigging bag, and guitar. Little did I know how each, would have an impact on me in the coming years.

I had also started playing in a progressive/county rock band the previous year and during the spring rodeo run, I had entered a rodeo in China Spring, Texas, just northwest of Waco about 15 miles on the way to Valley Mills. I can't recall who the producer was, but I entered the bareback and bull riding for a Saturday night, as at the time we weren't booked to play that date.

The band I was playing in was getting a lot of momentum and we were beginning to be booked almost every week. I was able to work the rodeos around our schedules. It wasn't easy, but I got it to work. Shortly after entering the rodeo in China Spring, our manager and bass player Bill Adkins called and said we were booked to play a 'Battle Dance' just north of Waco, at Elm Mott.

I called the rodeo secretary, but couldn't get traded out, so I wasn't sure what I was going to do. Then I learned that since we were going to be alternating with the other band, we were to play the first set from 9 PM to 10 PM, take a break, then we'd play from 11 PM to midnight.

I thought this might just work. My plan was to get set up at the dance hall, then drive out to the rodeo arena and get on my bareback horse then drive back to Elm Mott for the first set. After that, I'd drive back to China Spring in time for the bull riding then haul ass back to Elm Mott for the second set…if everything went right.

The rodeo was to start at 7:30 PM with the bareback riding so after we got set up and did our sound check I borrowed a car and drove to China Spring, not telling the rest of the band what I was doing. As the crow flies, the two towns are only about 10 miles apart with the Brazos River in between them. But, since the only place to cross the Brazos River is at Waco, I had to drive back down to the north side of Waco to cross, then haul ass back up to China Spring, a total drive of about twenty-five minutes one way.

I'd never been to China Spring, but finally found the arena and it was packed. I told the producer that I needed him to load my bucking horse as early as possible and he said he'd see what he could do. I got on my bareback horse, but he didn't have a good out so I got a re-ride, which was something I hadn't planned on.

I immediately told the producer I'd take the re-ride, but that I had to get on him right now. Fortunately for me, he was already loaded so they run him in. This horse bucked and I made a good spur ride, got off on the pickup man and ran back to the car. I left my riggin' bag and gear behind the chutes and drove back to Elm Mott. I'd made a deal with another contestant to grab my bareback riggin' and watch my stuff while I was gone.

I arrived back at the hall during the last song of the first band's set, just before they took their break. I still had my spurs on and my left arm was taped as I ran in, jumped up on stage and got ready to play our set. Bill Adkin's our bass player and manager looked over and said, "What the hell you been doing?" Of course he knew, so I played that hour's set and as soon as we went to break, I unplugged my amp and yelled over to Bill, "I'll be right back." I ran out to the parking lot, jumped in the car and drove back to China Spring.

I had asked the stock contractor to hold my bull as late in the performance as possible, and he did. When I arrived back at the arena the bull riding had already started and my bull was loaded in the alley so I grabbed my rope, changed my spurs, and chapped up.

I hadn't seen what was winning the bull riding up to that point, but I was next to last, and rode the big cross-bred bull. I gathered up all my gear and ran up to the rodeo secretary to see if I placed. All said and done, I'd won second in the barebacks and third in the bull riding.

I got back in time to play the second set and we even did a third set, well after midnight and into the early morning hours. In addition to free beer, I got paid for playing guitar as well as placing in two rodeo events all in the same night. Back then, gas was about sixty cents a gallon. Being single, I could go a long way on what I'd won riding bucking stock, and what I earned playing guitar. I thought I'd never see another broke day. Life was good.

I continued to rodeo until 1993 even though our band only played for a couple more years, but I still play guitar today. Five years after placing at the China Spring rodeo I married and moved 'my suitcase' there. We raised our family at there and I still continue to call China Spring, home.

BRENT FUTCH
SOME OLD RODEO COWBOYS

This year (2017) two cowboys who influenced me and inspired my desire to become a rodeo cowboy went home to be with the Lord. The first was Linwood Alan Parker from my hometown of Plant City, Florida. Alan was a Florida Cowboy's Association Champion Saddle Bronc Rider. Earlier in his career, he rode bulls, fought bulls, and had a clown act with trained Shetlands and mules.

He also rode bucking horses and did whatever else was required for Ralph Shaubacher's Wild West Show in the late 50's and early 60's. He also owned a horse sale barn in Thonotosassa called the 301 Livestock from the time I was in junior high school up until just a few years ago.

In his later years he also had a cow/calf operation that bordered the Futch family ranch, the Single R, where I was raised just east of Plant City. He was a top notch horseman and auctioneer, and auctioneered the Quarter Horse Congress in Ft. Worth and sold horses there for 7 figures, the highest being $2.35 million.

When I was a freshman in high school, I worked at the sale barn feeding, grooming and saddling horses for him to ride through the sale ring during the auction. One of the things about Alan that stood out to me is that he could step up on a $50 horse and ride him through the ring and make him look like a $500 horse. You'd get on that same horse after him and that horse would look like an idiot, making you look the same.

After a brief illness, Alan passed away on March the 25, 2017 at the age of 72. I attended his funeral in Lakeland where another good cowboy and man of the Lord I've always looked up to, Mike Fletcher, originally from Winnsboro, Louisiana, gave Alan's eulogy and did a jam up job of it.

A number of us who were involved in Alan's life got up and spoke, and the service lasted about 3 hours. His two son's Hank and Jacob gave heartfelt talks about their father's life, and the influences he had on theirs. What an outstanding memorial, going home party, and celebration of Alan's life.

That was on Sunday, April 2, 2017, and five days later at about 7:00 PM, I got the call from my younger brother Stephen that my Daddy, Raymond Chester Futch, had just passed away from an apparent heart attack. He was 82. One of the proudest things my father was of, was that he was a cowboy. He and his two older brothers, William and Alvin, grew up in 40's and 50's central Florida during and before the period of the screw worm eradication.

As teenagers, they had to rope every newborn calf in open pasture or in the brush and pull them up in their saddles or under their horses and doctor their navels with pine pitch which would prevent the Cochliomyia hominivorax (screwworm) fly from continuing to lay their larvae on the umbilical cord. The flesh eating screwworm maggot would kill a calf in a brief period.

The momma cows they roped these calves off of were not the type that took kindly to a 14 or 15 year old cowboy messing with their calves. They were scrub and Brahma influenced cattle that would just as soon hook the snot out of you and your horse as look at you. It was a fast start for these young men at becoming top hands.

Over the years, dad and his two brothers cow hunted on the Cone Ranch owned by their Uncle Julius Cone that bordered

Blackwater Creek, north of Plant City, the 25,000 acre Futch/Crum cow lease in the Everglades, and the Single R which was owned by my grandpa Ralph E. Futch and Uncle Louis Cone.

These men were called cow hunters because of the Florida ranch habitat which consisted of pine flat woods where in places palmettos were head high while on horseback. There were cypress creek swamp, sawgrass/cypress sloughs, and flat flag ponds (sometimes belly deep to a horse in water), and wait-a-minute vines so thick in places you couldn't ride through,much less drive a cow.

So, when gathering time came, that's what they did, they hunted cows. Not only was my dad a ranch, cow hunting cowboy, but he was also a rodeo cowboy. He was a bull rider and a steer wrestler. In the early 60's, he was also a stock contractor with a string of bulls and bucking horses.

His rodeo company was called Futch Brothers' Rodeo Company. He had bulls with names like Alley Oop, Diesel Smoke, Ground Fever, Snoopy, Wrong Way Willie, Whirly Bir,d and his most notorious, #19 Spider. Some of the bucking horses were named Baldy Lou, Widow Maker, Mickey Mouse, Shag, etc.

During that time, a legendary rodeo cowboy from Mansfield, Texas by the name of Johnny Clark came to Florida, entered the bull riding and bareback riding, and secured a contract with my dad to fight bulls at some of his rodeos. Johnny and Daddy became fast friends and my dad loved John Clark.

He always bragged on John, and said that he felt he could fight bulls every bit as well as he rode them. Johnny used an old tractor inner tube that he would roll at the bulls that would fight, and they would sometimes hook it 20 or 30 feet in the air. Dad said John would fight one of his bulls after a ride and that would sort of close out the rodeo.

Johnny had made several rounds with the bull by one horn or the other, and slapping him in the face and such. After a short pause in the fight, the bull who was relatively close, made a run at Johnny so he put a cleated shoe on the top of the bull's head between his horns and it catapulted him in the air. He did a spectacular back flip, landed on his feet, tipped his hat to the crowd, and closed out the rodeo. What an ending to the great entertainment event of rodeo.

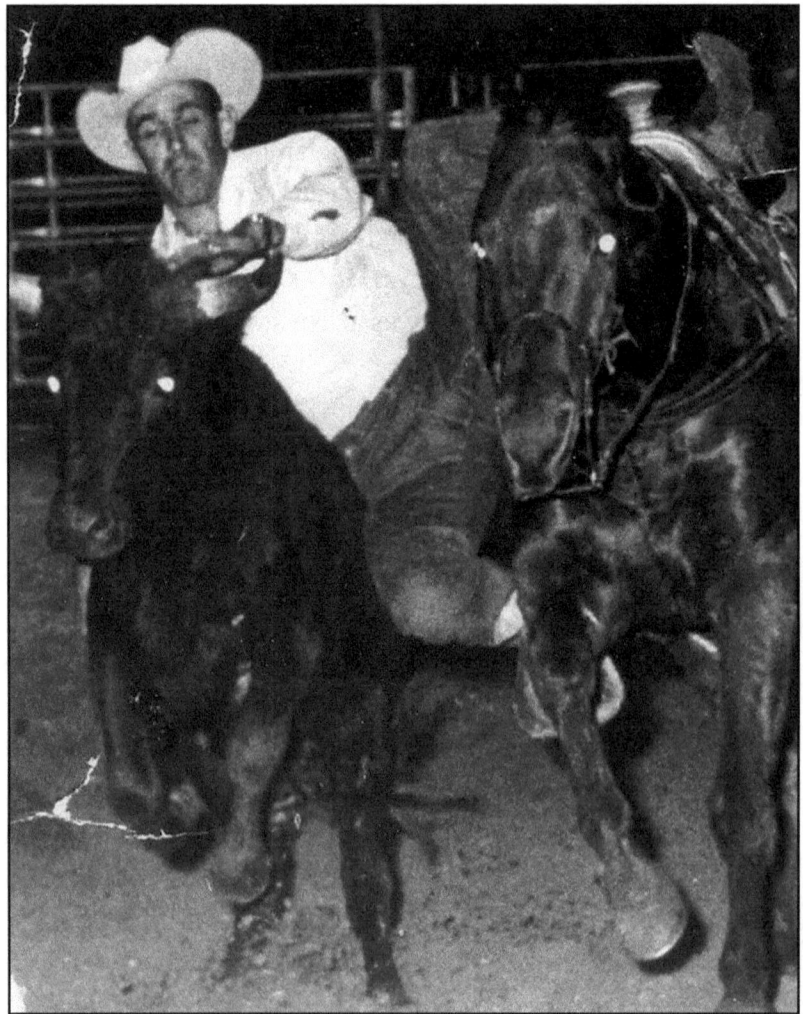

Photo of John Clark, credit Tom Woods Brent's dad doggin...

Another story dad loved to tell is about the time in the early 60's, when he and momma and the rest of us (my older brother Jim, me, and my younger sister Sherry; Julie and Stephen weren't born yet) went to Mansfield to look at some bucking horses dad was considering buying and visit with the Clark family.

A rodeo at the Ft. Worth Coliseum was coming up, and Clark called Dad and asked if he wanted to enter the bull riding. Dad said, "Yes, but enter me in the steer wrestling too." Clark said, "Look Raymond, you might be able to ride bulls with us, but these bulldoggers out here are sure enough tough to beat." Dad said, "Clark, just enter me."

A couple of days later, the rodeo and steer wrestling rolled around. Dad backed a horse he had mounted (he left his good bulldogging mare Peaches at home in Plant City) into the box and when he nodded, he ran one down and threw him in 4 flat to win the steer wrestling.

Then he rode a bull named Orange Crush that turned back in the latch and won second in the bull riding. I think Clark won first. The bucking horse deal never materialized and the horses never made it to Florida, but a new barrel horse my momma rode named Scooter Reed, did.

I shared this story on a Facebook rodeo page created by Tim Sparks called The IRA Project since Dad's passing and asked if anyone was in contact with Johnny on a regular bases to let him know the news. A couple of people stepped in. Ronnie Dallys daughter, Julie Milliken, had her dad call Johnny and let him know. Then a couple of days later, Johnny's daughter in law Charlene sent me the following message.

This is Charlene Clark, Johnny's Daughter in law.

I was told by Barry Adams to let you know that Johnny knows about Raymond's passing. He is sorry to hear and wanted to let you know.

Johnny told me to say, "Raymond was my employer, as well as a good friend. I stayed at his house every time I went to Florida. I would liked to have talked to him before he passed, but I won't be very far behind him and I'll talk to him in Heaven."

On another posted comment Charlene said, "He is telling me that once they were on the road in west Texas and a crop duster plane landed on the road and headed right to them. It scared them, and he said he needed toilet paper."

These men were three of my heroes growing up. There were many others, but the ones that influenced me the most were number one my daddy, then Alan for the following reasons. I grew up wanting to be a bull rider. I didn't care about being any other kind of rodeo cowboy, but a bull rider because my daddy was a bull rider. Well, I learned quickly that in order to be considered a bull rider amongst your peers, you have to make the whistle on a pretty regular basis. So I was only a bull getter on'r.

One day a really good friend of mine, and a saddle bronc rider (and bull getter on'r himself) that I went to high school with in Plant City named Ricky Rumore said, "Brent, we're gonna buck some horses at Alan's on Saturday. You ought to come on over and get on some broncs and see if you like it."

I went over to Alan's on Saturday and he loaned me his Salisbury 604 bronc saddle, chaps, a halter and a bronc rein, and the first one I get on a big, bay, blaze faced gelding Alan got from Ralph Shaubacher called Mohican. Mohican was an old retired bronc that jumped and kicked straight down the pen nice and slow for about four seconds, then he would get ill and start rearing then jumping backwards and kicking like he was trying to kick somebody. That's when we would jump off before he reared over backwards.

From that day forward, I was in love with riding broncs. I was 15 years old. For the next two years Ricky, Alan, another FCA Champion named Dennis Morgan, and I, got on broncs at Alan's arena on a regular basis, and he ran plenty of them under us. He would buy killer pen horses by the truckloads and if there were any of them that snorted and blew and acted a little broncy, we had a special place for that one.

Down the alley to the bucking horse pen and we'd get on them ASAP. Sometimes we would wait until the weekend, and other times we couldn't wait and would get on them right after the sale at midnight, on a school night, under one street light. I played hookie on Thursday's a lot. There were lots of wild broncs ran through there, and there were plenty of wrecks, but we survived.

I continued to enter the bull riding, but finally decided I didn't like the idea of being a bull rider as well as I thought I did, and concentrated my efforts on riding bucking horses. I continued to ride broncs until about 1981 or 82, and made it to the Southeastern Circuit Finals at Matt Dryden's in Marianna, Florida.

Before that, I made two trips to the National High School Rodeo Finals. The first was in Ogden, Utah in 1973, and the second was in Gallup, New Mexico in 1975. We got on Cotton Rosser's horses in Ogden, and Cervi's in Gallup.

I wish my rodeo career had lasted longer because I was just beginning to get it, and lift on my rein and beat them to the ground. But, in 1982, I decided to pursue a career in another field. I came back in 1985, and went to some SRA Rodeos of the Treadway's in North Carolina, but that didn't go so well. I wish I could do it all over again.

In closing, to the two men I am forever grateful. One is my dad Raymond C. Futch for putting cowboy in my blood, and also to Linwood Alan Parker, for presenting me with an opportunity and showing me some things about riding bucking horses. I love you both.

I don't currently cowboy for a living, but because of these men and my love for the whole cowboy persona, I will be a cowboy at heart for the rest of my life. But, the one thing I am most grateful for is that these two men (Alan and Daddy) both gave their lives to our Lord and Savior Jesus Christ, long years before they passed away. Thank you Jesus. Thank you men, I love you both. I will see you again in heaven and when I get there, we will twist some bulls and bucking horses, and bulldog some steers. Long live Cowboys!

TAIT CORTEZ
THEY THOUGHT I WAS JUST A ROOKIE

I traveled the Rodeo Circuit down in the southeast mainly, as it was closer to home. I don't toot my own whistle, but I did pretty good in the bareback riding and won my fair share. I'd gotten divorced and wanted to get my life back tighter, so I got hired on with a construction company that built restaurants. We built restaurants in a lot of places, but the one state I enjoyed working the most in, was Texas.

I ended up meeting a fella by the name of Damon Rogers who was an all-around hand, and was also one hell of a rodeo clown. Anyway, he came by the job site one evening when I was getting off work and asked if I wanted to go to a rodeo with him, so I jumped in his truck. I told Damon I'd ridden some barebacks, but that's about as far as it had gone. Well, we got to the rodeo and Damon ended up entering the team roping, and told me that the producer needed some more bareback riders.

He said Lester would pay the entry fees, and that they were giving buckles in each event. I said I don't have any gear with me and Damon started laughing as he led me back behind the bucking chutes and yelled at the top his voice, "This guy wants to ride a bareback horse, so who'll help him?" I was bombarded with guys helpin' me. I mean like guys loanin' me their stuff, helpin' me strap on my chaps, bucklin' my spurs, and even puttin' a riggin' on my horse.

One guy tugged it down for me and told me to hold out my arm as he tapped it up, and even slid a glove on my hand. When I climbed up on the back the chute and got down on the horse, there were like twenty guys around me giving me instructions, telling me what to do and what not to do. All of a sudden I felt someone grab my foot and say, "We're ready for you."

Tait Cortez [Tina Patrick photo]

I ran my hand in the riggin' and slid up, gave a big nod, and the horse was perfect. He came out high jumping, kicking, and circlin' around to the left, so I just layed back and tried to spur his head off. When the horn sounded I got off on the pickup man, and when I looked at the back of the chute where I had just left, all I saw were jaws droppin' from those guys. They thought I was just a rookie.

Tait Cortez [Tina Patrick photo]

When I got back to the chutes I told that bunch of guys that they were the best bareback teachers in the world. Anyway, I won the money and the buckle and yes, I did indeed buy a round of drinks for the teachers and Damon Rogers.

My dad was so proud and happy when I called home that I ended up giving him the buckle. He kept in a drawer in his bible so it would keep me safe. He wanted to keep it forever, so when he passed away I made sure he was wearing it when we laid him to rest. Rest in Peace, Dad.

WAYNE STRINGFELLOW
LIFE WITH THE WILD WEST SHOWS, BY TOM OAR

Wild West shows had been big entertainment in America and Europe in the late 1800's, with such shows as Buffalo Bill Cody's Wild West Show, and also the 101 Wild West Show, which ran until 1939. Numerous other traveling show companies were formed and entertained audiences in cities and towns.

Cowboys and cowgirls exhibited their skills which included bull riding and bronc riding, along with trick riding and roping. Some young cowboys got their training in riding that proved valuable later with the popularity of rodeos. Modern day rodeos are an evolution of the old Wild West Shows which were mainly in the Eastern United States, combined with the early contests that were the beginning of the more modern rodeos. Here's an account of what life was like in the Wild West Shows by Tom Oar.

In the 1950's, my brother Jack and I, had been traveling with our dad with a Wild West Show. Jack and I were just small kids, and we were trick riders. I had been trick riding from ages 7 to 14. Dad, Chike Oar, picked up broncs, clowned, and steer dogged. He was pretty much a company man, driving a truck, caring for the stock, and doing whatever else needed to be done.

We also had to set up all the pens when we got to the rodeo grounds. We worked for the 105 Ranch Rodeo which was owned by a young fellow named Jerry Partlow. Sometimes, my dad would cook for the whole crew, and we slept either under the truck, or sometimes in the back.

When traveling at night, Jack and I would throw our bedrolls in the back of the truck with our horses. If we needed to stop, we'd crawl under the horses to the back of the cab where we could knock on the back window to get dad to pull over. Our dad was really good with animals. In fact, he could park in the pasture and call the horses to load up on their own, which they would in their own order.

Jerry Partlow, the owner, had gotten his start in Iowa, where he broke horses for farmers. He ended up getting a train car load of unbroken horses and convinced another guy to go in with him to put on a rodeo. They had two bucking chutes and would bring in a few local beef bulls to ride, along with the wild horses. A local radio announcer got on board with the event, and Jerry rode all the broncs. Jerry, being the showman, would light a cigarette before each ride and would be blowing smoke with each jump.

The rodeo grounds were a mixture of car race tracks, pastures, and even cinder race tracks scattered across Pennsylvania, Ohio, and New York. The cinders were really tough on the bulldoggers, and the concrete curbs in the arena added a whole incentive not to buck off, as did the hard sod that wasn't tilled.

Most of the show coincided with local fairs, where we could have a crowd. In those days, everyone involved noted how many people were in attendance because it could make a difference whether we got paid or not. There were a few open rodeos, but without the Fairs, crowds were often poor. Of course, the money was good and we were pulling fifty dollars per week.

Part of the attraction was the four lady bronc riders that were there, including Jerry's wife Anna Bell. I got my first bronc saddle from Anna Bell. It was an old Turtle Association saddle, which I still have. Some of our buddies we traveled with included Bud and Dub Grant, of Grant Ropes, young trick riders and trick ropers who went on to be professional cowboys in rodeo, and their dad Wes Grant, who worked the Wild West Show as an announcer. Wes's wife Jeanie was also a trick rider with the boys.

It was a great life for us boys. Dickey and Ronnie Partlow, Dub and Bud Grant, along with Jack and me, would swim together, have tug a wars on horseback in the river, and just play the games that boys did back in those days. Jerry's company soon joined the RCA and the world of contested rodeos.

In 1958, when I was 16 years old, after my dad and brother had quit working the show, I called up Harold Hinsen who owned the Silver Dollar Rodeo to see if he could use a rider for his Wild West Show. He asked if I could ride saddle broncs and I allowed that I had always wanted to, but had only ridden bareback horses and bulls. He said that he already had folks that were doing that, but if I'd ride broncs, then I was hired.

So, with that being said, I hitchhiked to catch up with him and started getting on my first saddle broncs. His wife Delores "Mousey," was also a bronc rider, so the two of us handled that event. We had three saddles between us, and we would often change hats and chaps to look as if there were more riders.

I also got on two bulls each performance besides the three saddle broncs that I rode. The broncs paid $6.00 each and I mounted the bulls for $5.00 each. If there were two performances in a day, then I got on ten head of stock that day. At the end of three months, I had made $1,470.00 dollars, which was good money in those days.

A fellow working a job was only pulling about $2.00 per hour and I was doing better than that. We had a tack truck with bunks that we could use for sleeping, so we saved by not staying in motels. We were the first rodeo company to cross the bridge to the Upper Peninsula of Michigan, where we put on a show at Iron Mountain.

After that, we eased down into Wisconsin. At Eagle River, Harold wanted me to ride a bronc in the parade, but I didn't. I did fly my mother up from Chicago to spend a few days with me to enjoy the show. We didn't have insurance if we had gotten hurt bad, but Harold and Delores told me not to worry, that they wouldn't leave me in a hospital. There were lots of wrecks in those shows, but fortunately I never got hurt bad.

The Silver Dollar Rodeo Company soon went the way of contested rodeos, with the help of some of the Midwest Rodeo Association members, including past PIRA President, Bob Ink.

This was a help since we then had plenty of riders, rather than the few of us who were just getting paid mount money.

LANCE ANDERSON
HIS NAME WAS ASPRO

When I was asked to tell a few rodeo stories from my past, I thought what I could say?

I couldn't say what happened up north, or about my first trip to the States, so what could I say? Then it came to me. Go back to where it all started. Not my involvement in rodeo, as it's been a family affair for three generations and now that my daughter is involved, it's four generations.

Back in the day it was about 1973, my buddy John and I were following the rodeos, going to all the steer rides and bullock rides we could get to. My father Ron Anderson told me, "You're not ready for bulls until you ride every steer you get on," so that's what we did.

Anyway, it was entry time for the Labour Day Holiday in March and there were two rodeos on that day, Kilmore and Kyabram, both about an hour from my home. Kilmore had a second division bull riding and Kyabram had a second division steer riding, so Kyabram was our choice. John and I entered.

We were too young to drive so we caught the train and a bus. We arrived at Kyabram the night before the rodeo, rolled our swags out in the grandstand and settled down for the night, talking about what we might get on tomorrow. About 10 o'clock P.M. a large stock truck came in and backed up to the loading race at the back of the chutes.

It was Bert Hall a well-known stock contractor with a reputation for having great bucking bulls and horses, and from the grandstand we had a great view of the bulls coming down off the truck. They all ambled down the race, snorting and checking out their surroundings. All of Burt's bulls had a nose ring and attached to that was a rope that wrapped around their horns. Burt's theory was he could handle them better.

The last bull on the truck had a long chain wrapped around horns. Burt walked across the top of the truck, pulling the chain down the ramp then tethered this bull to a post in the yards. He was the biggest Brangus bull I had ever seen, and he had a giant set of horns. He was about 6 years old and well developed. His name was Aspro. John and I lay awake for hours talking about the bulls, and wondering who was going to get on Aspro. We were going to make sure we saw it all.

The next morning when it came time to pay our entry fees, we stood in a long line to pay up. Suddenly, guys started dropping out of line and we wondered what was going on. Pretty soon we found out. The second division steer ride was now the second division bull ride, and they were going to use the bulls that we saw unloading the night before.

I turned to John and said, "It's now or never," so we paid our entry fees and waited anxiously for the start of the rodeo. The draw went up and John was in the first section and I was in the second section. It was working out pretty good as we had to borrow a bull rope, because what we had wouldn't even come close to fitting around any of these bulls, but we were set to go.

Dad showed up so we told him the news. We could tell he was a bit nervous, but he never put a negative thought in our head. He said, "Well, we need to get someone who knows, to help you." Max Frame and Ken Coleman, both toughs of that time offered, so we were set. What possibly could go wrong?

As with today, the second division is a chute draw, and the chute boss called out John's name and said, "Chute Two." The chutes weren't loaded yet so we nervously waited for the bulls to run up. The first bull was a brindle with short horns, and he looked OK. The second bull was Aspro. John had drawn Aspro.

Sometimes ignorance is bliss. We didn't know Aspro had a reputation as long as your arm, and that he had been nominated for bucking bull of the year several times and John was getting on him. You didn't climb down on Aspro you climbed across him, because he was so tall in the chute.

Dad was up on the chutes giving John a positive talk, although dad was as white as a ghost. Max and Coley pulled John's rope and showed him how to take his wrap then John slid up on his rope and screamed as loud as he could, "Let him out!"

Old Bert was ready with his hot shot, but he almost fell off the chute when John screamed. Out came Aspro, with John looking like a pimple on a watermelon. He got about three jumps then bucked off, but he was pretty happy walking away, unharmed by Aspro.

I was getting ready for the second go-round when they called my name. I was also in chute Two. The bulls started to run up and it was looking good. A big old bull was in chute one, a smaller bull was in chute two, and Aspro was in chute three. I missed out getting on Aspro and felt pretty lucky, but I spoke to soon. The back sliders hadn't been pulled and Aspro pushed himself over the smaller bull, the sliders were pushed closed, and guess what I was getting on. Aspro was now in Chute Two.

Dad was even whiter then he was before, but still being positive about the situation because Max and Coley were there to give me a hand. I didn't make the eight seconds on Aspro that day, but I came very close. Not from any skill, I was just lucky enough to be in the right place at the right time. I will never forget the power of that bull, but he was quite smooth. He turned back into the gate and into my hand. At about 6 seconds I slid off the back end of him and landed on my feet.

I don't think I ever got on another steer again, and that day changed my life forever. It turned out that Aspro was actually owned by Lofty Cannard, and was being used by Bert Hall. I married Lofty's daughter seventeen years later, but in 1976 I was off to America with Max Frame and Ken Coleman as well as five other cowboys for the America Bicentennial, a long way from Kyabram.

A couple of years after that first ride, I was riding for a living. Four of us had entered the Ross Rodeo in Tasmania on Saturday and the Keith Rodeo in South Australia on the Sunday, and for this to work everything had to fall in place.

Back then, there were only two flights into Launceston on Saturday and two out Saturday night. It was imperative that we catch the last flight out on Saturday night or we wouldn't make the rodeo. It was a five hour drive to Keith from the airport and the rodeo started at 9 o'clock A.M on Sunday morning. We drove my old 1966 station wagon to the airport and backed it into a parking space that would give us a quicker getaway when we returned.

Well, the four of us had a great rodeo. Mitch won the bull riding, Clancy won the bronc riding, Bill placed in the bull riding, and I won the bareback riding. We hired a car in Launceston to get to Ross, did that rodeo, and everything was going as planned. We were going to make Keith.

After collecting our winnings, we jumped in the rental car and headed to the airport. We had heaps of time and actually had a couple of drinks, then got on the plane and took off to Melbourne. We arrived at about 5:30 o'clock A. M. and got our gear off the plane and loaded up the station wagon and we were set. The car had only been parked overnight and nothing looked amiss, so we started it up and took off to the toll gate to pay out, and we were on our way.

I bolted up to the boom gate and hit the brakes, but nothing happened as we shot straight through the boom and smashed it to pieces. I steered the car into the curb to stop it and with an almighty bang, we were stopped. What a mess. Anyway, I popped the hood to see what was wrong. While we were gone, some lovely people had stolen our master cylinder.

Unbelievable, but true. After clearing things up with airport staff, we called another buddy who came out with a trailer and picked us and the car up, then dropped my car off at his house. He loaned us his car, and apart from being a few hours behind schedule, we made it to Keith in time for the rodeo. So, as we used to say, "We walked away from another one."

TOM RAY
POPPED MY BALLOON

Hopefully, this will convey to youngsters what the all greatest cowboys believed. No participation trophies. I was raised by the best parents ever. My dad was a great cowboy and even a better man. My mother was great woman who worked along side dad and never complained. I grew up meeting dads great cowboy friends. From my first memory I wanted to be like those cowboys. I did a lot of normal kid things, but always just wanted to be a cowboy.

One summer after being away rodeoing, I entered the Belton, Texas, Forth of July Rodeo. I got my parents tickets so they could watch me ride, but I bucked off pretty damn quick. When I got home from the rodeo, everyone was already in bed. I got up pretty early that next morning so I could leave for the west coast.

When I walked into the kitchen, mom and dad were sitting at the table eating breakfast, just like they did every morning. Without even looking up, my dad said, "What happened to you?" A little stunned by his question, but knowing what he really meant I said, "What do you mean?"

He said, "Your name is in the Sports News sayin' you placed here, or you won there." Not to deterred, I began with the excuses like, "I thought he was going to left, but he went to the right. My rope was too loose," and whatever else I thought someone might believe.

Dad looked up and said, "No, that's not what happened. I could have had a balloon on each of your spur rowels and you wouldn't have popped either one of 'em." I had no reply so I gathered up my gear and said my goodbye's, and left.

I couldn't get what dad said out of my head. I kept on trying to come up with a plausible excuse to ease my hurt. However by the time I got to Austin, I finally faced the truth that he was right. The lesson was learned. Either try or stay home, so for the rest of that year I could for sure pop balloons. What dad said, was a wake call for me. Without effort you won't win.

JOHN CLARK
OUT OF THE DARK CAME OL' JOHN CLARK

That comment, "Out of the dark comes Ol' John Clark," was made many times through the years back behind the bucking chutes across the country during the IRA Glory Days. John Clark, the 1964 International Rodeo Association All-Around and Bull Riding Champion, and 1965 Bull Riding Champion, is a true legend of the Pro Rodeo world.

John Clark [Tom Woods photo]

John's daughter-in-law Charlene Clark recalled the time John was at a rodeo somewhere and the arena was a sloppy, messy, muddy swamp. John drew a good bull that turned back right in the gate and really bucked hard. When the horn sounded, John being as agile as he was timed his get-off just right, and reached up and grabbed the front of the chute and climbed right over the back.

IRA Champion John Clark and his son, Kelly Clark, at the Cowtown Coliseum in 1976.

John said, "I never set foot in the arena and won the bull riding. All the other guys were wet and muddy, but I never got a speck on me and was ready to go to the dance."

Rodeo Stories III

ABOUT THE AUTHOR

Chimp Robertson is a former bull rider, an author, song writer (songs recorded by Chris LeDoux) private pilot, artist, auctioneer, rancher, army veteran, and sky diver.

Chimp's other books include:

Killin' Time: A Collection of Short Stories
POW/MIA: America's Missing Men
Mortal Secrets: A Mystery Novel
I'll Be Seeing You: A Battle with Cancer
Tall Tales and Short Stories: A Family Legacy
Billy Howard and the Buckskin: A Western Novel
Billy Howard and the Palomino: A Western Novel
Billy Howard and the Appaloosa: A Western Novel
Billy Howard and the Pinto: A Western Novel
Rodeo Stories: True Cowboy Tales
Rodeo Stories II: True Cowboy Tales
Rodeo Stories III: True Cowboy Tales

Born and raised in Dalhart, Texas, he is retired and currently living in Hooker, Oklahoma where he is pumping wells, working at a feedlot, and team roping.

Contact:
www.chimprobertson.com
chimp.robertson@hotmail.com

www.ingramcontent.com/pod-product-compliance
Lightning Source LLC
Chambersburg PA
CBHW070724160426
43192CB00009B/1311